Security Engineering
for Service-Oriented Architectures

T0280288

Michael Hafner • Ruth Breu

Security Engineering for Service-Oriented Architectures

 Springer

Michael Hafner
Ruth Breu

Universität Innsbruck
Inst. Informatik
FG Quality Engineering
Technikerstr. 21a
6020 Innsbruck
Austria
m.hafner@uibk.ac.at
ruth.breu@uibk.ac.at

ISBN: 978-3-642-09847-5   e-ISBN: 978-3-540-79539-1

ACM Computing Classification (1998): D.2, H.3, H.4

© 2010 Springer-Verlag Berlin Heidelberg

Cover design: KünkelLopka GmbH, Heidelberg

Printed on acid-free paper

9 8 7 6 5 4 3 2 1

springer.com

To Jakob

To Korbinian, Magdalena, and Felizitas

Preface

The growing popularity of Service Oriented Architectures is mainly due to business and technology trends that have crystallized over the past decade.

On the business side, companies struggle to survive in a competitive environment that pushes them towards a tighter integration into an industry's value chain, to outsource non core business operations or to constantly re-engineer business processes. These challenges boosted the demand for scalable IT-solutions, with efforts ultimately resulting in a flexible architectural paradigm – Service Oriented Architectures.

On the technical side, middleware standards, technologies and architectures based on XML and Web services as well as their security extensions have matured to a sound technology base that guarantees interoperability across enterprise and application boundaries – a prerequisite to inter-organizational applications and workflows.

While the principles and concepts of Service Oriented Architectures may look evident and cogent from a conceptual perspective, the realization of inter-organizational workflows and applications based on the paradigm "Service Oriented Architecture" remains a complex task, and, all the more when it comes to security, the implementation is still bound to low-level technical knowledge and hence error-prone.

The number of books and publications offering implementation-level coverage of the technologies, standards and specifications as required by technical developers looking for guidance on how to "add" security to service oriented solutions based on Web services and XML technology is already considerable and ever growing. The present book sets a different focus. Based on the paradigm of Model Driven Security, it shows how to systematically design and realize security-critical applications for Service Oriented Architectures.

In this book we pursue two objectives. First, we show how systems and security engineering go hand in hand and are integrated right from the beginning in the requirements elicitation and the design phase – thereby guaranteeing a security implementation more closely aligned to the requirements as specified within the application context. Second, we apply the principles of Model Driven Security to Service Oriented Architectures. Model Driven Security is an engineering paradigm that aims at the automatic generation of executable software for target architectures. The automation of security engineering through proven and reliable mechanisms guarantees correctness and facilitates an agile and flexible approach to the implementation and high-level management of security-critical systems. We base our approach for Model Driven Security on the ProSecO method for requirements engineering and the SECTET-framework for the model-driven configuration and management of target infrastructures.

Contribution

The contribution of this book consists in the systematic elaboration of a conceptual framework for an extensible domain architecture for Model Driven Security. The aim is to provide a sound methodical and technical basis for the engineering of security-critical SOA scenarios.

The starting point is the business level view where functional as well as security requirements are specified in models in the language of the domain expert – bare of any technical details as much as possible. Following the principles of Model Driven Security, models are transformed into executable artefacts. They configure target architectures designed and implemented according to best practices in security engineering and integrating proven technical solutions. Model Driven Security thereby improves traceability of security requirements, starting at the business level accross levels of abstraction down to their technical realization.

Target Audience

This book addresses IT professionals from industry interested in the design and realization of security-critical applications based on Service Oriented Architectures. SOA as well as application security engineering are broad subject matters. As can be seen by the numerous publications in either field, both deserve special attention. This book presents a synthesis of various best practices, standards and technologies from both fields, and – guided by the engineering principles of Model Driven Security – shows how to realize SOA Security.

The book will therefore be useful to software architects who are interested in

1. application-level security issues in the context of Service Oriented Architectures,
2. how to identify security requirements during systems engineering,
3. how to model security-critical business applications and inter-organizational workflows,

4. how to realize security-critical applications and workflows targeting a Web services based reference architecture,
5. how to leverage principles and techniques of Model Driven Security for a systematic and correct implementation of a given specification.

Readers are expected to have basic knowledge about UML modeling tools and techniques, about the major principles behind OMG's Model Driven Architecture and some understanding of XML and Web services technologies.

Organization

Here is the way we organized this book. Part I presents the background to our work. Chapter 1 is a general introduction to security issues relevant to the engineering of Service Oriented Architecture. We give an overview of paradigms, technologies and standards that represent the technical and conceptual foundation of the SECTET-framework in Chapter 2 and introduce basic notions and concepts of security – streamlined towards SOA – in Chapter 3. We elaborate a frame of reference for terms and concepts related to *Model Driven Software Engineering* and its core concept the *Domain Architecture* in Chapter 4. In Part II, we show how to apply the concepts of *Model Driven Security* to a *Problem Domain* defined as "security-critical inter-organizational workflows". A motivating case study from e-government is introduced in Chapter 5. It will serve as a running example throughout the book and will be the object of a method for *Security Analysis* in Chapter 6. In Chapter 7, we build the first part of our Domain Architecture, the *Domain Specific Language*. The target SECTET-*Reference Architecture* for the enforcement of *Basic Security Policies* of the SECTET-Domain Architecture is detailed in in Chapter 8. *Model Transformations* complete the Domain Architecture; they are presented in Chapter 9. A set of tools for stakeholders planning the realization of an inter-organizational workflow is introduced in Chapter 10. We sketch the extensions to the existing structure of the Domain Specific Language to model *Advanced Security Policies* in Chapter 11. Part III consists of a single Chapter and demonstrates how to apply the SECTET-framework to a real-life scenario from healthcare.

Acknowledgments

We would like to express our deepest gratitude to all the people who contributed to the realization of this work. They are the many colleagues, students and researchers who contributed to this book through their work in the two projects – SECTINO and health@net: Berthold Agreiter, Muhammad Alam, Michael Breu, Frank Innerhofer-Oberperfler, Basel Katt, Markus Mitterer, Memon Mukhtiar, Matthias Farwick, Stefan Unterthiner. We are also indebted to our colleagues Barbara Weber and Joanna Chimiak-Opoka at Quality Engineering for various comments, also to Bernhard Rumpe for fruitful feedback to the scientific work this book is based upon. Very special thanks go to our co-operation partners from industry. Without them our ideas would never have found the ground to grow and stand the test of reality: Thomas Schabetsberger, Richard Mair, and Florian Wozak from health@net and Andrea Nowak and Mirad Zadic from ARCS Seibersdorf Research GmbH. The excellent cooperation with Ralf Gerstner from the Springer-Verlag is gratefully acknowledged.

This work was financially supported in part by the Fonds zur Förderung der wissenschaftlichen Forschung (FWF), the Österreichische Forschungs-förderungsgesellschaft (FFG), the ARCS Seibersdorf Research GmbH, and the Tiroler Zukunftsstiftung; the latter contributed through the project health@net. The support is greatly appreciated.

Innsbruck,   *Michael Hafner*
February 2008   *Ruth Breu*

Contents

Part I The Basics of SOA Security Engineering

1 Introduction 3
  1.1 Service Oriented Architecture 3
    1.1.1 Interoperability and Securitiy Issues in SOA 4
    1.1.2 Model Driven Security Engineering 5
  1.2 Problem Description 6
  1.3 Contribution 7
    1.3.1 ProSecO 8
    1.3.2 SECTET 8
  1.4 Related Work 9
    1.4.1 Model Driven Security 9
    1.4.2 Formal Systems Engineering 10
    1.4.3 Pattern-based Approaches 11
    1.4.4 Tools and Frameworks 11
    1.4.5 Workflow Management 12

2 SOA - Standards & Technology 15
  2.1 Service Oriented Architectures 15
    2.1.1 Principles of SOA 16
    2.1.2 Motivating Example 16
  2.2 Web Services 17
    2.2.1 Basic Definition 18
    2.2.2 Service Invocation 18
    2.2.3 Service Description and Discovery 20
  2.3 The Web Services Specification Stack 20
    2.3.1 Transport Layer 21
    2.3.2 Messaging Layer 21
    2.3.3 Description Layer 22
    2.3.4 Discovery Layer 22
    2.3.5 Quality of Service Layer 22

2.3.6   Web Services Security Standards 23
2.3.7   Services Composition Layer....................... 23

3   Basic Concepts of SOA Security 27
3.1   What Is (SOA) Security? 27
3.2   Security Objectives 29
3.3   Security Policies....................................... 30
      3.3.1   Basic Security Policies 31
      3.3.2   Policy Models..................................... 32
      3.3.3   Advanced Security Policies 36
3.4   Security Analysis 38
      3.4.1   Security Requirements 38
      3.4.2   Attacks 38
3.5   Web Services Security Standards 41
      3.5.1   Confidentiality, Integrity, and Authenticity 41
      3.5.2   Authentication 42
      3.5.3   Advanced Web Services Security Standards 44

4   Domain Architectures 47
4.1   Model Driven Software Development 47
      4.1.1   The Unified Modeling Language.................... 48
      4.1.2   The Meta-Object Facility.......................... 48
      4.1.3   Model Driven Software Development................ 49
      4.1.4   Model Driven Architecture 50
      4.1.5   Model Driven Security 51
4.2   A Definition of Model Driven Software Development 51
4.3   Domain Specific Languages 52
4.4   The Target Architecture................................ 54
4.5   Model-(to-model-)to-code Transformation 54
4.6   Domain Architecture................................... 56
4.7   Framework 57
4.8   Model Driven Security 57
      4.8.1   Definition 57
      4.8.2   Extensions to the Problem Space 57

Part II Realizing SOA Security

5   Sectino – A Motivating Case Study from E-Government ... 65
5.1   Problem Context 65
5.2   Project Mission 66
5.3   Expected Benefits 66
5.4   Scenario Description 67
      5.4.1   Requirements 68
      5.4.2   Security Requirements 69
5.5   Results.. 70

6   Security Analysis 71
    6.1   Overview 71
        6.1.1   Modularity 72
        6.1.2   Traceability 73
        6.1.3   Model-driven Configuration of Security Services 73
        6.1.4   Tight Integration of Functional and Security Aspects .. 73
        6.1.5   Security as a Process 73
    6.2   Functional System View 74
        6.2.1   Level of Interaction 74
        6.2.2   Level of Abstraction 74
        6.2.3   Functional Meta-models 75
        6.2.4   Global Functional Meta-model 75
        6.2.5   Local Functional Meta-model 77
    6.3   Security Analysis Process 79
        6.3.1   Security Concepts 79
        6.3.2   The Security Micro-process 81
        6.3.3   Elaborate Functional Model 82
        6.3.4   Define Security Objectives 82
        6.3.5   Identify Dependencies 83
        6.3.6   Security Requirements Engineering 83
        6.3.7   Threat and Risk Analysis 85
        6.3.8   Security Control Engineering 86
    6.4   Access Control 86
    6.5   Related Work 89
        6.5.1   Standards and Baseline Protection 89
        6.5.2   Security Management 89
        6.5.3   Security Analysis in the Software Process 90
        6.5.4   Formal Approaches to Security Requirements
                Specification 90

7   Modeling Security Critical SOA Applications 93
    7.1   The SECTET Domain Specific Language 93
        7.1.1   Domain Definition 93
        7.1.2   Global Worklfow 94
        7.1.3   Local Worklfow 94
        7.1.4   SECTET Model Views 96
        7.1.5   Security Policies 98
    7.2   The DSL Meta-models 100
        7.2.1   The Workflow View 101
        7.2.2   The Interface View 107
    7.3   Integrating Security into the DSL 114

8   Enforcing Security with the Sectet Reference Architecture 121
    8.1 Architectural Blueprint 121
    8.2 Components 122
        8.2.1 Service Components 123
        8.2.2 Security Components 123
        8.2.3 Supporting Security Components 126
    8.3 Communication Protocols 126
        8.3.1 Enforcing Confidentiality and Integrity 127
        8.3.2 Enforcing Non-repudiation 128
    8.4 Component Configuration 130
        8.4.1 Inbound Messaging - (Executable Security Policy File) . 131
        8.4.2 Outbound Messaging - (Executable Security Policy
               Files) 136
        8.4.3 Request for Compliance Check 138
        8.4.4 Response Request for Compliance Check 139
        8.4.5 Technology and Standards 140

9   Model Transformation & Code Generation 141
    9.1 Transformations in the SECTET-Framework 141
        9.1.1 The Generation of Security Artefacts 141
        9.1.2 The Generation of Services Artefacts 142
    9.2 Security Transformations 143
        9.2.1 Inbound Policy File 143
        9.2.2 Outbound Policy Files 144
    9.3 Services Transformations 145
        9.3.1 Global Workflow to Local Workflow Translation 146
        9.3.2 Global Workflow to WSDL Description 146
        9.3.3 Global Workflow to XSD Schema Template 148
    9.4 Implementing Transformation 149
        9.4.1 Template Based Transformations 149
        9.4.2 Meta-model Based Transformations 150

10 Software & Security Management 153
    10.1 Tool Chain 153
        10.1.1 Modeling 153
        10.1.2 Code Generation 154
        10.1.3 Build Tools and Integrated Development Environments 155
        10.1.4 The Realization Process 155
        10.1.5 The Engineering Process 156
    10.2 The Deployment Process 157

11 Extending Sectet: Advanced Security Policy Modeling 159
    11.1 Motivation 160
    11.2 Extending the DSL 161
        11.2.1 A New Security Objective 161

11.2.2 Advanced Security Policies 162
11.2.3 Introducing the RBAC Policy Model 162
11.3 Modeling Policies with Dynamic Constraints 164
11.3.1 SECTET-PL 164
11.3.2 Static RBAC 165
11.3.3 Dynamic RBAC 165
11.3.4 Rights Delegation 167
11.4 Integrating SECTET-PL into the SECTET- Framework 171
11.4.1 Metamodel Extensions 171
11.4.2 SECTET-PL - Abstract Syntax 173
11.5 Extending the Reference Architecture 174
11.5.1 Access Control, Delegation and Privacy Policies 174
11.5.2 Protocol Extensions 179
11.5.3 PDP Extensions 180
11.6 SECTET-PL Transformations 182
11.7 Modeling Advanced Use Cases with SECTET-PL 182
11.7.1 Break-Glass Policy (BGP) 182
11.7.2 4-Eyes-Principle 183
11.7.3 Usage Control (UC) 183
11.7.4 Qualified Signature 183

Part III A Case Study from Healthcare

12 health@net – A Case Study from Healthcare 189
12.1 Background 190
12.1.1 The Electronic Healthcare Record 190
12.1.2 National E-Health Initiatives 190
12.1.3 Technical Standards for Healthcare 191
12.1.4 The Austrian Data Privacy Law 191
12.2 health@net 192
12.2.1 Project Mission 192
12.2.2 Organizational Setting 193
12.2.3 Architectural Concept 194
12.3 health@net – Security Analysis 198
12.3.1 Introduction 198
12.3.2 Functional System View 198
12.3.3 Identification of Security Objectives 200
12.3.4 Engineering of Security Requirements 202
12.3.5 Conclusion 204
12.4 health@net – Security Concept 205
12.4.1 Phase 1: Service-level Security 205
12.4.2 Phase 2a: Static, Process-level Security 206
12.4.3 Phase 2b: Dynamic, Process-level Security 206
12.5 Realizing Security with the SECTET-Framework 207

12.5.1 Conceptual Background 207
12.5.2 Model Views...................................... 208
12.6 health@net - Phases 2a & 2b............................ 212
12.6.1 Use Cases 212
12.6.2 Security Architecture 213

Part IV Appendices

A   Mapping Tables 225
A.1 Mapping Table for Inbound Policy File.................... 226
A.2 Mapping Table for Outbound Policy Files 227
A.3 Mapping Table for BPEL Files 228
A.4 Mapping Table for BPEL Files (continued) 229
A.5 Mapping Table for WSDL Files 230

References... 231

Index 243

Part I

The Basics of SOA Security Engineering

1

Introduction

1.1 Service Oriented Architecture

The paradigm of Service Oriented Architecture (SOA) stands for an architectural concept that caters to the pressing need of today's companies for a flexible integration into an industry's value chain. The participation in a network of enterprises collaborating to deliver a service – a so-called inter-organizational workflow – requires a company to couple its internal workflows to those of its partners. A business producing consumer goods may wait for supplier parts needed for further processing, a content provider may be waiting for credit information from the customer's banking institution before initiating services delivery. Orders are posted over the internet, maybe even automatically by the company's enterprise resource planning system, order confirmations and invoices are delivered by mail. In a healthcare scenario, a doctor may issue an electronic prescription for medication and refer a patient to a radiologist by issuing an electronic referral; in e-government, a company may forward its financial statement to tax authorities whereas in public procurement the process of tendering heavily relies on electronic systems.

Every value-adding activity of one actor initiates a flow of information across domain boundaries: this requires the tight coupling of the processes of participating businesses in terms of the flow of digital information. Every time the information is received by the interaction partner, it triggers further activities in the partner's internal value creating process.

To facilitate the exchange of information – according to the concept of SOA – businesses expose well-defined interfaces to their services or applications. The interaction of geographically distributed information systems over these standardized communication interfaces realizes the merging of local processes to an inter-organizational workflow, a "virtual workflow", that is not necessarily orchestrated centrally and may eventually span over the entire value chain.

1.1.1 Interoperability and Securitiy Issues in SOA

In order to be able to cooperate over interfaces in such scenarios, the partners need to establish a common understanding along three strands.

First, there has to be an agreement on the technical underpinning up to a certain extent. The claim of platform independence always put forward in such cases has to be understood in relative terms. SOA are independent of programming languages, like Java, C# or C++ used to develop the applications, they are even independent of the runtime environments hosting the applications (J2EE, .NET, etc.). Nevertheless, machines still communicate over interfaces, which need to be described in a machine readable way: messages have to be understood by both interaction parties, common transport protocols need to be agreed upon. The ever growing hierarchy of standards - mainly from organization bodies like the OASIS and the W3C – addresses many inter-operability issues. It has been commonly agreed upon that the Web services specification stack corresponds to an efficient way to realize SOA (e.g., [148], [207], and [81]).

Second, all partners of a network, who want to realize a common business goal have to get a common understanding of how to organize the flow of information (and possibly goods or services). They may have agreed to use Web services standards and technologies, but still, they need to know which services they need to offer to their partners in order to comply with the role in the value creating process chain they agreed to comply with. The common understanding at this level of abstraction is captured through a "Global Workflow", which stands for a (non-legally) binding contractual agreement between autonomous business partners.

Third, the security concerns of all stakeholders have to be taken care of. Without a central instance of control for workflow co-ordination, security enforcement becomes a non-trivial task: peers need to formulate and advertise their securtiy policies in a generally understandable way. Additionally, they must find a way to enforce them on heterogenous platforms in their own as well as untrusted security domains. Until a couple of years ago, the slow pace of adoption of Web services could be explained with the lack of standards and mechanisms for the integration of security. This was meant to change with the advent of the Web services security specification stack. Web services security standards, like WS-Security, WS-Security Policy, WS-Trust etc., build on the three basic Web services specifications – SOAP, WSDL, and UDDI – and provide some guidance for the integration of security into B2B applications and workflows on top of these (cf. to Chapters 3 and 2). Nevertheless, they remain close to the technical level and hence almost unintelligible to domain experts and business analysts alike (e.g., a detailed account is given in [55], [56], and [106]).

The first point – technical interoperability – cannot be considered a major issue anymore: most standards have been approved by major organizations and represent a solid technical basis to build upon. The second point – the engineering of a virtual organization – is a big challenge but of rather practical relevance. In such cases, Model Driven Software Engineering possibly lends itself to be an efficent engineering approach. Still, this claim needs to be validated empirically. The third point – the intricacies of complex security technologies - addresses the focal point of interest in this book: we propose a framework facilitating the efficient and effective realization of security-critical peer-to-peer scenarios based on intuitive models. The framework is based on an engineering methodology we think the most appropriate to get a grip on the second and the third issue still open: Model Driven Security Engineering.

1.1.2 Model Driven Security Engineering

The semantic gap between the various notions of security specific to the phases of the development cycle (requirements analysis, design and implementation) often leads to a situation where the consideration of security concerns is postponed to the end of a software development project, or – at best but with a similar outcome – the realization is left over to developers with no little or no expertise in security. Even in case of a satisfying implementation of security requirements by security experts, usually endorsing a very technical notion of security narrowed to mechanisms, algorithms and protocols, the costs of continually adapting workflows to match changing business (and security) requirements are very often too high. Hence business processes remain static, optimizations are hardly feasible (e.g., [106], [109], and [110]).

When designing and implementing secure or trusted systems that fully meet security requirements in the context of business level security policy models, the systematic integration of security aspects into the engineering process is a key issue (e.g., [31] and [53]). The definition and implementation of security requirements can be seen as an iterative process that has to be executed in all phases of the development process (e.g., [55], [56]). Additionally, it has to take into consideration all architectural layers, constantly requiring the close cooperation of security experts, software architects and developers in order to guarantee a correct implementation. Taken that way, security engineering becomes a complex and costly endeavor.

Model Driven Software Development is particularly suited to cases, where a sheer unmanageable array of standards and complex technologies require highly specialized technical knowledge for the implementation (e.g., [132], [133]). Relying on Model Driven Approaches that integrate best practices, patterns, and an array of well-known security mechanisms, algorithms and protocols whose formal correctness was thoroughly proved (e.g., [125]), is a matter of cost-effectiveness for the development process and a boost to competitiveness by catering for flexible adaptation during run-time. The automatic generation of executable software for target architectures allows for an efficient and flexible approach to the implementation and high-level management of secure inter-organizational workflows [141].

Model Driven Security is an engineering paradigm that specializes Model Driven Software Development towards information security. Its claim is twofold: (one) to support the integration of security aspects at an early stage of the engineering process and (two) to alleviate the software engineer from some of the crucial problems associated with realizing security solutions aligned with the original specification (e.g., [106] and [26]).

1.2 Problem Description

The advent of new technologies and paradigms like Web services and Service Oriented Architecture may create huge opportunities for businesses and industries but also brings about new challenges that usually cannot be met only by relying on best practices and proven patterns. In this book, we consider those problem areas that represent serious challenges to businesses struggling to keep up with the requirements of a fast changing competitive and technical environment. These businesses co-operate by forming virtual organizations – a collaborative but decentralized, peer-to-peer style network [66]. We call these collaborations *inter-organizational workflows* (cf. [200], [50], [21], [141]).

Our problem description primarily relies on the exhaustive analysis of case studies elaborated during projects carried out with industry partners (especially from the healthcare industry and from e-government). The analysis draws heavily on feedback received during the many discussions with industry professionals and technical experts at conferences and meetings, it benefited substantially from competent reviews in the scientific publication process, and last but not least it is the result of a good deal of intuition and reasoning. The identification of real opportunities for an efficient integration of new technologies requires a systematic analysis of potential and may create the need for innovative methods and approaches. These are the challenges of interest to a scientific community.

Summarizing our introductory discussion, we identify the following problem areas:

1. **The notion of security.** There are huge differences between the notion of security as seen by security experts and developers on one side and domain experts, whose concepts and language we consider closest to the end user's world, on the other side. Technical people refer to security in terms of proven mechanisms, algorithms, protocols and implementations. They want to achieve a security goal by some technical means (e.g., encryption, decryption, hashing, etc.). But security in its application context is defined in more abstract terms. In this context, the definition of security is more obviously linked to the business goal. It generally aims at the preservation of a desirable but almost abstract state in order to be able to fulfil a business goal. A certificate based authentication mechanism and the four-eyes-principle may both be seen as a means to realize the security

requirement of authorization, but the problem is that these views refer to different levels of abstraction. The four-eyes-principle may generally be realized with certificates (for authentication and authorization) but there is more to it: when considered from a juristic point of view its correct realization may rely on additional mechanisms (e.g., for logging and auditing) and may even require a re-organisation of the business process.

2. **Increasing systems complexity.** Modern systems have to be seen as computing components distributed across open networks. Through their interfaces, components are continuously exposed to potential attacks from the outside world. Additionally, the act of interacting with communication partners itself is subject to a considerable amount of security threats. Messages carrying confidential data may travel through intermediaries; digital data can easily be forged, lost or stolen. Preserving a state of security in such a networked world is certainly no trivial task.

3. **Interoperability and cooperation in distributed environments.** In an open network, communication occurs between autonomous interaction partners, who may not even know each other beforehand. Collaborations under such circumstances need methodologies supporting collaborative software engineering. This adds complexity to the engineering process. Both partners have to dispose of some means to synchronise their engineering efforts. But they also have to agree on ways on how to secure their collaboration in order to prevent fraud and harm.

4. **Loose Coupling.** Today's competitive environment puts enormous pressure on businesses and organizations in terms of the degree of flexibility that is required to react to a fast changing competitive environment. This often requires the ability to re-use software and to re-arrange components to serve in different or multiple scenarios. Components have to be re-usable and easily configurable. The same holds for security. Being a context-dependent concept, security controls have to be easily adaptable to fit to the new situation and still properly realize security objectives.

Considering these problems, we elaborated an approach that claims to push the concept of security towards a better alignment to the needs of those whose stakes are at risk.

1.3 Contribution

This book has two main themes, one being the application of advanced methods of software engineering in an industrial context, the other being the integration of proven security solutions, mechanisms, and patterns into the software engineering and application management process.

The central aim is the application of one of the most promising approaches in software engineering - Model Driven Software Development - to the area of security engineering, thereby pushing the development of the emerging paradigm of Model Driven Security towards a more comprehensive and operational concept.

The conceptual framework for Model Driven Security is based on the ProSecO method for requirements engineering and the SECTET-framework for the model-driven configuration and management of security infrastructures. After a detailed presentation of the conceptual foudations, the ProSecO method and the SECTET-framework are applied to a case study from e-governement – our running example – and a case study from healthcare.

1.3.1 ProSecO

ProSecO is a process model for Security Engineering. It was elaborated with the goal to provide capabilities for the systematic analysis, assessment and management of IT security requirements and risks in an enterprise context. ProSecO is based on an enterprise modeling approach that integrates technical and business oriented concepts on different levels of abstraction. A key element of the approach is the provision of traceability of model elements, security requirements, threats and controls.

ProSecO delivers a set of models, a defined process and basic metrics to monitor the security management process. The process is targeted towards a collaborative security management in organisation, distributing the responsibility for security to various stakeholders in an organisation that possess the best knowledge of their area.

1.3.2 Sectet

SECTET is a framework for Model Driven Security. It supports business partners during the development and distributed management of decentralized peer-to-peer scenarios. It was primarily developped for the realization of decentralized, security-critical collaboration across domain boundaries – so-called inter-organizational workflows – but as will be shown in the case study of Chapter 12 it can also handle scenarios with no worklfow, as is the case with the distributed, virtual patient record.

The approach weaves three paradigms – each one pushed by a major standardization initiative – into an extensible framework for Model Driven Security. Based on a methodological standard (Model Driven Architecture), an architectural paradigm (Service Oriented Architecture) and a technical standard (Web services), SECTET realizes a domain architecture aiming at the correct technical implementation of domain-level security requirements.

The framework consists of three core components:

1. A **Modeling Component** supporting the collaborative definition of a security-critical peer-to-peer scenario at the abstract level in a platform independent context. The component implements an intuitive domain specific language, which is rendered in a visual language and is currently implemented as a UML 2.0 profile for various modeling tools. The modeling

occurs at a level of abstraction appropriate to bridge the gap between domain experts and business analysts on one side and engineers on the other side, roles chiefly involved in two different phases of the engineering process – the requirements engineering and the design phase respectively.

2. A **Reference Architecture** representing a Web services based target runtime environment for the local workflows and back-end services at the partner node. The workflow and security components implement a set of workflow and security technologies based on XML- and Web services technologies and standards.

3. A **Transformation Component** that takes model information and translates it into configuration code for the components of the target architecture.

1.4 Related Work

We identified five major areas of work related to ours.

The approach on Model Driven Security (Section 1.4.1) bears some similarity to the SECTET approach (e.g., use of MOF/UML modeling techniques, code-generation), but its primary focus is set on the generation of access control infrastructures for object-oriented applications.

The engineering of secure systems based on well-founded semantics (Section 1.4.2) primarily aims at the formal analysis and verification of security mechanisms, architectures and protocols.

Pattern-based approaches (Section 1.4.3) shift the emphasis on the application of proven concepts for the realization of secure systems, transformations and code-generation definitely taking a back-seat.

In past years two providers of frameworks for the realization of domain architectures – the key concept of Model Driven Software Development – established themselves as the key players in that field (Section 1.4.4). The SECTET framework relies on them for the implementation of the approach.

Last but not least the community researching and realizing workflow security is ever growing and is touching upon key-issues for the realization of security-critical, decentralized, inter-organizational workflows (Section 1.4.5).

Some of these approaches bear similarities to the one presented in this book; we built on those ideas, where it made sense, adopting and extending the concepts so to realize our vision (e.g., the use of security patterns in the design of the Target Architectures). Other approaches are rather orthogonal and are prime candidates to complement and extend our approach (e.g., the formal analysis and verification of security policies in complex healthcare scenarios).

1.4.1 Model Driven Security

In an innovative work coining the term Model Driven Security [45], the authors present a model driven approach whose basic idea is close to that of our framework. The work introduces the concept of Model Driven Security for a software development process that supports the integration of security requirements into models at the design level using UML/MOF. The models form the input for the generation of security artefacts.

However, the approach focuses exclusively on the generation of access control infrastructures in the context of server-based application logic and targets object-oriented platforms (.Net and J2EE).

Based on a general schema for constructing languages, the modeling languages presented are semantically well-founded, and integrate a security model for access control generalizing Role Based Access Control. In terms of abstraction, the visual modeling language SecureUML directly addresses the software developer.

By comparison, firstly, our framework caters to a completely different application context. We aim at supporting the realization of security-critical inter-organizational workflows. Secondly, we raise the level of abstraction. Instead of addressing the needs of software and secutity engineers in the traditional development process of object-oriented applications, we consider security from the perspective of domain and security experts during the engineering but also the management process. Security concerns are identified and defined in terms of a language comprehensible to those bound to work with it.

In [59], the authors extend their approach towards a tool-chain for software modeling and code generation based on formal analysis techniques leveraging the theorem proving environment HOL/OCL. Going beyond mere code generation, the framework supports type-checking and facilitates a formal analysis of the UML/OCL model. The extension is implemented using a functional language.

1.4.2 Formal Systems Engineering

In [125], the author presents UMLSec, a formalized verification framework for UML models enriched with security properties. UMLSec is grounded on formal semantics and primarily aims at the formal analysis and verification of security mechanisms, architectures and protocols. The pluggable framework architecture facilitates the development of tools supporting the generation of test-sequences and – in some limited way – code-generation for object-oriented programming languages.

The framework stores models using an XML-based format (XMI) in a Meta Data Repository, which is then queried using Java Metadata Interfaces by different analyzers. These analyzers perform static as well dynamic analysis on the UML models for security properties like confidentiality and integrity.

The approach is actually orthogonal to ours and the level of abstraction is very close to the technical level. As explained in the previous section, SECTET caters to the needs of a specific domain, namely security-critical, inter-organizational workflows. With SECTET we raise the level of abstraction: our objective is to develop an intuitive language for the realization of security requirements in distributed systems. Inuitive in our case means, that the language should abstract as much as possible from the technical and architectural details.

Compared to UMLSec, which only provides rudimentary tool support, SECTET primarily facilitates the systematic generation of security artifacts (policies, message templates for various protocols etc.) specified during the early phases of software development. Another goal is the administration of security during run-time.

1.4.3 Pattern-based Approaches

In [172], the authors present an approach for the application of pattern-based software development to recurring problems in the domain of security. The basic idea is to capture expert-knowledge and make it available to developers as a pattern to be used during software design and development.

The focus is set on productivity improvements during the development process by re-use of best-practices and proven solutions. The approach provides an in-depth view at the concept of patterns applied to security. It supports the development-process through an ontology based repository of expert security knowledge. This facilitates the systematic analysis of the relationship between various security patterns. Although the authors use patterns to systematically capture knowledge about security issues at the model level, and thereby successfully demonstrates a way to boost efficiency, the semantics remain close to the technical level (application code, design, and architecture). Transformations are not addressed in any way (model-to-code or model-to-model).

1.4.4 Tools and Frameworks

Depending on the application context, work in this area can be split into two categories. Workflow frameworks apply model driven approaches to workflow engineering, whereas generic frameworks provide powerful tools to implement domain architectures, consisting of a domain specific modeling language, a set of transformation functions for code generation, and a target runtime architecture.

Workflow Frameworks

In a seminal publication [137], the author describes an implementation, where a local (executable) workflow is modeled in IBM's UML case-tool Rational Rose [8]. The various UML Class and Activity Diagrams are exported via XMI-files to an integrated development environment (e.g., the Eclipse IDE [2]) and automatically translated into executable code for a BPEL-engine (e.g., [7] and [9]) based on Web services. Nevertheless, the approach does not provide any facilities for the integration of security requirements at the modeling level nor does it support the specification of global workflows by means of peer-to-peer interactions as suggested by the concept of abstract processes (as in e.g., [34]). Additionally, the models do not raise the level of abstraction, but provide simply a visual means for the process definition.

By now, commercial grade tools for the "visual programming" of executable processes based on that approach are widely available (e.g., [7] and [9]).

Generic Frameworks

MDA-frameworks are UML-based modeling tools such as e.g., MagicDraw UML [5] providing the plumbing technology for the realization of domain architectures. Based on meta-models they support the definition of expressive modeling languages and the specification of model-to-model and model-to-code transformations as well as the definition of templates for code generation. Nevertheless, these frameworks do not specify any domain specific language (DSL) supporting the domain expert in modeling context specific issues.

AndroMDA [1] is an open source MDA-framework that provides metadata handling facilities through the Apache Velocity template language. The framework uses the NetBeans metadata repository (MDR) for storing metadata and a set of cartridges for accessing the MDR [6]. A major drawback of the framework is the complexity involved in defining extensions.

openArchitectureWare (OAW) is an open source framework that provides a more generic solution for domain specific engineering [157]. The reason is that it is open to other modeling frameworks like the Eclipse Modeling Framework or tools like MagicDraw UML. Its template language XPAND provides an intuitive way to generate any kind of data from specified models.

The SECTET framework leverages these technical frameworks, and defines languages for problems specific to various domains (e.g., the engineering and administration of security-critical inter-organizational workflows in e-government and healthcare).

1.4.5 Workflow Management

Inter-organizational Workflow Management Systems

A big community deals with inter-organizational workflow management systems, whose outstanding common feature is a central instance of control. The number of efforts dedicated to the analysis of issues specific to inter-organizational workflows is growing rapidly (e.g., [129], [22], [101], and [68]). The main efforts chiefly revolve around modeling issues.

Lately, these efforts took a direction picking up some of the issues relevant to our approach: [49] provides a methodical comparison of WSDL- and ebXML-based approaches and comes to the interesting conclusion of the incompatibility of the two approaches. In [50] the authors analyse security and workflow semantics related issues that arise during the modeling of business-to-business protocols.

As we do not aim to contribute a novel approach to this field, we rely on existing approaches. For example, we use UML 2.0 for modeling workflows and experiment with various workflow management systems based on Web services technology.

Workflow Security

In the area of workflow security, literature traditionally focuses on scenarios with a central instance of control, where process execution is controlled by a workflow management system.

Research in this area started with the analysis on how to enforce access control through mandatory or discretionary security (e.g., [39], [38], and [38]). The formalized approaches were soon implemented and integrated into workflow management systems (e.g., [118], [51], and [144]).

Alternative approaches analyse the application of RBAC to workflow management (e.g., [206]) and process models (e.g., [211], and [210]) and even apply concepts like RBAC to distributed scenarios (e.g., [93], [94], and [209]).

Security extensions at a low level of abstraction for workflow management systems are treated in [118], [38], [206], and [102]. In an interesting contribution, [112] proposes an approach for integrating security at different levels of abstraction in the system development cycle, but the full potential of a model driven approach, linking abstract domain-level models to their technical implementation, is not yet exploited.

A number of approaches deal with secure document exchange and workflow management in a centrally organized environment. Among these are the Author-X system [51], PERMIS [69], and Akenti [197].

Often central control may be appropriate, but in many of today's application scenarios a peer-to-peer style communication architecture is imperative in order to guarantee an appropriate level of security (e.g., a patient's privacy in electronic healthcare, a citizen's anonymity in electronic voting and a bid's confidentiality in an electronic tendering scenario). We consider this to be SECTET's main domain of application.

2

SOA - Standards & Technology

This chapter gives a brief overview of paradigms, technologies and standards that represent the technical and conceptual foundation of the SECTET-framework. Section 2.1 introduces the paradigm of Service Oriented Architecture (SOA) and presents a motivating example for subsequent sections: Section 2.2 lays out the technical underpinning of SOA – the concept of Web services, and Section 2.3 covers the standards in the Web Services Specification Stack. Web Services Security Standards will be covered extensively in Chapter 3 after having introduced issues around SOA security.

2.1 Service Oriented Architectures

The concept of Service Oriented Architecture (SOA) has emerged as a powerful architectural paradigm catering to the needs of today's companies to constantly keep up with a fast changing competitive environment. Rapidly evolving technologies force businesses to focus on core competencies and outsource many of their activities. Market forces promote scenarios where companies have to cooperate closely in order to be able to achieve a common business goal. Businesses have to cope with ever changing customer requirements. These challenges make the ability to flexibly reorganize a company's business processes a decessive key to success.

On the other hand, mature markets push companies to merge, to acquire one another, or to collaborate even more tightly in order to reach the critical size to survive. What in earlier days was achieved by a process within a single company became a complex process involving many actors, very often with no central point of control – a form of industrial organization called "Virtual Enterprise" [65]. SOA basically caters for issues that arise when the integration of heterogeneous business environments is on the agenda.

2.1.1 Principles of SOA

SOA is based on principles that support a flexible approach for the realization of distributed systems that interact across domain boundaries, be they inside the company or scathered among a multitude of business partners co-operating in order to accomplish a common business goal.

The concept of SOA is based on the notion of services. Services package application functionality and make it available through interfaces. Because a component's functionality is specified through its interface, and thereby hides implementation detail, it is said to be *loosely coupled* with other systems that may access its services. This abstraction separates service description from the execution environment.

Service description can occur at different layers of abstraction and is often referred to as service meta-data. Meta-data describes the services in terms of quality of services, security requirements, business functionality etc. in a machine readable manner (e.g., XML). Meta-data makes services discoverable by other systems over a network and facilitates a concept known as *dynamic binding*, where the exact implementation is determined at run-time. The use of wide spread XML-standards for service description fosters interoperability of loosely-coupled systems in distributed environments.

Being accessible through a public interface, services are *composable*, which means that they may be a functional part of some other service. The raise of abstraction level for service description allows to narrow the conceptual gap between its implementation and its actual business function. This supports a business-purpose oriented combination of several services to a complex service composition or an orchestration of several services into a process.

2.1.2 Motivating Example

Figure 2.1 shows a simplified SOA Scenario modeling the service offering of a provider of online tax services. The example should illustrate the concept of SOA and the use of Web services standards and technologies in subsequent sections. It also establishes the context for the introduction of basic concepts of SOA security in Chapter 3.

The scenario describes the processing of a company's annual statement for filing a tax return with tax authorities. The process is offered as an online service by a provider of tax services (called Tax Advisor in Figure 2.1) and relies on external services (e.g., the retrieval of tax files stored with public authorities) offered by a third party, which in our case is the Municipality.

According to the process definition the company initially submits its annual statement to the Tax Advisor through a Web service call. The Tax Advisor retrieves the company's tax files from its own database. In case the files are not present he relies on external services to access his client's files. In

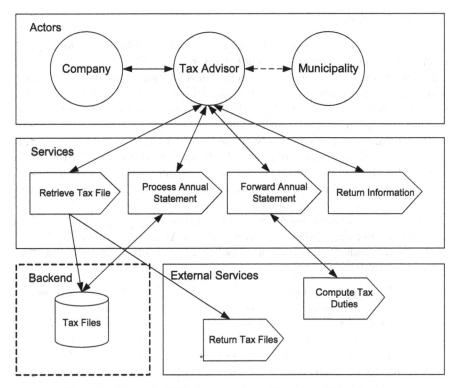

Fig. 2.1. Example SOA Scenario for a Provider of Tax Services

our example, they may be stored with the Municipality. Once processed, the declaration is forwarded to the Municipality which returns the amount of due taxes. The Tax Advisor finally notifies the Company.

2.2 Web Services

Service Oriented Architecture and Web services are often referenced to as interchangeable concepts, but they represent two distinct concepts. Web services specifications and technologies define the technical concept for services implementation and interaction, whereas the concept of Service Oriented Architecture represents an associated architectural paradigm expanding the focus towards the realization of a decentralized systems architecture that delivers application functionality. In this sense, SOA supports the end-to-end integration of services across domain boundaries. SOA may be realized using other technologies as well (e.g., CORBA [196] or Enterprise Java Beans [3]).

2.2.1 Basic Definition

The term *Web services* commonly refers to a set of technologies for a platform neutral and language-independent interaction. The concept specifies a software interface that defines a collection of operations that can be accessed over some kind of network through standardized XML messaging. Web services use protocols based on the XML language to describe an operation to execute or data to exchange with other Web services.

The beginnings are commonly pinned down to the year 2000, with the introduction of the cornerstone standards specifications SOAP [103][104], WSDL 2.0 [70] and UDDI [47]. The specifications soon became industry-wide standards for interoperability among software components, and, since then, many companies and organizations have been involved in the process of open standards development, struggling to specify enhancements that raise the level of inter-operability. The Web services Architecture Working Group of the World Wide Web consortium (W3C) has developed the following definition for a Web service:

> *A Web service is a software system designed to support interoperable machine-to-machine interaction over a network. It has an interface described in a machine-processable format (specifically WSDL). Other systems interact with the Web service in a manner prescribed by its description using SOAP-messages, typically conveyed using HTTP with an XML serialization in conjunction with other Web-related standards [10].*

This definition states that a Web service can be seen as an application that is accessible through its application programming interface (API), which is specified in the machine-processable XML-based format Web Services Description Language (WSDL) [70].

2.2.2 Service Invocation

A Web service interacts with other services through an invocation mechanism based on the communication protocol SOAP. SOAP messages leverage XML for the representation of data and are usually conveyed over HTTP [205], and TCP/IP [150].

Figure 2.2 shows the structure of a SOAP message based on XML. The SOAP structure acts as an envelope consisting of two part. The header carries transport related meta-information and information on sender and recipient, whereas the body "wraps" application data such as method calls, parameters and/or responses to corresponding queries.

Figure 2.3 exemplifies the submission of a company's annual statement to a tax advisor offering online tax services. The company submits its annual statement through a Web service call by passing company data wrapped in the message body as a SOAP message. The application at the tax advisor's end knows how to retrieve relevant data and may return a response.

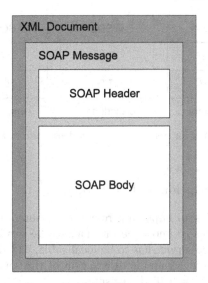

Fig. 2.2. Example SOAP Message Based on XML

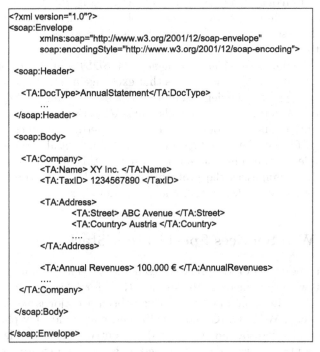

Fig. 2.3. Example SOAP Message for a Company Submitting an Annual Statement to its Tax Advisor

Fig. 2.4. Protocol Stack for Service Discovery, Description, and Invocation (taken from [91])

2.2.3 Service Description and Discovery

Service discovery plays an important role in distributed environments. A service requester only has to know the interface of the service at the provider's side, implying that the service has to be localizable. This is basically achieved by publishing a machine readable description of the service with a publicly available repository – a so-called "registry".

Meta-data describe services and need to be searchable and discoverable. The *Universal Description and Discovery Interface (UDDI)* is the most widely used specification of such a registry. It provides a highly functional and flexible approach for searching, discovering, and publishing Web services. UDDI functionality is accessed over SOAP. A search query for a specific service returns a link pointing to a WSDL document.

The *Web Services Description Language (WSDL)* is an XML format that describes services as a set of endpoints that exchange messages. The standard specifies a language for the definition of abstract service functionality, as well as syntax and structure of service calls. Service operations and messages are defined abstractly and then bound to a concrete network protocol and a specific message format (late binding, cf. p. 16). A potential service requester should be able to "consume" the service based on this information.

Figure 2.4 summarizes the protocol stacks used for the three phases of Web services discovery, description and invocation.

2.3 The Web Services Specification Stack

Since the introduction of Web services technology, which is commonly dated to mid 2000 with the release of the specifications for XML-messaging (SOAP and WSDL 1.1), interoperability has always been a major issue. Various organizations (e.g., W3C, OMG and OASIS) and major industry players (e.g., IBM, SUN and Microsoft among others) are putting considerable efforts to standardize a uniform way of how to describe, access, and locate services that are distributed over a network. The result is a stack of open specifications that build upon the basic protocols (cf. Section 2.2.1). They are categorzied according to their level of abstraction and to their functionality (Figure 2.5).

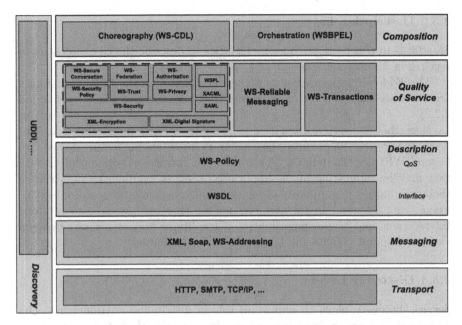

Fig. 2.5. The Web Services Specifications Stack

In the remainder of this section, we give a schematic overview of the specifications in the stack.

2.3.1 Transport Layer

A Web services platform is a transport neutral messaging architecture. This means that Web services can be accessed using any common communication protocol (e.g., HTTP, HTTPS, TCP/IP, etc.) or even use proprietary ones.

2.3.2 Messaging Layer

This layer defines the technical underpinnings for realizing the most basic messaging functionality, comprising the *eXtensible Markup Language (XML)* [54] and the SOAP protocol - both covered in Sections 2.2.2 and 2.2.3.

WS-Addressing [204] goes a step further: it specifies transport-neutral means to communicate addressing information. By including HTTP-specific data in the XML message itself (i.e. a standardized SOAP header), the message carries its own dispatch meta-data. This shifts network-level transport funtionality to convey dispatch information to the message level: the responsibility of network-level transport is reduced to delivering the message to a dispatcher capable of reading that meta-data. Once that message hits the dispatcher, the job of network-level transport is done. Therefore this standard facilites end-to-end message identification, especially usefull for long-running asynchronous interactions that span arbitrary periods of time.

2.3.3 Description Layer

Standards in this layer provide the facilities to describe the characteristics of services in an abstract way.

The *Web Services Description Language (WSDL)* is the XML format that describes services as a set of endpoints that exchange messages (cf. Section 2.2.2).

Nevertheless, services often need to be decorated with more refined descriptions. *WS-Policy* [40] provides the framework for extending feature description beyond WSDL's capabilities. The framework specifies additional meta-data that may be interesting in the application context: endpoints can advertise their capabilities (e.g., quality-of-service) and constraints imposed on service usage (e.g., security) in the form of policies that are attached to services. Intersections and/or incompatibilities of conditions and constraints between various endpoint policies can be identified and evaluated.

2.3.4 Discovery Layer

Service discovery plays an important role in distributed environments. The *Universal Description and Discovery Interface (UDDI)* is the most widely used specification for Web services discovery (cf. Section 2.2.3).

In some cases it may be requested to address the query directly to the service endpoint, bypassing the registry. The *WS-MetadataExchange* ([42]) specifies three protocols (request-response message pairs) to retrieve the meta-data for the interaction with a specific service endpoint. Based on these protocols the bootstrapping mechanism faciliates the incremental retrieval of a Web service's metadata: a WS-Policy file describing the capabilities, requirements, and general characteristics of Web services, one or more WSDL files specifying abstract message operations as well as concrete network protocols, and a couple of XML-Schema files specifying the structure and the contents of XML messages received and sent by Web services [159].

2.3.5 Quality of Service Layer

On top of the transport, messaging and description layers, which specify the fundamental mechanisms for Web services interactions, various organizations have proposed extensions for different purposes related to the description of quality-of-service features. The extensions cover the three areas: security, reliability of message delivery and transactional support ([131], [52], and [64]). We subsequently sketch those standards related to reliability of message delivery and transactional support.

WS-ReliableMessaging defines concepts and protocols for the realization of a message exchange that satisfies specified delivery assurances like in-order delivery, at-least once delivery and at most once delivery of messages [52].

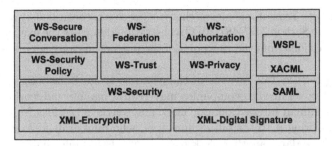

Fig. 2.6. The Web Services Security Specifications Stack

WS-Coordination specifies a protocol for the coordinations of actions of distributed Web services based applications. An application service can trace a message through its coordination context that is attached to a message specifically addressed to an endpoint reference [62]. The context can be propagated through standardized messages between cooperating services.

Nevertheless, as a mere coordination framework this specification needs to be complemented by two other standards for the coordination of transactions among Web services: *WS-AtomicTransactions* [64] and *WS-BusinessActivity* [63] are specific protocol extensions to *WS-Coordination* on how to reach the overall outcome agreement.

2.3.6 Web Services Security Standards

The world of Web services standards, recommendations and drafts has grown considerably in the last years. IBM and Microsoft have published a roadmap [143] related to the further evolution of the framework towards specifcations focusing on security related issues. The impressive set of Web Services Security Standards (Figure 2.6) addresses issues around the establishment of trust between peers, the definition of security policies, the enforcement of access control, etc. We will introduce these standards in Chapter 3 after having covered SOA specific secerurity issues.

2.3.7 Services Composition Layer

A business process defines the execution order of interrelated tasks - may they be automated or require human intervention. Businesses provide value-added services through composition of elemental Web services using service composition languages. A composition consists of multiple invocations of Web services - often scattered across many domains - in a specific order. It takes the form of either an *Orchestration* or a *Choreography*.

An *Orchestration* describes the execution order of Web services (control flow) and how the services interact with each other by exchanging messages (information flow). In the context of Web services, an orchestration describes an executable process in a machine readable format, which in most cases is an

XML language. Executable means that the process is controlled by a *Workflow Management System (WfMS)*. An Orchestration describes the execution order of the interactions from the viewpoint of the partner in charge of implementing the process.

Example: the Tax Advisor in the example scenario in Section 2.1.2, offering the tax services to companies may realize his internal workflow based entirely on human interaction: one clerk may retrieve the files from the local archive and bring it to the offical in charge, who may draft a tax declaration based on these data, another clerk may claim missing information from local authorities, and so on. Or, alternatively, he may choose to automate the whole workflow (or parts of it as not all activities may be offered as electronic services) by orchestrating service calls with a WfMS. In that case, the messages (e.g., request for retrieval of tax files) and documents (e.g., annual statement, tax declaration) are sent from one service to the next triggering some manual or automated processing.

The *Business Process Execution Language for Web Services (WS-BPEL)* [36] is the de-facto standard for Web service orchestration. WS-BPEL is an XML-based language to compose workflows based on "atomic" Web services. It provides mechanisms to define executable business processes, which can be executed by a WfMS (i.e. a BPEL engine) and, with limitations, abstract business protocols. The latter represent process descriptions that only specify the mutually visible message exchange behavior of each of the parties involved in the protocol, without revealing either the implementation behind or their internal process logic.

BPEL provides the means to specify workflow activities (e.g., invoke, receive, reply) for a WfMS that orchestrates the execution of Web services in a specific order defined by the flow of control. *BPML* [35] and *ebXML* [71] are alternative languages to specify executable processes. BPML is quite similar to WS-BPEL as it supports Web services standards, but it is considered as semantically weaker.

Since we strongly focus on Web services, we consider WS-BPEL as the most appropriate top-layer standard to model local workflow processes in our context. The specifications of local processes in Chapter 9 are based on the semantics of WS-BPEL.

A *Choreography* is a non-executable business protocol that describes the sequence of interaction activities (control flow) between business partners in terms of message exchange behavior of each of the parties involved in the protocol (information flow) in a "peer-to-peer" fashion. As opposed to abstract business protocols of WS-BPEL, a choreography is not limited to messages exchanged with the WfMS executing the workflow but involves the viewpoint of all peers. This means, that there is no central control of workflow execution. A Choreography can be seen as a virtual workflow that emerges through interaction of executable processes.

Example: The motivating scenario in Section 2.1.2 may be extended and adapted to cover the viewpoint of all participants (i.e. the Company, the

Municipality and possibly a further party e.g., a Notary offering notarization services) including services interaction that may not concern the Tax Advisor (e.g., the Company may need to access a notarization service as a result of company bylaws changing prior to annual statement submission).

Collaboration protocols like *BPSS* [71] and *WS-CDL* [126] provide the means to formally specify collaborations in distributed environments by offering a global view on collaborating services. *ebXML* comprises a powerful set of standards for the specification of these collaborations called B-2-B protocols but it is not compatible to the Web services concept. In Part II of this book, the specifications of peer-to-peer style compositions – so-called "Global Workflows" (cf. Chapter 7) – are based on the semantics of WS-CDL.

3

Basic Concepts of SOA Security

This chapter presents the basic notions and concepts of security. We will elaborate on these in later chapters in context of a motivating case study from e-government in Chapter 5 and an extensive case study from healthcare in Chapter 12.

Based on the many meanings of security we elaborate a definition of security appropriate to the context of distributed and decentralized systems in Section 3.1. We move on to define security concerns in context of such systems in Section 3.2. We introduce the key concepts facilitating the expression of these concerns in terms of security "needs" of an asset: either when engineering and managing security-critical systems (as Security Policies in Section 3.3) or when evaluating them in light of the three driving forces defining the state of a system's security: Vulnerabilities, Threats and Security Controls (as Security Requirements in Section 3.4). We close with Section 3.5 introducing Web Services Security Standards as a means to realize SOA Security.

3.1 What Is (SOA) Security?

Common knowledge defines Security as a state of freedom from risk or danger. It can also mean a state free from doubt, anxiety, or fear. Computer security narrows the focus to computing systems. It describes a field of computer science dealing with risk, threats and mechanisms related to the use of computing systems. Even seen in that context, the definition of security comes in (too) many flavours. For example, Garfinkel et al. define computer security in a very broad sense, emphasising the notion of a system's availability [96]:

> "A computer is secure if you can depend on it and its software to behave as you expect."

However security obviously does not only describe a desirable state, where systems function as intended. It also encompasses amongst other things - the notion of actively taking measures to preserve this state through security measures. Gollmann gives a complementary definition [100]. Accordingly, security

> *". . . deals with the techniques employed to maintain security within a computer system."*

Nevertheless, these two definitions – even taken together – fall short on one important point. Nowadays, computing systems cannot be viewed anymore as isolated hosts offering computational functionality to human users. Rather, modern computing systems are loosely coupled components distributed over a network and communicating with each other: they are heterogeneous, distributed, and inter-connected. For one, it is evident that a system which is connected to other systems is exposed to a considerable amount of additional security threats. Nevertheless there is another quality in todays computing architectures. Computer systems are not conceived as centralized architectures anymore. A Service Oriented Architecture represents an inherently decentralized computing concept. Hence, an appropriate understanding of the concept of security needs to take into account the system, its context and dependencies between both.

Therefore, the first dimension we need to add to reach a working definition of security for our goals is the dependency of a system on its "surrounding" or context – which in our case refers to distributed and decentralized architectures.

Once we identify all relevant dependencies of a system's well functioning on its context, security can be analysed properly and implemented correctly. These dependencies make security a relative attribute, which may best be understood in terms of how much it contributes to achieve a specific category of "needs". As a consequence, the second dimension we add to our definition of computer security is the relationship to specific goals – in terms of security needs – to be reached.

Accordingly, we define security as (extended and adapted from [100], [53], and [162]):

> *". . . the sum of all techniques, methods, procedures and activities employed to maintain an ideal state specified through a set of rules of what is authorized and what is not in a heterogeneous, decentralized, and inter-connected computing system."*

Going beyond the requirements of traditional, monolithical computing systems, this definition of Security addresses the specificities of Services Oriented Architectures in three dimensions:

1. the architecural blueprint of SOA: SOA infrastructures realize security-critical business processes involving many partners and spanning multiple security domains – this significantly augments the number and complexity of security requirements to be met,

2. the organizational aspect of SOA: partners want to stay in control over their part of the workflow, thereby imposing a decentralized, peer-to-peer style architecture, and

3. the administrative challenge of managing and enforcing SOA security: parties may not know each other prior to engaging in a buisness relationship. Some partners may even stay (at least partially) unknown to each other when interacting.

Taken together, these three dimensions clearly justify the need for the definition and analysis of security challenges and concepts in light of SOA. We will take our definition of security as a starting point to clarify relevant concepts of SOA Security in the next Section.

3.2 Security Objectives

Security Objectives provide a categorization of the most basic security needs of an asset. [12] defines a Security Objective as:

> *"... a statement of intent to counter identified threats and/or satisfy identified organisation security policies and assumptions."*

Security Objectives are also called security properties, security aspects, security concerns or security states [172]. Literature categorizes them according to various taxonomies. For example, Bishop identifies three basic aspects of computer security: confidentiality, integrity and availability, whose interpretation vary according to the context in which they arise [53]. Menezes et al. list as many as seventeen basic objectives for information security, among them common objectives such as confidentiality, integrity, identification, and authorization [142]. They also identify signatures, timestamps, and receipts as security objectives, which in conventional terms are rather seen as mechanisms, means to realize a specific objective. However those security objectives are derived by the four cryptographic goals: confidentiality, integrity, authentication and non-repudiation. Eckert identifies six basic security objectives (Authenticity, Confidentiality, Integrity, Availability, Accountability, and Anonymity) [78].

For our purpose, we identify three broad categories of generic Security Objectives according to the basic goal that is pursued for a given asset. We rely on the taxonomy given in [53] and define the three objectives accordingly:

1. Confidentiality is the goal that data should be readable to actors with appropriate permission.

2. Integrity is the goal that data and information should not be altered if not explicitly allowed.

3. Availability is the goal that assets have to be available to authenticated and authorized individuals when needed.

The definition is deliberately kept abstract so to emphasize the independence of any technical, architectural and application level context.

We define other security objectives as mentioned in literature (e.g.,[142]) as *Security Policies* which realize one or more of the three generic Security Objectives. For example Authenticity actually refers to the Integrity of information identifying the sender; a Break-Glass-Policy (BGP) specifying emergency access to sensitive information realizes Confidentiality but also Availability: it aims at making information about who accessed what information availiable (e.g., through logging) in case of a security incident. An introduction into Security Policies is given in the next Section.

In part II, Chapter 7 extensively covers Basic Security Policies realizing exactly one objective whereas Chapter 11 covers Advanced Security Policies realizing a combination of the three basic objectives.

3.3 Security Policies

Security Objectives provide a generic categorization of goals that – when strived for – may contribute to reach a certain kind of security need. Security needs may take either of two forms depending on the context of their use: we subsequently introduce the concept of *Security Policy*, and the next section introduces *Security Requirements*.

A Security Policy realizes a specific Security Objective (or a combination thereof). A Security Policy is defined as [53]:

> *"... a statement of what is, and, what is not allowed."*

We define Security Policies as semi-formal models. Formal in the sense that they can be expressed in a machine-readable way so to configure security mechansims, informal in the sense that we do not provide a mathematical definition. This may give raise to legitimate criticism: policies may not be formulated unambiguously. However, our apporach focuses on applicability and usability in an industrial context. A formal policy may add a considerable degree of precision and even be the only way to prove the policy's correctness at a specific level of assurance. But this usually comes at a price too high with regard to general applicability. We define an effective policy as based on the common consensus and interpretation of the community supposed to use it. Nevertheless, formal models can be integrated in the framework as needed: in later chapters we will integrate models with a proven formal underpinning (e.g., for Role Based Access Control) to support the definition of complex policies.

We differentiate between *Basic Security Policies* and *Advanced Security Policies*. The latter are based on a formal *Policy Model*. We will present the four most prominent Policy Models before introducing Advanced Security Policies.

3.3.1 Basic Security Policies

A *Basic Security Policy* considers one of the Security Objectives (Confidentiality, Integrity, and Availability) in isolation.

Confidentiality Policy

A *Confidentiality Policy* specifies system states where only those entities which are authorized can access information. Such a policy realizes the Security Objective of Confidentiality. Nevertheless it relies on authentication and authorization as a means to realize access control. Whereas authentication is the mechanism to establish and verify an entity's identity, authorization realizes a specific security model on how to grant various privileges to authenticated entities. This is the reason why both – authentication as well as authorization – where not defined as Security Objectives but are mere means to an end. Security Policy Models are covered in Section 3.3.2, Security Mechanisms in Section 3.4.2,

SOA are message based systems. The use of open and machine processable standards makes the messages particular prone to manipulation and unauthorized disclosure. In such systems communication is secured through the use of cryptography. Confidentiality is realized through the encryption at the message-layer. The possibility to encrypt various parts of a message with different keys allows end-to-end security, keeping the message parts confidential and accessible only to the intended recipient even if travelling over intermediaries (or stored with them temporarily). In SOA, a Confidentiality Policy is enforced through standards like XML-Encryption, XML-Digitial Signature and WS-Security (Please, refer to Section 3.5).

Note that we do not interpret such a policy in the sense of guaranteing what is commonly known as an *Information Flow Policy* based on complex mathematical models (e.g., Bell-LaPadula or Biba and Clark-Wilson for Integrity [53]). As we will see in later chapters, we define this policy as preventing the unauthorized disclosure of information in a basic, distributed SOA scenario, where peers exchange documents.

Integrity Policy

An *Integrity Policy* identifies authorized ways in which information may be altered and subjects authorized to alter it. Integrity comes in two flavors: data integrity ensures that data are not compromised and can thus be trusted over a specific period of time, whereas integrity of origin guarantees that information about a recipient is correct. Both are implemented with the same cryptographic primitive: digital signature.

Like message confidentiality, integrity is realized through the application of cryptographic primitives at the message level. In most cases only parts of a message are signed. Besides boosting performance (leaving uncritical parts unsigned) this also caters to the fact that a message travelling over many intermediary may be subject to many transformations (e.g., adding application-level information during process execution). A message may therefore not pass an integrity check even after a single transformation. This means that integrity must be realized at a level of granularity below the message level (e.g., elements, or parts of a message). An Integrity Policy is enforced through standards like XML-Encryption, XML-Digitial Signature and WS-Security (Please, refer to Section 3.5).

Availability Policy

An *Availability Policy* specifies system states where the provision of a specific resource has to be guaranteed. Availability is not only an important aspect of reliability, guaranteeing the existence of a resource. In security, the aspect of availability is interpreted in the sense of non-repudiation: someone may use a resource, access information, or call a service as needed under specific conditions, and that use must not be deniable.

Non-repudiation is an important security requirement for the realization of SOA executing mission-critical processes. Electronic transactions have to comply with a plethora of legal regulations. In scenarios where partners mostly unknown to each other engage in a business relation, the digital signature is a means to realize a legally binding commitment which holds before court. For example, the Austrian E-Government Law [158] puts the digital signature on a par with its "handwritten" equivalent and specifies requirements for its realization in distributed architectures [91].

In SOA, a *Non-repudiation Policy* is basically implemented through an exchange of signed and time-stamped messages documenting transactions (e.g., the Company sending its annual statement to the Tax Advisor) leveraging standards like XML-Encryption, XML-Digitial Signature and WS-Security (Please, refer to Section 3.5). The variant of our implementation realizing Non-repudiation of Reception as well Non-repudiation of Sending is covered extensively in Chapter 8.

3.3.2 Policy Models

In an industrial context, security concerns usually go way beyond what we cover with the category *Basic Security Policy*. The electronic realization of security-critical processes is tightly coupled with concerns about how to best realize security in compliance with the many provisions, regulations and laws imposed by regional, national, international and industry legislations.

Security Models abstract from specific policies and their particular characteristics. A Security Model represents the formal foundation for an *Advanced Security Policy* with complex characteristics and dependencies between its statements. This model-based abstraction allows a systematic analysis of a policy's correctness and supports systematic reasoning about its properties.

We subsequently analyse four of the most important Policy Models with respect to their ability to cope with complex *Authorization Policies* – which are covered in Chapter 11. Authorization restricts access to authenticated entities holding the privileges to perform an action on a resource. Authorization Policies define the rules of what is allowed and what is not. They are enforced at the various service providers' endpoints through a security infrastructure acting as a single point of entry – a so-called Policy enforcement Point– into the security domains. Prior to granting access to a resource the requester is authenticated and then assigned privileges according to the underlying Security Model. The infrastructure decides by checking upon assigned privileges captured in executable XML policies whether to grant access or not.

In SOA, the administration of these endpoints is a crucial issue. Endpoints not only need to be aware of the technology used to enforce security at the interaction partner's end (e.g., by advertising their technical security requirements through machine-readable policies with WS-Security Policy, cf. to Section 3.5.3), but they also need an efficient concept to dynamically manage these privileges.

The efficient administration of Authorization Policies in distributed environments is a pivotal criteria for the choice of an appropriate Security Model.

Discretionary Access Control (DAC)

In DAC based systems, users in possession of an object are considered to be the owners of the resources. They have full control over the resource. This enables them to use objects they own as they wish, and, for example, to delegate access rights deliberately to any further user [117]. The latter in turn becomes an owner as well and may proceed as he likes.

This notion of *Resource Ownership* makes the DAC model unsuitable for exclusive use in many distributed systems. For example, in a SOA based healthcare scenario, medical data is created by users of healthcare information systems in the domains of various collaborating partners. Evidently, none of those can actually claim ownership of the data. Those to whom the data may be of most value (or, alternatively, those who may suffer the greatest loss when used inappropriately) – the patients – have no control at all.

As a sideline we would like to point out, that the debate about ownership of sensitive medical data is currently gaining momentum in light of technological advances facilitating storage, dissemination, and duplication of sensitive data (e.g., [76], [28] and [139]). The outcome is very likely to be linked to an appropriate definition of the concept of ownership. Ownership can obviously be interpreted in various ways: does the radiologist who actually produced the x-ray own the artefact, the hospital which is bound to store the document for a specific time period, is it your doctor who ordered the x-ray, or is it your insurance who paid for it. The issue is far from resolved and for the time being the intuitive answer may be rooted in the fact that medical data actually is of most value to the individual concerned – the patient – and that he should be empowered to determine its appropriate use. So in our context, an appropriate security policy model will be evaluated with respect to its abilities to integrate this viewpoint.

The administration of policies based on DAC in distributed environments is evidently almost infeasible.

Mandatory Access Control (MAC)

In MAC based systems, users and their rights are enforced by a central mechanism (e.g., the operating system) and administered by a central authority (e.g., the system adminsitrator). Users do not have the ability to override the policy.

MAC is traditionally associated with multi-level secure systems. The concept of MAC is realized by assigning security labels to data elements at very fine-granular levels, thereby expressing their security sensitivity and assigning clearance levels to subjects. In MLS, less-sensitive information can be accessed by higher-cleared individuals, and higher-cleared individuals can share "sanitized" documents – where sensitive information that the less-cleared individual is not allowed to see is removed– with less-cleared individuals.

MLS was the concept of choice in the mainframe era, where many users had to be granted simultaneous access to sensitive information. It is still in use today in operating systems, however, in many SOA scenarios MAC is of limited use: e.g., inter-organizational healthcare scenarios involve many actors accessing resources scattered over multiple domains and the centralized administration and enforcement architecture of MAC is incompatible with SOA-based Systems which advocate loose coupling with decentralized control.

Role Based Access Control (RBAC)

RBAC enforces access control according to access policies, which define a number of roles and assign permissions to roles [169]. Subjects are assigned one or more roles. A role hierarchy defines inheritance relations between roles. The principal motivation of RBAC – this is to provide administrative convenience – can be further strengthened by using RBAC to manage RBAC ([170]). Many approaches analyse the application of RBAC to workflow management (e.g., [38], [206]) even taking distributed scenarios into account (e.g., [93] and [94]).

The limitations of the basic RBAC model become obvious especially when used in context of Service Oriented Architectures.

Firstly, in practice authorization can generally never be granted exclusively based on permissions assigned to roles as in static RBAC. Rather, access rights depend on a set of dynamic constraints: the right to call an operation of a specific Web service may primarily depend on the caller's role but may be further confined by attributes of the system's environment (e.g., a principal may access a service only between 9.00 a.m. to 5.00 p.m. on working days), of the service call himself (e.g., authentication mode) or on the content of resources (e.g., a principal with role Tax Advisor may only access the files of Clients he is mandating). Dynamic constraints define the conditions under which a role has the right to access services.

Additonally, the level of granularity necessary for the definition of access rights in security-critical SOA scenarios goes well beyond what is possible with basic RBAC. A requester's permissions may not only be restricted at the services level (e.g., the right of a princpal to call a service that may return a document) but his access rights may have to be further limited at a finer level of granularity (e.g., the permission to only read specific parts of the document). Constraints on permissions support the specification of access rights at various level of granularity.

The framework we are going to present in this book – SECTET – handles these points of criticism by supporting the dynamic constraints through SECTET-PL, a language with predicate logic conditions (cf. Chapter 11).

However, the limitations of RBAC much further: for example, it does not cater for the notion of continuity in access control. This means that it does not support the revocation of access rights once granted. The set of suggestion for improvement is ever groving (e.g., [28]). With these limitations in mind, we will replace the RBAC model with an extended security model – the UCON$_{ABC}$ model in Chapter 12. It is briefly introduced subsequently.

UCON$_{ABC}$

UCON$_{ABC}$ is a comprehensive policy model for usage control. It extends traditional access control models in two respects [160]:

1. continuity of access decision, and
2. mutability of attributes.

Continuity of access decision means that the decision to access an object is not only verified before but also during access and may result in the revocation of permissions, whenever conditions are not met. For example, a Tax Advisor should be allowed to retrieve and read a Client's tax file only as long as he his mandating that client. Once his mandate lost, he should not be able to read the tax file anymore. Policy conditions in UCON consist of subject, object and environment attributes.

Mutability of attributes refers to subject or object attributes changing as side-effects of accessing a resource. This may additionally result in a change in ongoing or subsequent access decisions. This facillitates for example a policy, where access is confined by access history. For example, a Chartered Accountant working for a Tax Advisor should not mandate a Company that stands in direct competition to any of his former clients (a so-called Chinese Wall Policy [53]).

Policy statements in UCON consist of *authorizations, obligations* and *conditions*. Authorizations refer to predicates based on subject or object attributes. Obligation actions are directives to a subject to perform additional actions before or during access. Predicates exclusively based on environment attributes such as system time, device type etc., are categorized as conditions. Authorizations, o*B*ligations and *C*onditions are collectively referred to as the building blocks of UCON$_{ABC}$. UCON conditions can be used to express static constraints (e.g., duration, purpose) as well as dynamic constraints (e.g., number of times to access a resource, location-dependent access).

In a similar manner to RBAC, UCON uses the concept of server-side reference monitoring for access control and trust management. However it also leverages technologies of client-side reference monitoring to enforce usage control and digital rights management. It divides access rights into functional categories like *Viewing* a resource or *Modifying* a data object (e.g., a Physician has privileges to view and update the Patient's medical record).

3.3.3 Advanced Security Policies

Many industry scenarios impose complex security requirements. In this section we introduce scenarios requiring some *Advanced Security Policies*. Some of these use cases already stand as candidates for near future integration into various industry-concerted initiatives (e.g., "Integrating the Healthcare Enterprise (IHE)"-projects [4]) whereas others represent more an educated guess based on discussions with experts on what the industries – especially e-government and e-health – may be needing in a couple of years. All of them are extensively covered in Chapter 11.

Dynamic Access Control Policies

In many security-critical scenarios, permissions to execute services cannot be assigned statically. Instead, they are associated with a set of *Dynamic Constraints*. Such constraints refer to subject, system or object attributes and are evaluated at runtime.

Referring to our running example, a dynamic constraint could state the following: *"A Tax Advisor can modify any tax file records of Clients he is mandating."* It is evident, that this condition has to be checked at runtime as the undelying facts can change over time.

Delegation of Rights Policies (DRP)

DRP allow a user to delegate her rights to other legitimate users of the system in specific situations with defined limitations. For example, in healthcare a patient referral corresponds to such a policy: *"A Primary Care Physician delegates her rights to access an online Patient file to a Radiologist."*

In other scenarios the patient himself could want to grant access to the specialist using the delegated rights of the primary physician [130]. DRP may be further restricted: the rights of the delegatee may depend on additional information such as her legal status, credentials, purpose, duration etc.

Break-Glass Policy (BGP)

BGP is an authorization scheme granting access in case of emergency. An example policy from healthcare could state the following: *"An attending Physician can bypass routine access control restrictions to a Patient's medical records in order to provide timely treatment."* Hence, treatment can occur without any delay due to administrative or technical complexities (e.g., [173, 116]). As an additional safeguard against misuse access could be logged providing evidence in case of abuse.

4-Eyes-Principle

The *4-Eyes-Principle* is a form of *Multiple Authorization*. It requires two users with a common interest to access the system simultaneously. This principle supports monitoring of the data access, e.g., when one user accesses data the other user monitors it (e.g., [182]). In a healthcare scenario, the 4-Eyes-Principle could state that *"The Patient needs to be present when a Physician accesses her records."*

The physician's access is logged during the visit by some trusted *Proxy Service*. Enforcement of the 4-Eyes-Principle is usually performed indirectly and supported with storing the access record into a logging database for future auditing. Logging and auditing capabilities permit the patient to set her privacy preferences based on access history and support the identification of potential abuse.

Usage Control Policies (UCP)

A UCP is an extension of access control because it does not only control data access but also how accessed data may or may not be used or distributed afterwards. In a healthcare scenario a usage requirement could state that *"Access to tax files is allowed for 5 times only and should last for at most 48 hours, after its first access."*

Qualified Signature

In many e-government applications, a system signature is not legally binding. For example, filing your income tax return online with a typical e-government application, the "technical" signature provided by your application or even the security gateway at the organization's domain boundaries is not sufficient when submitting a document. In such a case legal regulations may stipulate that the signatory be a natural person (e.g, the Austrian E-Government Law [158]). This requirement extends the concept of digital (system) signatures to the *Qualified Signature*, requiring the signatory be a natural person.

Privacy Policies

In healthcare, a patient is still to be considered the owner of his records. He retains legal rights over his medical records. Patients concerned about who may read their records could want to define a "Privacy Policy" restricting access to data even if scattered over many repositories.

In public procurement, Anonymity of Bidders is guaranteed by a specific security protocol and in most cases requires a trusted third party. Anonymity of Bidders can be considered a variant of a Privacy Policy.

3.4 Security Analysis

A *Security Policy* is enforced through one or more *Security Controls*. The dependency between policies and controls needs to be constantly evaluated in the light of Security Objectives targeted, underlying assumptions, and looming threats: this is done during *Security Analysis* – an on-going evaluation process.

3.4.1 Security Requirements

In contrast to a *Security Policy* which is used for the management of security (e.g., during runtime) as a set of statements of what is allowed, and what is not, *Security Requirements* focus on the early stages of enigneering, the elicitation phase.

A Security Requirement is a detailed context-dependent explication of a Security Objective. It breaks a Security Objective down into several more detailed descriptions based on the results of *Security Analysis*.

Security Requirements also play a role when defined in context of systems evaluation: security evaluation techniques (e.g., TCSEC [16], ITSEC [11], CC [12]) guarantee that a system may qualify as a trusted system when meeting specific Security Requirements under specific conditions. Standardized, these methodologies provide a measurement of trust based on specific security requirements and evidence of assurance.

We will perform a detailed Security Analysis in the context of use cases for e-government and healtcare systems in Chapters 6 and 12 respectively.

3.4.2 Attacks

Attacks can inflict some kind of loss or harm on computing systems. At its very core computer-based security revolves around three main forces: *Threats, Security Controls* and *Vulnerabilities*.

Potential attacks may be the same for SOA as for traditional information systems inside a particular partner node (e.g., malicious software, buffer overflows, trojans, denial of service attacks, cryptoanalysis). They may be based on the same vulnerabilities (e.g., missing user awareness, flawed code and/or design, wrong administration etc.), and can thus be countered by the same security mechanisms.

Nevertheless, the properties of SOA open the door to a category of specific threats. These threats have to be countered with dedicated technologies catering to the specificities of SOA. As we will see, most of these technologies – the so-called security controls – are based on SOA and Web services standards. We will cover threats and securtity controls specifically in context of SOA subsequently.

Threats and Vulnerabilities

A *Vulnerability* is a flaw in a system's design or its implementation. It is a weakness that might be exploited to cause a system to malfunction, ultimately resulting in some harm or loss. However, a vulnerability may remain undetected and not be exploited at all.

A *Threat* is a specific set of circumstances that bears the potential to cause loss or harm. A threat remains a potential violation of security. It materializes into an attack when a subject (a person or another system) exploits a vulnerability and attacks the system.

Threats can be divided into four broad classes (cf. [53] and [178]):

1. deception which corresponds to the acceptance of false data
2. disclosure resulting in unauthorized access to information;
3. disruption preventing correct system operation;
4. usurpation leads to the unauthorized control of some part of a system.

In the following we give examples attack vectors that may be launched in the context of SOA architectures and specifically leverage technical vulnerabilities, rooted in the implementation of underlying technologies (as in [91]).

XML-specific Attacks. The use of XML for messaging makes the infrastructure particularily prone to attacks targeting those components processing the messages (be they part of the security- ot the services infrastructure). XML-bombs (XML documents with endless recursions), X-Path injections (a technique used to exploit Web services by crafting malicious XPath queries as user-supplied input) and schema poisoning (a modifications of a message's grammatical structure (XML Schema) leading to inconsistencies) may at least render the infrastructure unavailable and at worst compromise the whole system opening access to unauthroized users. Here, a validation service acting as a security proxy or "filter" to any application service can efficiently counter the threat.

Service Scanning. Reconnaissance (aka footprinting) is the activity necessary to a successful operation against a target (e.g., an application, a host in a network, or a service). It refers to information-gathering behavior that aims to profile the target in order to identify efficient attack tactics. It is evident, that in SOA publicly available information on services (methods, parameters etc.) in their WSDL files could be used for a systematic analysis for weaknesses, for example through automated tests – so-called fuzzying.

Compromised Services. In a distributed scenario service information needs to be retrieved through a service repository. The service repository may hold information on a manipulated, compromised service. This threat can only be countered by authenticating the service provider and checking upon his trustworthyness.

Replay Attacks. One of the most evident attacks on SOA is based on a central property of Web services: their statelessness. As a consequence of that, an attacker could simply intercept a message from an earlier call for a service request and replay it to that service at a later point in time. In case service requests are coupled with costs (e.g., retrieving a Tax File from a Municipality) this has the potential to inflict serious damage.

A system providing a service never remembers which messages already where processed. This necessitates a mechanism to firstly, authenticate a message, e.g., through a digital signature and a timestamp and, secondly, to provide some application level state information. The latter could be implemented through the security infrastructure which keeps status information on messages received and would simply dismiss a replayed message.

For an exhaustive account on technical attacks on SOA architectures, the interested reader may refer to [177].

Most of these attack vectors leverage technical vulnerabilities. However, the Security Analyses in Chapters 6 and 12 will basically cover application layer threats like **Eavesdropping** through compromised communication channels (e.g., the channel between the Tax Advisor Server and and the Municipality Application Server may be compromised) and **Unauthorized Access** due to faulty configuration (e.g., access to the service sendAnnualStatement is not properly configured; services may thus be accessible to companies offering tax sevices which are not anymore actively involved in the scenario).

Security Controls

A *Security Control* is broadly defined as any managerial, operational, and/or technical safeguard put into place to mitigate identified risks. This rather general definition especially applies when performing a Security Analysis (e.g., during requirements engineering).

For our purposes – when designing, implementing or managing a security-critical system – we narrow down the definition to any technical, architectural, or mathematical concept that counters a specific Threat in order to enforce a Security Policy.

In the context of SOA, Web Services Security Standards leverage these techniques, algorithms and mechanisms, and thereby abstract from specific implementational details (e.g., application programming interfaces, management architecture, protocols etc.).

We hence differentiate between *Technical Security Controls* and *Web Services Security Standards*.

Technical Security Controls are generally categorized according to their security function (e.g., Identification and Authentication, Access Control, Audit and Accountability and Systems and Communication and many more [168]). Each one leverages one or more technical, architectural, or mathematical concept (e.g., public- or secret key cryptography for confidentiality through encryption, for integrity, identification and authentication through digital signatures, message protocols for the establishment of trust and accountability, the use of reference monitor for access control etc.). Technical Security Controls accross various layers and tiers (application, operating system, networking, middleware, database etc.) are extensively covered in literature (e.g., [53], [162], [78]).

Henceforth, we will only cover Technical Security Controls in context of their integration into Web Services Security Standards in the next section (Section 3.5) as well as in later chapters when designing and realizing enforcement architectures for various policies in the use cases (Chapters 8 and 11).

The integration into the various Web Services Security Standards and specifications is also extensively covererd in literature, e.g., in [167], [156], and [114]. For a good overview covering these security standards see e.g., [143].

3.5 Web Services Security Standards

3.5.1 Confidentiality, Integrity, and Authenticity

Basic security objectives targeting message security, like Confidentiality, Integrity of data and Integrity of origin (authenticity) are covered by the three basic security standards: *WS-Security*, *XML-Digital Signature*, and *XML-Encryption*.

OASIS proposed an extension of the SOAP message structure to enable the addition of security features to Web services based messaging: *WS-Security* is the basic building block for secure interactions in scenarios on top of Web services technology [37]. The specification describes how to embed security tokens in the header of SOAP messages. These tokens may be used by senders and/or recipients to digitally sign and encrypt the message or parts of it. WS-Security also specifies how to embed these encrypted and signed parts within the SOAP message.

Example: Figure 3.1 shows how the security infrastructure at the Company's side would first encrypt the application relevant data to some cipher value with a symmetric encrytpion scheme (triple-DES-cbc) and then embed that value as an encrypted string according to the standards XML-Encryption and XML-Digital Signature. The symmetric key is encrypted with the recipients public key based on an RSA encryption scheme.

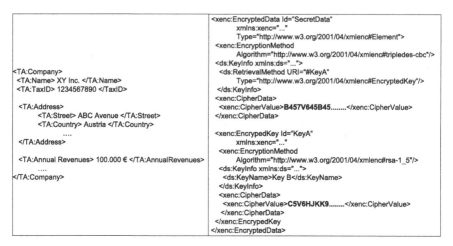

```
                                          <xenc:EncryptedData Id="SecretData"
                                             xmlns:xenc="..."
                                             Type="http://www.w3.org/2001/04/xmlenc#Element">
                                          <xenc:EncryptionMethod
                                             Algorithm="http://www.w3.org/2001/04/xmlenc#tripledes-cbc"/>
                                          <ds:KeyInfo xmlns:ds="...">
<TA:Company>                                 <ds:RetrievalMethod URI="#KeyA"
  <TA:Name> XY Inc. </TA:Name>                  Type="http://www.w3.org/2001/04/xmlenc#EncryptedKey"/>
  <TA:TaxID> 1234567890 </TaxID>           </ds:KeyInfo>
                                          <xenc:CipherData>
  <TA:Address>                               <xenc:CipherValue>B457V645B45........</xenc:CipherValue>
      <TA:Street> ABC Avenue </TA:Street>  </xenc:CipherData>
      <TA:Country> Austria </TA:Country>
          ....                             <xenc:EncrypedKey Id="KeyA"
  </TA:Address>                               xmlns:xenc="..."
                                          <xenc:EncryptionMethod
  <TA:Annual Revenues> 100.000 € </TA:AnnualRevenues>  Algorithm="http://www.w3.org/2001/04/xmlenc#rsa-1_5"/>
          ....                             <ds:KeyInfo xmlns:ds="...">
</TA:Company>                                <ds:KeyName>Key B</ds:KeyName>
                                          </ds:KeyInfo>
                                          <xenc:CipherData>
                                             <xenc:CipherValue>C5V6HJKK9........</xenc:CipherValue>
                                          </xenc:CipherData>
                                          </xenc:EncrypedKey>
                                          </xenc:EncryptedData>
```

Fig. 3.1. Application Data Encrypted According to XML-Encryption and XML-Digital Signature

In the example, the second cipher value refers to the symmetric key encrypted with the recipients public key based on an RSA encryption scheme. Upon reception and once decrypted, the recipient (Tax Advisor) uses this key to decrypt the first cipher value. This means that the interaction partners are relying on a hybrid crypto scheme to secure their communication. The advantage over using pure public key cryptography lies in better performance during encryption and decryption.

WS-Security in turn relies heavily on the underlying XML-standards *XML-Digital Signature* [43] and *XML-Encryption* [119] for the signing and encryption of XML documents. Both standards specifiy a process for encrypting or signing arbitrary application data and representing the result in XML format.

Example: Figure 3.2 shows how the security infrastructure at the Company's side would then embed the XML structure with the cipher value in the SOAP message structure according to WS-Security before calling the Tax Advisor's service and thereby sending the document.

Vendors and Open Source Initiatives are beginning to offer reference implementation of these standards. For example, *Web Services Security for Java (WSS4J)* [89] is a prototypic extension of the Apache Axis SOAP engine [189] that implements the standard.

3.5.2 Authentication

The process of authentication binds an identity to a subject. Authentication is a technical means to achieve the premises to any non-anonymous interaction.

Authentication is integral to many policies as an implicit prerequisite. For example, an Authorization Policy stating that a Tax Advisor can access his Client's tax files implies the existence of an underlying authentication

```
<?xml version="1.0"?>
<SOAP:Envelope
  xmlns:SOAP="http://schemas.xmlsoap.org/soap/envelope/">
  <SOAP:Header>
   <wsse:Security>
    <xenc:ReferenceList>
     <DataReference URI"#bodyID"/>
    <xenc:ReferenceList>
   <wsse:Security>
  <SOAP:Header>
  <SOAP:Body>
   <xenc:EncryptedData Id="bodyID"
       xmlns:xenc="http://www.w3.org/2001/04/xmlenc#"
       Type="http://www.w3.org/2001/04/xmlenc#Element">
   <xenc:EncryptionMethod
       Algorithm="http://www.w3.org/2001/04/xmlenc#tripledes-cbc"/>
   <ds:KeyInfo xmlns:ds="http://www.w3.org/2000/09/xmldsig#">
    <ds:RetrievalMethod URI="#KeyA"
       Type="http://www.w3.org/2001/04/xmlenc#EncryptedKey"/>
    </ds:KeyInfo>
    <xenc:CipherData>
     <xenc:CipherValue>B457V645B45........</xenc:CipherValue>
    </xenc:CipherData>
   </xenc:EncryptedData>
  </SOAP:Body>
</SOAP:Envelope>
```

Fig. 3.2. Encryted XML Embedded in SOAP Message According to WS-Security

mechanism checking the identity of the requester. Before a request can be evaluated and access granted or denied the requester has to be authenticated. In our context authentication is neither a Security Objective nor a Security Policy. It is considered a technical concept.

Authentication may generally be performed based on:

- something the subject may know (e.g., pin, password, pass phrase, shared secret),
- something the subject may possess (e.g., key, card, token), or
- physical attributes of the subject (e.g., biometrics).

In SOA, authentication occurs at the application- or the SOAP layer instead of relying on transport- and HTTP-layer authentication schemes (e.g., SSL and TLS). The reasons are, for one, that transport layer security is limited to point-to-point interactions, and two, that applications cannot directly retrieve security context information (username, role and/or password of requester) from the transport layer.

Leaving authentication to the application inevitably leads to interoperability problems: in a distributed, heterogenous environment the various applications at the endpoints will, in all likelihood, implement proprietary solutions. Securing communication between all peers turns into a nightmare.

Thus, the most efficient way to realize authentication in SOA, is the integration of security mechanisms in the SOAP message structure. However, SOAP does not provide a specific security model for its protocol. Instead, it supports security extensions inside the SOAP headers for various security models and mechanisms. WS-Security is designed to incorporate existing security mechanisms for authentication (e.g., X509 certificates, Kerberos tickets, username tokens etc.). The way on how to embed a specific format is defined in token profiles.

Nevertheless, WS-Security does not support much beyond its capability to integrate security tokens. These tokens, incorporating security claims, need to be verified, policies need to be advertised, tokens may need to be mapped from one technology to another etc. This is covered by Advanced Web Services Security Standards building on top of the three basic standards.

3.5.3 Advanced Web Services Security Standards

In this section we briefly introduce advanced Web services standards. The specifications cover application level security concerns that go much beyond what can be covered trough the standards presented in the last section. We confine ourselves to a verbal description without giving code examples as the relevant standards will be covered in-depth as needed in the second part of the book.

The *Extensible Access Control Markup Language (XACML)* is an OASIS standard supporting the specification of authorization policies to access (Web) services [147]. The standard defines a language for the formulation of policies and describes the messages for related queries between components of the security infrastructure. It specifies functionalities needed for the processing of access control policies and defines an abstract data flow model between functional components. The *Role Based Access Control Profile of XACML 2.0* extends the standard for expressing policies that use Role Based Access Control (RBAC) with a scope confined to core and hierarchical RBAC [29].

Example: The Tax Advisor may want to control access to his local services by his employees or external parties through a reference monitor acting as a security proxy to Web services. Every service call would be intercepted, the requester authenticated through some credentials (e.g., message signature), and his rights would be checked against a machine-readable policy stored in XACML format. Once access granted, the service request is forwarded to the application.

XACML is closely related to the *Security Assertion Markup Language (SAML)*, which is the XML-based framework for exchanging security assertions [67]. SAML is integrated into XACML as a profile [30]. It supports the integration of further security-related information – so-called assertions – into the SOAP header.

Example: In a slightly more complex scenario involving many parties, the Tax Advisor may only want to authenticate once (e.g., with an identitiy providing third party), to get an assertion in the form of an Authentication Statement and have this information propagated automatically through tokens when accessing services of further parties (e.g., Municipality, Notary etc.). These parties can check up with the party that issued the assertion.

The *XML Key Management Specification (XKMS)* describes how developers can integrate access to Public Key Infrastructures in order to secure inter-application communication especially in SOA environments [113]. The specification describes how to use XML- and Web services based interfaces and protocols to third parties providing "expensive" cryptographic services. XKMS consists of two parts - the XML Key Information Service Specification (XKISS) and the XML Key Registration Service Specification (XKRSS). The specifications define specific protocols that can be used for the exchange of messages between an XKMS client and an XKMS server implementation.

Example: The Tax Advisor could rely on XKMS messaging to retrieve certificates from a trusted third party (e.g., certificate authority) to verify the signatures of parties he needs to authenticate.

WS-Trust [33] is based on the security mechanisms of *WS-Security* and defines an extensible model for establishing and maintaining trust relationships across security domains. In SOA, trust is usually realized through the issuance, exchange and validation of security tokens, services offered by a Security Token Service. WS-Trust also defines necessary extensions to the SOAP message structure as well as the protocol bewteen parties relying on and offering the services.

Example: Any peer in the said scenario may need to get some credentials in the form of security tokens from a Security Token Service for authentication with his partners. The format for requesting the tokens is described in WS-Trust. Another example would be the request to a Security Token Service to map from one format (e.g., username token) to another (e.g., Kerberos ticket).

WS-SecureConversation offers features for the establishment of a context for secure communication similar to the concept of HTTPS [32]. Instead of leveraging transport layer security it is based on application-level messaging. It is a protocol that uses a concept based on public keys for the exchange of session keys for message encryption and signature. It thereby provides enhanced efficiency.

WS-Federation realizes the concept of federated security, which allows a set of stakeholders to define a virtual security domain [41]. The specification standardizes the way companies share identities with each other. This is the case whenever authentication and authorization systems are spread across corporate boundaries. Together, *WS-Trust* and *WS-Federation* provide a model to create and broker trust within and across federations.

Example: The Tax Advisor may want to communicate (over Web services interaction) with regular partners in a more efficient way. He could do so by establishing and sharing a security context with e.g., the Municipality. This would also allow him to derive much more performant session keys to secure communication. This increases the overall performance and the security of subsequent exchanges.

4

Domain Architectures

In this chapter, we establish a frame of reference for terms and concepts related to *Model Driven Software Development (MDSD)*. The core concept of MDSD is the *Domain Architecture*. It represents the conceptual framework for the realization of engineering activities according to the paradigm of MDSD.

This chapter is organized as follows. We start with an explanation of how the present work relates to existing approaches, like the OMG's Model Driven Architecture, and extends the concept of MDSD towards *Model Driven Security* (Section 4.1). We give a precise definition of our understanding of Model Driven Software Development (Section 4.2), followed by a definition of three building blocks (Sections 4.3, 4.4, 4.5) of the abstract concept of a Domain Architecture (Section 4.6). The Domain Architecture is usually implemented with a framework for MDSD (Section 4.7). Taking a special focus on security engineering, we specialize the concept of a Domain Architecture to Model Driven Security (Section 4.8).

4.1 Model Driven Software Development

Meta-modeling is a key activity in Model Driven Software Development (MDSD). Meta-models specify the abstract syntax – the language – of the concepts that need to be modeled. MDSD aims at facilitating transformations, taking models as input (source) and generating either code or models as output (target). Transformations from source to target models are defined on the basis of source and target meta-models. Code generation uses code templates defined on the basis of meta-models of the target language. In the sections to follow, we provide a brief sketch of those concepts. We will need them for the realization of the SECTET-approach.

4.1.1 The Unified Modeling Language

The Unified Modeling Language is the software industry's de-facto standard for software modeling. It is a wide-spread graphical language for modeling object-oriented systems. Many tools implement the standard and define profiles for various specific modeling purposes.

The specification differentiates between the abstract syntax and the notation of a language. The abstract syntax defines the language elements used to build models. It is independent of the notation (also called concrete syntax) which defines the graphical representation of these syntactical elements. UML supports the description of structural and behavioral aspects of a software system by different model element types and corresponding diagram types.

Generally, the advantages of using UML 2.0 for MDA are the following (adapted from [92]):

1. Separation of abstract and concrete syntax
2. Extensibility trough profiling mechanisms
3. Platform independence
4. De-facto industry standard
5. Object constraint language (OCL) tightly integrated

In our work, we use the version 2.0 of UML ([195] and [193]) for the modeling of various aspects of security-critical scenarios. For example, Activity Diagrams are used to specify inter-organizational workflows (e.g., the interaction between the Company, the Tax Advisor and the Municipality in our example in Section 2.1.2 on page 16) as well executable processes (e.g., an executable BPEL Process for the Workflow Management System of the Tax Advisor). Class Diagrams are used for the modeling of service interfaces (e.g., the Web service sendAnnualStatement offered by the Tax Advisor), documents (e.g., the annual statement sent to the Tax Advisor) and role models (e.g., the roles Junior Clerk, Senior Clerk and Chartered Accountant inside of the Tax Advisor's domain).

Nevertheless, we use the mechanisms of the Meta-Object Facility for the integration of the various models into one "language". The modeling of security-critical scenarios as well as the integration of all models at the meta-level is covered in Chapter 7.

4.1.2 The Meta-Object Facility

Meta-models describe possible model structures. They define the language elements, also called the abstract syntax, and the context-dependent meaning, the static semantic, of a modeling language. The abstract syntax of a modeling language needs to be modeled with a meta-modeling language, which itself also needs to be defined. Seen in this way, the notion of meta-model is actually a concept that has to be understood in relative terms; theoretically, the cascade could be set forth endlessly.

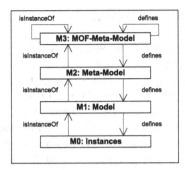

Fig. 4.1. The Four Levels of the MOF Meta-model

The OMG's Meta Object Facility, which is at the core of the MDA approach, uses models for specifying metadata; these models are called meta-models. The modeling framework of MOF - actually a subset of the UML - supports the definition of modeling languages. The OMG provides a mapping of the meta-model to XML (XML Metadata Interchange [152]). Together with application programming interfaces in various languages this can be used to build repository infrastructures, with model elements that can be accessed and processed with various languages (Java Metadata Interface). The MOF Metadata architecture is a reference model for meta-modeling. It identifies four model levels (Figure 4.1).

The instance level (M0) and the model level (M1) are those concepts familiar to the developer of object-oriented software systems. In M1, the developer defines classes, that are instantiated to objects at the M0 level.

The M2 level provides the means to model concepts needed for the M1 level. For example, the object-oriented concept of a class and its related attributes is defined at the M2 level through class elements defined in the MOF meta-model. M2 level elements are themselves instances of the MOF meta-meta-model class elements (M3).

The UML is a modeling language that is defined and formalized at the M2 level. For example, the UML concept of a class and its attributes and their relationship is defined at the M2 level in the UML Infrastructure [193].

We will use the MOF for the integration of all models at the meta-level (cf. Chapter 7). Our work is based on version 1.4 of the MOF [154].

4.1.3 Model Driven Software Development

The paradigm of Model Driven Software Development (MDSD) evolved as a response to challenges imposed by productivity and risk management issues in the ever changing complex area of software engineering. Its primary purpose was to alleviate the burden by offering tools and methods to counter the problem at its roots: streamlining of the software engineering process, switching to open software architectures and supporting the management of dependencies between components [180].

Whereas at the beginning of the 90ies, software engineering was heavily dominated by the paradigm of Computer Aided Software Engineering and Fourth Generation Languages, the last years of the decade saw the emergence of tools supporting the new paradigm of Object Oriented Software Development, which among other things brought about the Unified Modeling language. Powerful modeling tools and integrated development environments supported the new notation and promised a significant gain in productivity by offering wizards that could generate code skeletons for classes and even code for graphical user interfaces out of customizable blueprints.

But still, the tools did not live up to the promise; they were too inflexible in terms of change management. The propagation of changes in the design of a component could not be propagated through all the levels of abstraction. These circumstances led to the emergence of the OMG initiative "Model Driven Architecture", whose basic premise is the promotion of standards and methods for the engineering of software systems guaranteeing a minimum level of portability and Interoperability.

4.1.4 Model Driven Architecture

The main idea behind Model Driven Architectures (MDA) is the switch of focus from technical detail to more abstract concepts – so called models – that are principally more stable, more intuitive, and would change less. In software engineering, a model is an abstract representation of some system structure, function or behaviour. This basically means that through the use of models, MDA addressed a much broader audience. Additionally, the concepts were valid for a much longer period of time.

In MDA, a concept is basically captured through models at various levels of abstraction. The OMG's paradigm of Model Driven Architectures specifies three levels of abstraction:

- The Platform Independent Model captures the domain level knowledge and abstracts from implementation details of the target architecture.
- The Platform Specific Model (PSM) describes the system on its intended platform (e.g. BPEL4WS) by integrating platform specific syntax and semantics.
- The Implementation Specific Model (ISM) represents the reference architecture that acts as the runtime environment at local partner nodes.

Applying the MDA approach means capturing abstract domain-level specification in a PIM, transforming the PIM into a PSM through Model-to-model Transformation and / or transforming either the PIM directly or the PSM into an ISM through Model-to-code Transformation.

We extend the MDA approach towards Model Driven Security in the sense that we integrate security requirements at the abstract level into the PIM.

The PIM and the PSM are mapped onto each other and finally translated into configuration artefacts for the runtime environment.

4.1.5 Model Driven Security

The growing popularity of standards related to Web services, workflows and security during the past years fostered the implementation of powerful infrastructures supporting interoperability for inter-organizational workflows. The paradigms of Model Driven Software Development and specifically Model Driven Architecture (MDA) made it possible to realize their full potential [92].

The OMG is promoting the approach of MDA and the use of related standards like UML and MOF as a means for the reduction of development costs and the improvement of application quality. Model Driven Security Architectures (e.g., [45]) extend the MDA approach in the sense that the Platform Independent Model integrates security requirements and the Platform Specific Model specifies a target reference architecture acting as the security infrastructure for the runtime. Security requirements map to executable (XML-) artifacts onto the platform.

4.2 A Definition of Model Driven Software Development

Model Driven Software Development (MDSD) is a technology and standards independent engineering methodology based on the concept of *Models*[1]. Models describe system aspects significant to a particular problem, in that way abstracting from the system under study up to a certain level. Models can be defined as [174]:

> *"a set of statements about some system under study."*

The degree of abstraction depends on the problem's nature. Useful modeling requires the application of abstraction techniques like *Reduction*, which is the selection of relevant properties, *Generalization*, which is the selection of relevant similarities between otherwise different elements to form an entity, and *Classification*, which is the identification of different types or concepts.

The concept diagram in Figure 4.2 depicts the concepts and notions used in MDSD and the relation between them. For an engineer, a *Problem Space* structures the real world, by focusing on a specific set of problems (e.g., how to model security-critical worklfows in e-government). It allows him to express the issues of concerns with a spezialized terminology tailored for his world of expertise – his *Domain*. The *Solution Space* is related to the Problem Space

---

[1] This is why we use MDSD instead of MDA, which is associated to an array of specifc standards (e.g., UML and MOF), for the clarification of our concepts.

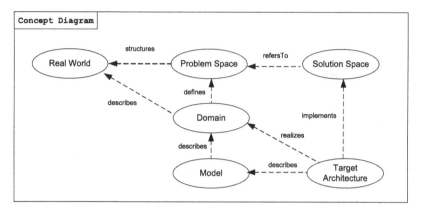

Fig. 4.2. Concepts of Model Driven Software Development

as it offers the means to design solutions (e.g., security architectures, management procedures etc.) to those problems. In the engineering world, the solution often corresponds to a specific system design or even implementation, which is called a *Reference* or a *Target Architecture.*[2]

Models are used to reason about problems in a specific Problem Space, and to design solutions in the language of the Solution Space. The Problem Space is formally captured through one or more *Domains*. A Domain can be defined as [180]:

> *"... a field of application delimitated by a specific area of interest.".*

Accordingly, the knowledge about the "area" (aka Domain) is systematically captured through ontologies, which are abstract representations of entities relevant to the envisaged context.

4.3 Domain Specific Languages

Key-aspects of a Domain's Problem Space are expressed with the help of a graphical or textual modeling language in a formal way. More specifically, a *Domain Specific Language* (DSL) is a [203]:

> *"... concise, precise and processable description of a viewpoint, concern or aspect of a system, given in a notation that suits the people who specify that particular viewpoint, concern or aspect.".*

The concept diagram in Figure 4.3 shows the main dependencies of the concept and notions of Model Driven Software Development around its central term: the *Domain*.

---

[2] We use the term *Reference Architecture* in context of the SECTET-framework.

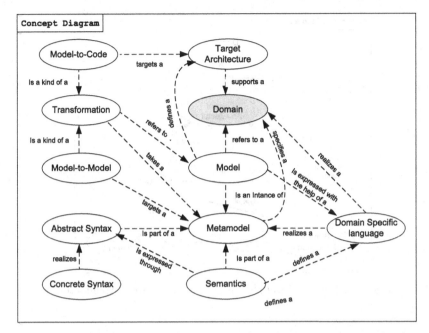

Fig. 4.3. Relationship of Core Concepts in MDSD (Adapted from [180]

A *Domain* is defined with the help of one or more meta-models. Also
known as the domain's abstract syntax, a meta-model defines the elemental
syntactical blocks for capturing a particular problem or scenario in a formal
way in terms of a model. A model is a particular instance of the meta-model.

The *Concrete Syntax* defines possible notations for the use of the language,
which can be either graphical or textual.

The *Semantics* of a language capture its meaning in context and define
criteria for an expression's or a model's well-formedness. Semantics either can
be defined formally or should at least be documented in some informal, verbose
way. The degree of formality is not to be mistaken by the differentiation
between textual or symbolic languages, which are often thought to be the only
means to a rigorous formalization, and visual and diagrammatic languages,
relying on visual formalisms.

All three concepts together form a *Domain Specific Language* corresponding to a modeling language that captures key-aspects of a Domain's Problem
Space in a formal way. A DSL for our example from Section 2.1.2 would allow
a security engineer to capture all security aspects relevant to security-critical
worklfows in e-government. In Chapter 7 we will show how to elaborate the
DSL for that specific Domain.

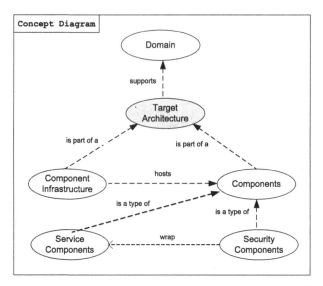

Fig. 4.4. Relationship between Domain and Target Architecture

4.4 The Target Architecture

The *Target Architecture* (TA) represents the target (runtime) for the realization of the Domain (Figure 4.4). TA implements application functionality and supports non-functional requirements, like performance, scalability, and security. The building blocks of a TA are components, modular software entities, which are accessed through an interface.

We generally differentiate between *Service Components*, which implement application functionality, like the workflow engine or modular Web services and *Security Components*, which enforce Security Objectives specified as Security Policies. The component infrastructure provides the technical underpinning of the TA and acts as a middleware integrating the components.

In Chapter 8 we will design a Target Architecture for the enforcement of security at the partners' nodes .

4.5 Model-(to-model-)to-code Transformation

MDSD aims at facilitating transformations, taking models as input (source) and generating either code or models as output (target). The concept of *Transformation* links a source Domain to a target Domain. Figure 4.5 shows the types of transformations along two dimensions.

Horizontal Transformations take a source model and transform it into a target model thereby staying at the same level of abstraction.

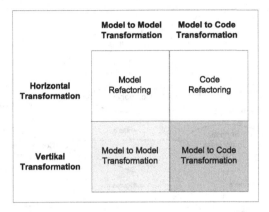

	Model to Model Transformation	Model to Code Transformation
Horizontal Transformation	Model Refactoring	Code Refactoring
Vertikal Transformation	Model to Model Transformation	Model to Code Transformation

Fig. 4.5. Transformation Types in Model Driven Software Development

As an example, Horizontal Transformations are performed for refactoring purposes – a controlled technique of software engineering where code elements (or model elements at the same level of abstraction) are rearranged in order to improve the design. It can be seen as an informal activity – also phrased as "cleaning up" the code – without changing the code's external behaviour or the intended purpose in case of model refactoring [90].

Vertical Transformations transform a source model into a target model whose level of abstraction is closer to the Reference Architecture, resulting either in a Platform Specific Model, with some semantics of the technical platform captured in the models or an Implementation Specific Model, which corresponds to executable code (Please refer to Section 4.1.4 and [151] for more information on PIM, PSM, and ISM).

In the case of Model Driven Software Development, a transformation primarily links the Domain to the Target Architecture (Figure 4.5). We differentiate between *Model-to-code Transformation* and *Model-to-model Transformation*. Both take an instance of the source meta-model as input. Model-to-model Transformation generates a model based on a target meta-model, whereas Model-to-code Transformation produces platform and implementation specific generated *Code Artifacts*, in our case by taking templates that capture the idioms of the Target Architecture and filling in relevant parts.

We will use Model-to-model Transformation to generate some model elements for executable BPEL processes out of the specification of an inter-organizational workflow modeled as a UML Activity Diagram in Chapter 9. Model-to-code Tansformation will be used for the generation of the executable Security Artefacts also in Chapter 9.

Generated code can be adapted manually to a *Modified Artifact*. Both artefacts – Modified and Code Artifacts – configure components of the RA (Figure 4.6).

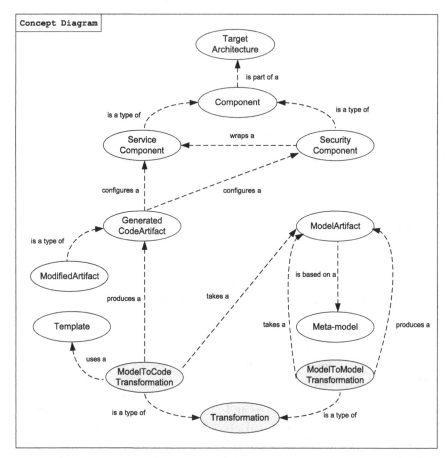

Fig. 4.6. Relationship between Main Concepts of Model Transformation

4.6 Domain Architecture

A *Domain Architecture* consists of the Domain Specific Languange consisting of the domain's meta-models (cf. Section 4.3), the Target Architecture (cf. Section 4.4) and all the transformations (cf. Section 4.5).

We define a Domain Architecture as a ([165]):

> "... *generic, organizational structure or design for software systems in a domain. The domain architecture contains the designs that are intended to satisfy requirements specified in the domain model. A domain architecture can be adapted to create designs for software systems within a domain and also provides a framework for configuring assets within individual software systems.*"

4.7 Framework

A *Framework* consists of a suite of tools supporting the realization of extensible and adaptable concepts. A framework for Model Driven Software Development supports the implementation of Domain Architectures by providing tools for one or more of the following tasks:

1. extending the meta-models of the Domain Specific Language
2. building the models (e.g., graphically like UML tools)
3. testing and validating the models and the transformations
4. specifying mappings between model elements and transformations
5. modifying generated artefacts
6. deploying the configuration artefacts
7. monitoring the Reference Architecture
8. versioning and release management

As an example, the Domain Architecture for securitiy-critical inter-organizational workflows in e-government is implemented with the SECTET-Framework (cf. Chapter 5).

4.8 Model Driven Security

4.8.1 Definition

The goal of *Model Driven Security (MDS)* is the definition of a generic framework supporting the systematic transformation of models integrating security requirements to executable artefacts for configurable security architectures. An MDS-framework realizes an extensible Domain Architecture for security-critical (application-) scenarios.

4.8.2 Extensions to the Problem Space

Figure 4.7 shows the extensions to the Problem and Solution Space of Model Driven Software Development resulting in Model Driven Security.

Modeling Extensions

First, the extension introduces the abstract concept of Security Concerns into the *Problem Space*. If security is considered as the condition of absolute protection against harm, loss, and danger, we can define a *Security Concern* as the sum of all known and unknown threats to the state of security in terms of a specific security target. An example Security Concern may be related to the threat that an unauthorized third party may read the Company's tax file due to some leaks, flawed security administration, or missing awareness on the Tax Advisor's side.

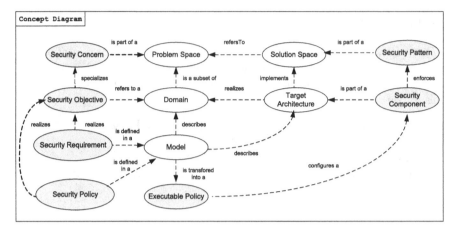

Fig. 4.7. Conceptual Security Extensions for Model Driven Security

A *Security Objective* specializes the abstract notion of Security Concern by setting a domain specific context (e.g., confidentiality of a tax file sent from the Municipality to the Tax Advisor in an inter-organizational workflow).

A *Security Policy* – or a *Security Requirement* in the context of a Security Analysis – ultimately realizes a Security Objective based on a specific security concept (e.g., realizing confidentiality by granting access to confidential data to authopized peers based on their roles). The enforcement of a Security Policy is guaranteed by mostly technical mechanisms of the Reference Architecture (cf. Section 4.8.2).

Enforcement Extensions

The transformation process takes a Security Policy and produces *Security Artefacts*. The latter configure *Security Components* that provide all services needed for the enforcement of one or more specific abstract *Security Patterns* – a concept currently getting a lot of attention as a promising approach to efficient security engineering.

A security pattern can be defined in the following way [172]:

> *"A security pattern describes a particular recurring security problem that arises in specific contexts, and presents a well-proven generic solution for it. The solution consists of a set of interacting roles that can be arranged into multiple concrete design structures, as well as a process to create one particular such structure."*

Patterns can potentially be identified at any level of abstraction, and, could thus be considered as an omnipresent concept in Model Driven Security. Model Driven Security integrates the concept, but it does so by applying the concept to the technical layer. Secure solutions are designed based on

Security Patterns, hence capitalizing on best practices in the area of security engineering.

For example SECTET's Target Architecture is realized according to the proxy pattern [172]: every service request is intercepted by a kind of security filter implementing and enforcing the Security Policies. The design of the SECTET Target Architecture is discussed into details in Chapter 8.

Part II

Realizing SOA Security

In Part II, we show how to apply concepts of Model Driven Security to a Problem Domain defined as "security-critical inter-organizational workflows in e-governement". This domain refers to a category of scenarios that feature specific patterns in their architectural design and thereby exhibit commonalities in the nature of arising security concerns.

The goal of part II is the specification of an extensible software framework that supports the realization and the management of SOA-based workflow scenarios according to the stated paradigm. The specification was implemented as the SECTET-Framework for Model Driven Security. The framework implements a concept known as a *Domain Architecture* – a concept introduced in Part I Chapter 4.

Part II is structured as follows. We start with Chapter 5, where we introduce a motivating case study from e-government. This will serve as a running example throughout Part II.

In Chapter 6 policy modeling is complemented by a *Security Analysis* in context of the Problem Domain. Functional aspects of target systems are modeled at various layers of abstraction thereby facilitating a comprehensive analysis of security requirements and related risk. Advisable security controls can be identified and serve as a starting point to the generation of executable security services or artefacts.

In Chapter 7, we start building the first of the three blocks of the SECTET-Domain Architecture, the Domain Specific Language (DSL). The design of the DSL is implemented for a UML-based modeling tool and sample policies are specified.

In Chapter 8, we present the Web-services based Reference Architecture responsible for the enforcement of security policies at peer nodes. It represents a blueprint for a runtime environment for functional as well as for Security Components.

Chapter 9, bridges the gap between the policy models and the Reference Architecture by introducing the Model-to-Code Transformator. The transformator takes the models as input and generates code for the configuration of the Reference Architecture based on rules.

Chapter 10, discusses practical matters on how to manage the software and security policies in a distributed, de-centralized environment.

We close Part II, with Chapter 11, where we show how the three building blocks of the SECTET-framework can be extended to cope with a category of advanced security requirements and policies – among them *Dynamic Access Control Policies, Rights Delegation Policies*, the *Qualified Signature*, and *Usage Control Policies*. This Chapter does not describe a full implementation but rather addresses key issues in Model Driven Security Engineering, many of them subject to current scientific research. Nevertheless, we sketch a viable path to proof-of-concept prototypes, that might be useful, but at least relevant in an industrial setting.

5

Sectino – A Motivating Case Study from E-Government

In this chapter, we introduce a motivating case study from e-government. We will illustrate the methodology for the systematic design and realization of security-critical inter-organizational workflows with a portion of a workflow-scenario drawn from the e-government use case "Municipal Tax Collection". The case was elaborated within the project SECTINO, a joint research project between the research group Quality Engineering at the University of Innsbruck and the Austrian Research Centre Seibersdorf Research GmbH. The case will serve as a running example throughout Part II.

The scenario describes the Web services based interaction between a tax payer (the *Company*), a business agent (the *Tax Advisor*) and a public service provider (the *Municipality*). The document flow between the actors will have to comply to security policies based on basic security requirements like *Confidentiality*, *Integrity*, and *Non-repudiation*. More advanced, complex security requirements will be introduced in Chapter 11.

5.1 Problem Context

The project SECTINO, was a joint research project between the research group Quality Engineering at the University of Innsbruck and the Austrian Research Centre Seibersdorf. SECTINO started in May 2004 and ended in April 2006.

One of the project's main goals was the analysis of security issues that may specifically stem from the migration of a traditional paper-based workflow to a flexible and manageable e-government based solution. Flexibility and usability in that context meant a "use-friendly" solution supporting the intuitive configuration and management of ever-changing scenarios. The solution finally lay in a model-driven approach, where the necessary run-time artifacts for the target architecture were generated through model transformation.

5.2 Project Mission

The mission statement of the project SECTINO was phrased as follows :

> *"The development of a framework supporting the systematic realization and management of e-government related workflows with a special emphasis on security requirements."*

The project's vision was formulated with a focus on the domain of e-government but the framework was to be generic enough to be applicable to a broad array of scenarios from other industries. The ideas are currently applied to the healthcare industry. The project deliverables were defined as:

1. a method for the systematic design of security-critical, inter-organizational workflows.
2. a proof-of-concept prototype that allows for the systematic mapping of design artefacts to runtime code.
3. a reference architecture for the implementation of secure workflows across domain boundaries (based on Web services standards and technologies).

5.3 Expected Benefits

The project results were expected to lead to the following benefits:

1. *Early integration of security* into the engineering process: developers would not need to care about the integration of security during the development phase. Security requirements can be identified in the Analysis Phase and specified as Security Policies in the context of the business scenario. This should ideally happen in the language of the domain experts - through an intuitive graphical modeling language. The resulting models are directly configuring security components of a target architecture.
2. *Correct implementation* of security: the framework would automatically transform the models into executable code artifacts configuring the security components relying on proven security mechanisms as public key encryption, digital signature and logging etc.. This would guarantee the correct implementation of the Security Requirements.
3. *Flexible model-level adjustments:* changes of Security Requirements during development or adjustments to Security Policies during run-time would only require model-level adjustments. The framework would take care of reconfiguring the security components thereby supporting a flexible and iterative approach to security engineering.
4. *Abstraction from technology* would be achieved through a generic architecture for SOA security: security components provide complex security services based on standard security technologies and mechanisms. They

enforce security requirements by wrapping services or application components. Through their modularity the components can be added to the target architecture and configured as needed e.g., once the service components are implemented.

5.4 Scenario Description

In Austria, wages paid to employees of an enterprise are subject to the municipal tax. According to the traditional process, corporations have to send an annual statement via their tax advisor to the municipality. They get back a tax assessment with the amount of due taxes. Communication is done through traditional mail. As a motivating running example running throughout part II as we realize our approach, we will consider a simplified "electronic" version of the workflow: it describes the collection of municipal tax as a service offered. In this scenario the interaction occurs through the exchange of digital documents. The process had to be realized in a peer-to-peer fashion.

The workflow-scenario "Municipal Tax Collection" (Figure 5.1) describes a collaboration interaction between three participants: a tax-payer (the Client), a business agent (the Tax Advisor) and a public service provider (the Municipality). The latter is responsible for collecting the tax. It checks the declaration of the annual statement, calculates the tax duties and returns a tax assessment notice to the tax advisor, who informs his client. The example illustrates various aspects of the relationship between the externally observable choreography, capturing the message exchange between all roles and related internal process orchestrations of the individual collaborating partners' nodes.

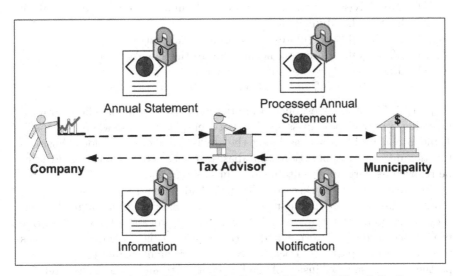

Fig. 5.1. The Online Version of the Process Municipal Tax Collection

5.4.1 Requirements

In our case, the stakeholders in this public administration process agreed to implement a new online service, which offers citizens and companies to submit their annual tax statements using Web services.

Legal Constraints and Assumptions

Due to various legal considerations, the process was realized in a decentralized, peer-to-peer fashion. The workflow specification should integrate various Security Requirements like Integrity, Confidentiality and Non-repudiation. We assume that there is no central control of the inter-organizational workflow. The workflow is designed by representatives of the partners involved in the collaboration effort. Actions are allocated to specific partners in the Global Workflow. Every action corresponds to some business logic implemented at a partner node.

Use Cases

The distributed process involves three types of actors: the local governmental authorities (Municipality), the citizens and/or the companies (Company) and a group of business agents providing legal and financial consulting services (Tax Advisor). The collaboration process was roughly specified as follows:

1. The Company sends an annual statement to its Tax Advisor;
2. The Tax Advisor does some internal processing on the document (e.g., formatting, complement legal data etc.);
3. The Tax Advisor forwards the processed annual statement on behalf of his client to the Municipality;
4. The Municipality calculates the amount of tax duties;
5. The Municipality returns a notification to the Tax Advisor;
6. The Tax Advisor processes the notification;
7. The Tax Advisor informs the Company about its tax duties.

Steps 1, 3, 5 and 7 correspond to interaction activities in the choreography, involving a peer-to-peer message flow between participants, whereas steps 2, 4 and 6 can be identified as being the "links" to the actors' local business functionality (e.g., applications, databases, services etc.), which would later be realized as parts of executable local processes.

Figure 5.2 shows the use cases. The grey shaded bubbles, outside the boxes, represent use case requirements local to every partner. Once agreed upon, they are of no further relevance to the realization process of the collaborative process scenario. They correspond to those parts of the scenario the role has to provide to its partners. Local process steps remain opaque to interaction partners. The use cases inside of the box capture those functionalities related

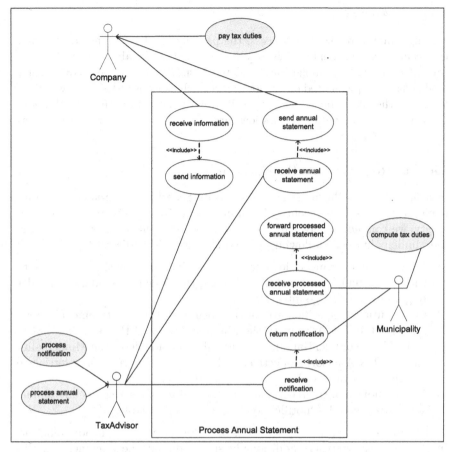

Fig. 5.2. Use Cases for the Process "Municipal Tax Collection"

to the interactions between the roles – also called the public part of a local process. Every interaction consists of two parts, one initiating the sending of a document and one waiting for reception of the document. The latter then triggers the local workflow at the partner's node. Notice: the sum of all public process parts is called Process Annual Statement; it is a subset of the inter-organizational workflow scenario "Municipal Tax Collection".

5.4.2 Security Requirements

In this section we give an example of how a first iteration of a Security Requirements specification may be carried out. A comprehensive analysis is performed in Chapter 6.

Security Analysis

Throughout the realization process, the participants have to make sure that the security requirements, wich were first defined at the abstract level, in the context of an inter-organizational collaboration, are reliably and consistently modeled and implemented on the lower levels (this means at the local workflow level and the component level). Security related aspects within the development of inter-organizational workflows are tackled by the Security Analysis as presented in Chapter 6.

Security Requirements Specification

In a first step, the business analysts specify Security Requirements guaranteeing basic end-to-end security in an inter-organizational workflow. For simplicity, we confine ourselves to the interaction between the Tax Advisor and the Municipality. The following requirements were identified:

1. Integrity: all exchanged documents have to be signed by the sending party with a "System Signature" when leaving the domain boundaries in order to guarantee message integrity.
2. Confidentiality: specific parts of the document "annual statement" - flowing from the Tax Advisor to the Municipality - and the returned "notificationT are confidential, and should only be readable to the Municipality and the Tax Advisor, respectively. This concerns information referring to the annual income and the tax identification number.
3. Non-repudiation: the reception and the sending of the documents "annual statement" and the "notification" must not be deniable.

In many e-government applications, a technical signature is not sufficient. In our case, the partners additionally specified that the document "notification" sent by the Municipality has to be signed personally by at least two clerks (which corresponds to a "Qualified Signature" according to the Austrian E-Government Law [158]). Although we may integrate advanced security requirements, like the Qualified Signature at the meta-model level, we primarily focus on the three basic end-to-end security requirements for our running example. The set of supported security requirements is extended in Chapter 11.

5.5 Results

At the end of the two years term, the project efforts materialized into a proof of concept demonstrator proving the applicability of the concept of Model Driven Security in an industrial context. Basic Security Requirements were identified, Security Policies could be specified for documents flowing between various independent partner-roles in an inter-organizational worklfow. Security Policies were confined to Confidentiality, Integrity, and Non-repudiation.

6

Security Analysis

This chapter is devoted to the continuous security analysis of service oriented systems during design and operation. We present the ProSecO framework which offers concepts and a process model for the elicitation of security objectives and requirements, evaluation of risks and documentation of security controls. The goal of ProSecO is to provide the analyst at any time during design and operation with information about the security state of the system.

Core ideas of ProSecO are the interweaved elicitation and documentation of functional and security properties based on system models, and the clear separation of business oriented and technical information. The kind of information ProsecO handles is in wide parts informal and non-executable. In this respect it complements the SECTET-framework which focuses on executable artifacts.

This chapter is structured as follows: we first give an overview in Section 6.1, then present the Functional System view tailored towards the functional aspects of service oriented systems in Section 6.2. Section 6.3 presents the ProSecO security micro-process, whereas Section 6.4 focuses on the specific aspect of access control. Finally, in Section 6.5 we give an overview of related work.

6.1 Overview

An important step towards the systematic design of secure applications is the tight integration of security in the whole development process. In too many real-world projects security is conceived as a mere technical aspect and security controls are designed in an ad-hoc way. This causes major drawbacks for the resulting system.

First, threats originating in the social or organizational context of the system may not be adequately covered. Examples of such threats are social engineering attacks where the attacker uses human interaction to compromise the system.

Second, the realized security solutions may not be in line with the requirements. Since most security controls have an impact on factors like user flexibility, system performance and budget a thorough analysis of requirements and possible security controls is an important step in a systematic design process.

Third, compliance plays a crucial role for many security-critical systems. For instance, in the e-government and e-health area privacy protection and authentication are connected with strict legal regulations. Moreover, regulations like Basel II and the Sarbanes Oxley Act have an increasing influence on applications in e-business. As a consequence the validation of compliance requirements plays an important role in many service oriented applications. A prerequisite for such a validation are interconnected requirements and solutions.

For the kind of systems we consider the following assumptions are characteristic.

- The networks of stakeholders and services are highly dynamic, both concerning stakeholder types, stakeholder instances and the workflows to be run. For example, a healthcare network may start with the exchange of health data among hospitals, other stakeholders like general practitioners and pharmacies may join the network in a later stage.
- The stakeholders are heterogeneous in their organizational structure, security requirements and security infrastructure, e.g., comparing hospitals with continuously administrated security infrastructures and general practitioners with ad-hoc systems.
- There may be a high number of stakeholder instances (e.g., millions of patients, thousands of hospitals) requiring complex infrastructures and effective engineering techniques.

From these basic assumptions and requirements we derive two goals for the security analysis of service oriented solutions.

6.1.1 Modularity

Modularity strives for a subdivision into independent layers, views and concepts, so to harness system complexity. This is relevant in three aspects.

- Different levels of abstraction can be analyzed independently of each other (e.g., separating organizational requirements from technical requirements).
- Different subdomains can be analyzed independently of each other (e.g., separating the analysis of the organizational structure of hospitals and general practitioners).
- The notions of requirements, risks and controls are clearly separated and may be considered independently of each other.

6.1.2 Traceability

Traceability traditionally aims at establishing the chronological interrelation of uniquely identifiable entities in a verifiable way. We differentiate two cases.

- Security aspects can be traced along the levels of abstraction starting with general security objectives (which may be derived from legal regulations) and arriving at the implemented security controls. Security controls may range from organizational rules (e.g., four eyes principle) to technical components (encryption, firewalls).
- The analyzer is provided with aggregated information about the state of the security analysis process at any time.

6.1.3 Model-driven Configuration of Security Services

In this Section we focus on the requirements engineering aspect and present the security analysis method ProSecO targeted towards the design of security-critical inter-organizational applications. ProSecO is based on the following two major principles.

6.1.4 Tight Integration of Functional and Security Aspects

In most process models security requirements are treated in an unstructured way as non-functional requirements. The key idea of our method is that we put any security related aspect in the context of the functional system view (e.g., specifying which data objects have to be kept confidential or which actions are non-repudiable). The *Functional System View* describes the system at different levels of abstraction ranging from business processes to the functional and technical architecture. The elements of the Functional Model (e.g., business processes, information objects, components) drive the security analysis through their interrelations.

6.1.5 Security as a Process

We conceive security as a process accompanying the whole lifecycle of the system. The aim of this process is

- to elicitate security requirements
- to detect threats and evaluate risks
- to design and to implement security controls meeting the requirements and counteracting the risks

Security related activities are condensed in the ProSecO *security micro-process*. Each instance of the micro-process is associated with a part of the functional model and analyzes security aspects of the associated model elements. In this respect the security analysis may focus on subsystems (e.g., concerning specific stakeholders) or on specific levels of abstraction (e.g., the business level).

During systems development instances of the security micro-process are integrated with the software development process. This means that the development of functional artifacts like the software architecture is enhanced by security related activities with the goal to develop an adequate security solution.

As soon as the system gets productive the security micro-process is used to monitor the system as part of the organizations' security management process. The goals in this phase are to detect security leaks, react to changed requirements (e.g., new legal regulations) or to adapt configurations of the security architecture.

6.2 Functional System View

For describing the functional aspects of a service oriented system in a modular way we use two orthogonal concepts for layering – the *Level of Interaction* and the *Level of Abstraction*.

6.2.1 Level of Interaction

The Level of Interaction determines if the focus of modeling is global or local. The *Global View* describes aspects related with the interaction of the system's stakeholders (i.e. autonomous partners in the network), whereas the *Local View* describes aspects related with the behaviour and structure of a specific stakeholder.

The Global View is in many applications developed by consortia of the stakeholders involved. Examples of such consortia are confederations in certain businesses (e.g., chemical industry, paper industry), public initiatives (e.g., in health care or e-govenment) or other initiatives among business partners (e.g., cooperations with suppliers in e-procurement). The goal of such consortia is to enact ways of seamless cooperation through interaction of IT services. In this respect core issues of the Global View are to agree on the steps of a common business process, on the kind of data exchanged and on the services offered.

On the other side the Local View is attached with a specific stakeholder and focuses on more fine–grained aspects relevant to take part in inter-organizational processes.

6.2.2 Level of Abstraction

The Level of Abstraction determines the basic concepts used to describe the system. ProSecO distinguishes three basic levels of abstraction. The *business level* focuses on business processes, business objects and the organizational structure, the *application level* is concerned with executable components and services and the *physical level* describes the technical infrastructure.

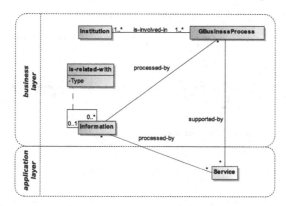

Fig. 6.1. Global Functional Meta-model

6.2.3 Functional Meta-models

Functional models in ProSecO are sets of interrelated model elements according to the ProSecO *Functional Meta Model*. The meta-model defines the concepts to describe certain aspects of a Functional Model (e.g., services, information objects, roles) and their interrelationships.

Following the categories described above the ProSecO meta-model consists of two parts – the *Global System Meta Model* and the *Local System Meta Model*. Each of these parts is layered based on the levels of abstraction.

The interdependencies between meta-model elements are both within and across layers and have the aim to support traceability from the business domain down to the technical infrastructure. These interdependencies are essential for the security analysis in driving the analysis of requirements and risks along the different levels and views.

In the following we present the meta-model elements of the ProSecO Functional Meta-model in more detail.

Figure 6.1 shows the Global Functional Meta-model, Figure 6.2 the Local Functional Meta-model. The main concepts and their interrelations are explained below.

6.2.4 Global Functional Meta-model

Institution (Business Layer) An institution instance represents an autonomous partner in the service oriented application. In the subsequent sections we also use the term *partner role* as a synonym for an institution.
Examples: The institutions *Company, Tax Advisor* and *Municipality*

Information (Business Layer) Information is an abstract concept to specify information types. Information classes may be related in various relation types such as association, composition or inheritance.
Examples: The information types *Annual Statement* and *Notification*

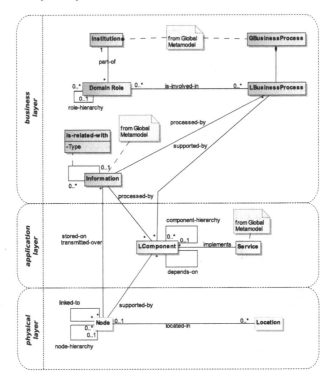

Fig. 6.2. Local Functional Meta-model

Global Business Process (Business Layer) A Business Process is a type of interaction between stakeholders. A Global Business Process models the interaction of institutions from an external point of view.

Global Business Processes are related with the institutions involved and the information types processed during the interaction.

Example: The Global Business Process *ProcessAnnualStatement* describes the process of processing an annual statement of a company as an interaction of the company, the tax advisor (considered as an institution) and the municipality.

Service (Application Layer) Services are executable components available in the network. Each service is associated with the information types it processes (e.g., as input or output).

Examples: The services *sendAnnualStatement* and *sendNotification*

The ProSecO Meta-model defines the structure of functional model elements but does not constrain their representation. This means that Functional Models may be represented both in textual or graphical ways. The ProSecO Meta-model is intended to provide a starting point for the security analysis and not as a complete meta-model for the development of service oriented applications. For the latter goal the meta-model has to be enhanced by de-

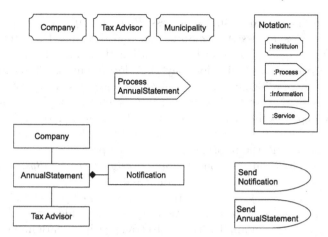

Fig. 6.3. Sample Global Functional Model

tailed structural and behavioural information. In particular, business processes may be defined based on business process notations such as BPMN [14].

Figure 6.3 shows as an example the Global Functional Model in the tax advisor case study. Notice the difference between the institution *Tax Advisor* and the information type *Tax Advisor* in the model. The institution models the tax advisor as a stakeholder taking part in the global business process whereas the information type *Tax Advisor* models the static information about tax advisors available at the business level.

ProSecO does not require complete Functional Models as input for the security analysis. The identification of interrelationships across layers is part of the initial steps within the security analysis process and may involve only a part of the model (e.g., starting from a specific business process or an information type).

6.2.5 Local Functional Meta-model

The Local Functional Meta-model describes the concepts used to model the properties of a specific stakeholder in the inter-organizational system. According to the definitions in the Global Functional System Model these stakeholders in the sequel are called *institutions*.

Domain Role (Business Layer) A domain role represents an actor in the fine-grained view of an institution.
Examples: The roles *Junior Accountant* and *Senior Accountant* at the Tax Advisor institution.

Local Business Process (Business Layer) A local business process models a fine-grained interaction of an institution as part of a global business process. A local business process is related with the global business process it is part of, the information types processed and the roles involved.

Example: The local business process *ProcessNotification* is part of the global process *ProcessAnnualStatement* and describes the internal steps of the municipality to issue the notification of an annual statement.

Local Component (Application Layer) A local component represents an application residing on the institution's domain. A component may be related with the service it implements, may be part of other components or may depend on other components and processes information objects. Moreover, local components are linked with the local business processes they support and the information types they process.

Example: The local component *MunicipalityInformationSystem* supporting the persons in charge at the Municipality.

Node (Physical Layer) A node represents technical or physical objects that are either used to store information objects (e.g., file server, USB stick, plain paper), to run applications or to transmit information. The concept of a node may be hierarchically composed and nodes may be linked with other nodes. Moreover, nodes can be linked with the components they run.

Example: The node *MunicipalityApplicationServer*

Location (Physical Layer) A location instance describes a physical location (e.g., a server room, an office) and is associated with the residing nodes.

Figure 6.4 shows a sample schematic Local Functional Model in the tax advisor case study. The model contains the local process *ProcessNotification* and the information types from the Global System Model. The relevant applications are the local *MunicipalityInformationSystem* and the Mail System for direct communication with the tax advisor and the company. Lastly the infrastructure is modeled consisting of the workstations and servers. A firewall acts as a boundary between the internal network and the Internet.

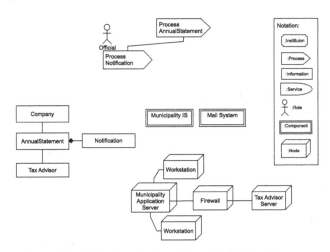

Fig. 6.4. Sample Local Functional Model

In the model of Figure 6.4 the business processes are not yet connected with applications and technical objects at the physical layer, as these dependencies are elaborated during the security analysis process.

6.3 Security Analysis Process

Core of the security analysis process are the classical actions of security analysis (as, e.g., described in the ISO 27001:2005 standard). These actions comprise

- elicitation of security requirements
- identification of threats
- evaluation of risks and
- security control engineering.

We extend this core process in two directions. First, all core actions are performed in the context of some model element and the security related information (requirements, threats, controls) is attached with these model elements. To this purpose we introduce a meta-model for the security related concepts, the *ProSecO Security Meta-model*. Each of the concepts in this meta-model is provided with a state indicating the state of analysis. For instance, a security requirement may be *pending* or *evaluated*.

Second, we conceive the core process as a micro–process that is coninuously executed on a defined part of the Functional Model. In order to support modular analysis the Functional Model is divided into sub–models with a responsible for each sub–model. For instance, there may be a responsible for the Global Functional Model and responsibles for each Local Functional Model. In this view we obtain a set of security processes concurrently executed by the sub–model responsibles on their sub–models.

In the rest of this chapter we first present the basic security concepts as a core of the analysis process. Then we give an overview of the ProSecO micro–process followed by a presentation of its subsequent steps.

6.3.1 Security Concepts

The goal of the Security Analysis Process is to attach the model elements of the Functional Model in a systematic way with security related information. Below we present the core security concepts and their interrelationships.

The ProSecO Security Meta-model is shown in Figure 6.5. In this meta-model the class *ModelElement* represents any model element of the Functional Meta-models. More precisely, *ModelElement* is considered to be a supertype of all classes in the Functional Meta-models.

Security Objective A Security Objective describes a general security goal to the system. Security Objectives in many cases originate in legal

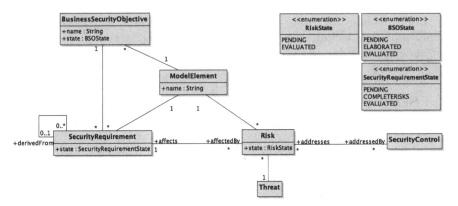

Fig. 6.5. Security Meta-model

requirements and general availability, integrity and confidentiality requirements. For the purpose of the Security Analysis, Security Objectives are
associated with model elements of the business layer (business processes
or information types).

Security Requirement A Security Requirement is a detailed context-dependent explication of a Security Objective. It breaks a Security Objective
down in several more detailed descriptions. The context of a Security
Requirement is derived from the model element for which it is defined.
Security Requirements are linked to Security Objectives to depict their
paths of inheritance.

Threat A Threat is the description of an adverse event that is considered as
potentially having a negative impact. A Threat by itself is not interesting
for our analysis, it only becomes relevant, if we further identify a targeted
model element and a related security requirement. Once the threat has
been assessed and estimated regarding its impact, it becomes a risk.

Risk A Risk is therefore defined as a triplet consisting of a targeted model
element, a related security requirement and a threat that potentially un-
dermines the requirement, including an assessment of its severity. Moreover, every risk is evaluated in the context of the currently implemented
security controls.

Security Control A Security Control is any measure or safeguard that has
been put in place to mitigate the identified risks.

During security analysis the system is described by a set of interrelated
model elements, where these model elements either adhere to the Functional
Model Types of Figure 6.1 and Figure 6.2 or to the Security Meta-model of
Figure 6.5. We call each such set of interrelated model elements a *Security
Model*.

6.3.2 The Security Micro-process

The task of the Security Analysis Process is to support the security analyst in developing, evolving and analyzing Security Models. At each point of time the Security Model should represent the current state of the analysis process, e.g. recording analyzed requirements, pending risks or implemented controls.

To facilitate the security analysis we divide the Functional Model in sub–models (*domains*) that will be analyzed by stakeholders which have the best knowledge and the responsibility of the domain. Good candidates for domains are the Global Functional Model and Local Functional Models attached to specific institutions, for large institutions it may be advisable to additionally separate abstraction levels or business processes.

Each domain responsible continuously executes the security micro-process on his domain which leads in the global view to a concurrent execution of security micro-processes. Since each security micro-process may modify the state of related security information (e.g. adding new requirements and threats) and the model elements of different domains may be interrelated the micro-processes are not independent but interact with each other.

As an example, if the responsible for the global business process *ProcessAnnualStatement* introduces the requirement *"Company related information has to be kept confidential"* then a trigger is set to the responsibles of the institutions (Company, Tax Advisor, Municipality) and the institution responsibles have to check if the requirements are fulfilled at the application and technical layer.

Figure 6.6 depicts in a schematic way domains, responsibles and the interplay of security micro–processes.

The actions of the security micro–process are shown in Figure 6.7. Within the processes the Security Model is elaborated, i.e. new model elements are added and security related information is created and modified. Each process

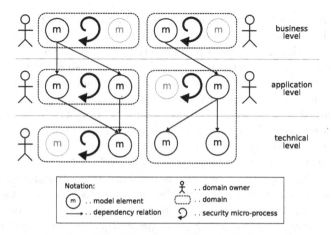

Fig. 6.6. The Overall Picture of Security Micro-processes

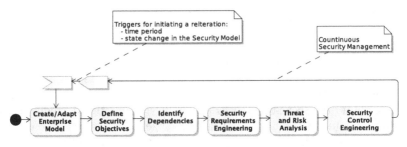

Fig. 6.7. The ProSecO Analysis Process

is repeatedly executed, where each iteration is initiated by a set of triggers. These triggers are mainly time events (e.g. the security process is executed periodically) or a state change in the Security Model. Relevant state changes may be the creation of new model elements (e.g. new business processes or services), the identification of new requirements or threats and the implementation of security controls.

In the sequel we will describe each of the actions of the security micro–process in more detail.

6.3.3 Elaborate Functional Model

The first step in each micro-process is the *creation* – or in the case of a reiteration cycle the *adaptation* — of the domain.

For instance, new services may be added and linked with other model elements or the technical infrastructure is changed. In this step it is not yet necessary to complete the links to other model elements.

6.3.4 Define Security Objectives

With the creation of the Functional Model we have identified important assets at the business level, the application level and the technical level. The next step in the security management process is the definition of high level, abstract security objectives to direct the required detailed modeling efforts to the right areas. A security objective can be based on legal requirements or on business considerations. Security objectives are useful for establishing a clear goal that is understandable at all levels. Typically such a Security Objective is attached to a model element of the business level (e.g. a business process, a business information). But depending on the context of analysis it is also suitable to attach an abstract security objective to a low level technical object.

The security objective's purpose is not only the communication of the goal of a security management effort, but it also serves as a guidance on the formulation of concrete security requirements. It is possible to define many security objectives per domain. New security objectives are associated with the state *pending*.

Fig. 6.8. Sample Security Objective

As an example (cf. Figure 6.8) we attach the security objective "Compliance with the E-Government Act" to the global business process *ProcessAnnualStatement.*

6.3.5 Identify Dependencies

With the definition of security objectives we have defined the areas of interest in the Functional Model. Each of the model elements that has a security objective attached is the root element of a separate scope called a *dependency graph*. The dependency graph is a non-cyclic graph of model elements. The dependencies are identified following a top-down-approach along the levels of abstraction of the Functional Meta-model. In the case of a global business process we

- identify associated local business processes
- identify the institutions and roles involved in the processes
- analyse processed information and
- the services supporting the processes
- relate the services with the implementing components
- relate these components with the hosting physical nodes and their location

Figure 6.9 shows a sample dependency graph starting with the global business process *ProcessAnnualStatement* leading to the local business process *ProcessNotification*, the *Annual Statement* information type, the institutions involved, the supporting services *sendAnnualStatement* and *sendNotification* together with the implementing components and nodes at the Municipality's domain.

6.3.6 Security Requirements Engineering

During security requirements engineering a general security objective attached with some model element is broken down into concrete requirements based on the model element's dependency tree. Security requirements engineering is done in a top-down way where the security requirements of lower level model elements inherit the security requirements of upper level model elements.

In our case study (cf. Figure 6.10) the security objective *"Compliance with E-Government Act"* attached to the process *ProcessAnnualStatement* is broken down to three more detailed security requirements (SR1, SR2, SR3) referring to confidentiality, integrity and non-repudiation. The dependent model elements (information types, services) and their children inherit these requirements.

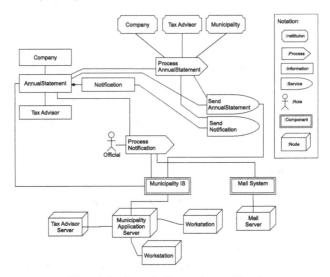

Fig. 6.9. Sample Dependency Graph

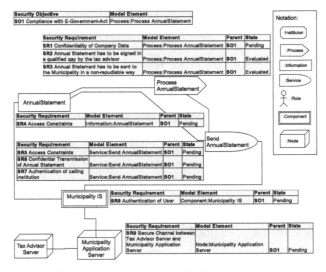

Fig. 6.10. Sample Security Requirements

The inherited requirement SR1 *"Confidentiality of company data"* is refined in the context of the information types to access constraints (SR4) which will be discussed in more detail in Chapter 6.4. Moreover, SR1 is refined in the context of the service *sendAnnualStatement* into the requirements *"Confidential Transmission of Annual Statement"* (SR6), *"Authentication of calling person"* (SR7) and an access control requirement to the service *sendAnnualStatement*. This access control requirement (SR5) states that only the institution *Tax*

Advisor can access this service given that it is registered at the municipal area of the hosting Municipality.

At the application and technical level SR1 is refined into the requirement *"Authentication of User"* (SR8). At physical level SR6 is refined into the requirement of a secure channel (SR9).

As a result of the elicitation of security requirements we obtain a non-cyclic graph of security requirements, where each requirement is attached with some model element and the parent-child relationships are induced by the dependency relations between the attached model elements. Note that security requirements at the same level are connected by a logical "and" which means that a parent security requirement enforces the fulfilment of all children security requirements.

At the stage of definition the state of a security requirement is set to *pending*. The state of the corresponding security objective is set to *elaborated*. If all security requirements related with a security objective are set to *evaluated* also the state of the security objective is set to *evaluated*. If the state of all security objectives is set to *evaluated* we call the whole Security Model *evaluated*.

6.3.7 Threat and Risk Analysis

While the security requirements state what properties have to be guaranteed, threats and risks state what kind of attacks may occur and what damage may be the consequence. Similarly to security requirements we associate each risk with some model element.

For a systematic threat analysis at the application or technical level threat catalogues such as the Baseline Protection Manual [61] or EBIOS [175] can be used. In this respect the drivers of threat analysis are the model elements at lower level of abstraction exposed to attacks from outside or inside the network.

In the second step threats are elaborated to risks. Each risk evaluates a threat in the context of a model element, an attached security requirement and relevant security controls. This means that we only consider threats related to security requirements. Moreover, the evaluation is based on the current set of related security controls.

For the evaluation itself we use a qualitative approach estimating the probability and the impact of the damage. For an approach which uses key figures for evaluating risks we refer to [163].

In the case study (cf. Figure 6.11) we consider two sample threats: TH1, *"The channel between the Tax Advisor Server and the Municipality Application Server is compromised"*, is evaluated to be of low probability in the context of the implemented security control of an SSL connection and of high impact. TH2, *"The access to the service sendAnnualStatement is not properly configured"* (e.g., accessible by tax adivsor institutions not active any more), is evaluated to be of high probability and medium impact.

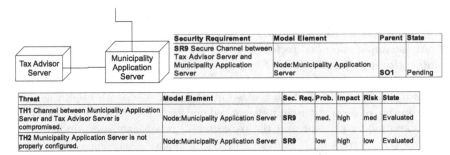

Security Requirement	Model Element		Parent	State
SR9 Secure Channel between Tax Advisor Server and Municipality Application Server	Node:Municipality Application Server		SO1	Pending

Threat	Model Element	Sec. Req.	Prob.	Impact	Risk	State
TH1 Channel between Municipality Application Server and Tax Advisor Server is compromised.	Node:Municipality Application Server	SR9	med.	high	med	Evaluated
TH2 Municipality Application Server is not properly configured.	Node:Municipality Application Server	SR9	low	high	low	Evaluated

Fig. 6.11. Sample Threat and Risk Analysis

Concerning the state model a risk is first *pending* then *evaluated*. Security requirements qualify if the related list of risks is handled to be *complete*. As soon as all risks related with a security requirement are evaluated the state of the requirement is set to *evaluated*. Upward propagation of state information in the dependency graph takes place when all subordinate security requirements are set to *evaluated*. Moreover, a security requirement which has been re–set to *pending* or *complete* also causes an upward propagation.

6.3.8 Security Control Engineering

In the final step of the micro-process the security controls are chosen and documented in the security information network. Generally, security control engineering is a complex task ranging from the choice of appropriate countermeasures (including alternatives), their correctness check, analysis of cost-effectiveness compared to the reduction of risks, analysis of remaining threats and the whole procurement- and roll-out-process.

At this place we only consider the small part of documenting implemented security controls. Each security control is related to the set of risks it reduces. Consequently, the risks have to be re–evaluated which means that the states of the related risks are re–set to *pending* and this state change is propagated up in the dependency graph as described above.

6.4 Access Control

The specification of access control requirements deserves special attention due to several reasons. First, access control in general is more complex and fine-grained than other security requirements. Second, access control can be based on a variety of concepts like role-based access control [87, 171], discretionary or mandatory access control.

In the context of the ProSecO Functional Model access control requirements can be attached to model elements of any abstraction layer, ranging from the business layer (access to information types) and the application layer (access to components) to the physical layer (access to nodes and locations). Though we do not impose restrictions on the type of access control we support a seamless process of dynamic role-based access control [58]. This process includes informal access right descriptions as presented in this chapter, formal access permission predicates (Chapter 11) and their translation into executable artifacts.

The basic idea of dynamic access control is to specify state and data dependent conditions under which a *role* has the right to execute an *operation* on some *resource*.

Role In the context of the ProSecO Functional Model a Role in the sense of role-based access control may either be an institution or a (human) domain role within an institution. As an example we may specify which information objects are accessible by the tax advisor as an institution or by the Senior and Junior Accountant as domain roles within this institution. A different example is the University as an institution and Professor, Secretary as domain roles within the institution. Roles may be arranged in a hierarchy specifying super- and subroles.

Permission A Permission is the condition under which a given role has the right to call the operation of some resource.

In the Functional Model we may attach permissions to

- *information types* specifying the conditions under which a role has the right to create, read, write or delete information objects
- *services* specifying the conditions under which a role has the right to call a service
- *components* specifying the conditions under which a role may call this component
- *nodes* specifying the conditions under which a role may access this node
- *locations* specifying the conditions under which a role may have access to this location

In our tax advisor case study we have a closer look on the access rules at the business layer of the Global Functional Model. This means that we specify the conditions under which an institution has access to a given information type. Figure 6.12 depicts the structure of information types with the central class *AnnualStatement* associated with the *Company*, the assigned *Tax Advisor* and the *Notification* if available.

An access permission to an information instance may not only depend on the role and on the kind of access (create, read, write, delete) but also on conditions on the information instance itself. As an example, a tax advisor has full access to the data of his client company, a municipality has write access to not yet issued notifications belonging to annual statements of companies in the municipal area.

The full set of access permissions of the institutions *Tax Advisor* and *Municipality* with respect to the information types of Figure 6.12 is given in Table 6.1.

In the next step these informal access permissions are modeled by predicates in the context of services. These predicates are transformed in the subsequent step into executable artifacts based on the XACML standard. For more information we refer to Chapter 11.

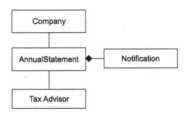

Fig. 6.12. Structure of Information Types in the Tax Advisor Case Study

Table 6.1. Access Permissions in the Tax Advisor Case Study

institution → ↓ information type	**Tax Advisor**		**Municipality**
Company	R/W: C:	client company –	R/W/C: all companies in the own municipal area
Tax Advisor	R/W: C:	own data –	R/W/C: all tax advisors registered in the own municipal area C: –
Annual Statement	R/W/C:	associated with own clients	R: all instances in the own municipal area W/C: –
Notification	R: W/C:	associated with own clients –	R: all instances related with companies in the own municipal area C: related with company in the own municipal area and notification not yet created W: elated with company in the own municipal area and notification not yet issued

6.5 Related Work

Related work exists in several directions which we categorized along the following line.

6.5.1 Standards and Baseline Protection

In the area of security management there exist a number of standards and collections of best practices like the ISO 2700x series and the German Baseline Protection Manual [61] of the BSI (Bundesamt für Sicherheit in der Informationstechnik). The focus of these frameworks is seucurity management in organizations and enterprises, thus IT related aspects rather refer to landscapes of productive IT systems than to the software engineering process.

ISO 27002 is a specification for an information security management system employing a Plan-Do-Check-Act (PDCA) model. The Baseline Protection Manual offers a process for analyzing basic security requirements for the technical infrastructure in organizations and provides detailed catalogues of threats and security controls. Both the ISO 2700x standards and the BSI Baseline Protection Manual do not support security analysis in software projects. They can be applied to the security analysis of services which are already deployed and productive and need continuous surveillance and configuration, however there is no methodological assistance for such an analysis.

6.5.2 Security Management

In addition to the before mentioned standards there is a variety of approaches from the discipline of security management underlining the importance of managing information security from a business point of view.

In the area of security requirements engineering the OCTAVE method [27] uses a three phase approach to identify and manage information security risks. This comprises the identification of critical assets, threat analysis and security strategy planning. OCTAVE provides strong support for the overall process and management aspects whereas our approach focuses on the systematic integration of modeling artifacts and security analysis. In this respect OCTAVE could perfectly be used complementarily to our approach.

An approach that is following a model-based risk analysis is CORAS [164]. CORAS uses UML models mainly for descriptive purposes to foster communication and interaction during the risk analysis process. A strength of CORAS are the methodological foundations on which it is built, like Failure Trees, Event Trees, HazOp and Failure Mode Effect Analysis (FMEA), that help to identify vulnerabilities and threats. To depict the identified assets, sources of threats and threats CORAS uses adapted diagrams inspired by UML. Our method uses text-based representation of threats and security requirements but supports a security analysis process driven by the functional system properties.

Suh and Han [183] use a business model to identify business functions in order to evaluate the relative importance of information assets for these functions. The authors focus solely on the security requirement of operational continuity. Our approach in contrast is not restricted to a single set of requirements but allows the definition of all security objectives that are relevant for the analysed organisation.

6.5.3 Security Analysis in the Software Process

Besides the security management methods there are a couple of approaches focusing on security analysis in software development.

In [185] a tool based method for threats modeling in software projects is presented. The authors basically use attack trees and data flow diagrams to analyze threats and vulnerabilities of systems. In [95] a basic process for security analysis is defined and the notion of misuse cases is introduced to describe possible attack scenarios. Misuse cases correspond to our notion of threats and the concept of providing data bases of general misuse cases is valuable also in our approach. Both [185] and [95] do not provide a separation of abstraction layers, in particular do not distinguish business oriented and technical concepts.

In [166] extensions of a Business Process Notation through security related concepts is defined. These concepts include confidentiality, non-repudiaton and integrity and are attached to model elements of business processes (such as actions or object flow). In this respect the approach is based on security patterns and resembles the SECTET -framework (cf. Chapter 7), but is not equipped with a transformation framework. At the level of business processes the introduced symbols are not expressive enough to describe all kinds of security requirements.

In [111] a framework for security requirements elicitation and analysis connected with functional requirements is presented. This framework does not distinguish different abstraction levels. Finally, the ST–Tool [83] is a security analysis method targeted towards the design of multi-agent systems. The starting point of an analysis in the ST–Tool is an interconnected functional model which is step by step extended by security requirements. Similar to [166] the ST–Tool does not support the explicit specification of security requirements which is necessary for expressing non-standard security requirements. Such non-standard security requirements are typical e.g. in payment processes and applications in health care and e-government.

6.5.4 Formal Approaches to Security Requirements Specification

A set of further approaches deals with the specification of security requirements in the context of formal methods. The motivation is to provide frameworks for the (tool-supported) correctness proof of security solutions. UMLsec

[125] and SecureUML [133, 44] define extensions of the UML. Other approaches are PCL [74] and the SH Verification Tool [13] for security protocol verification. So far our framework does not provide verification facilities and rather focuses on pragmatic security analysis and model-driven software development. In future steps the integration of a formal foundation is planned.

7

Modeling Security Critical SOA Applications

In this chapter, we build the first part of our *Domain Architecture*, the *Domain Specific Language* (DSL). We show how to define a language to model security-critical inter-organizational workflows. The language is implemented as a profile for a popular UML modeling tool and supports the modeling of *Basic Security Policies*. Every one enforces one of the three basic Security Objectives *Confidentiality*, *Integrity*, and *Non-repudiation*. The language will be extended to support *Advanced Security Policies* in Chapter 11.

This chapter is structured as follows. We begin with an informal description of the *Problem Domain* in Section 7.1. We identify relevant *Model Views* and draft an informal specification of the features for the DSL. In Section 7.2, we first develop the modeling language for the specification of decentralized inter-organizational workflows – called *Global Workflows*. The language is based on meta-models, which define the structure of the language – its syntax and semantics. Security Policies are considered an integral part of the *Domain Architecture* ("first class citizens"). Beginning with the modeling language, we show how to extend the *Domain Architecture* to cope with security concerns. In Section 7.3 *Security Policies* are integrated into the DSL in a platform- and technology-independent context.

We exemplarily show how to model the use case "Municipal Tax Collection", introduced in Chapter 5 and associated Security Policies as we go along.

7.1 The Sectet Domain Specific Language

7.1.1 Domain Definition

The SECTET-framework caters to the needs of a specific *Domain*. In our case, it is defined as the area of *security-critical, inter-organizational and distributed workflow scenarios*. A distributed workflow scenario can be thought of as a network of peers interacting by exchanging documents and/or accessing

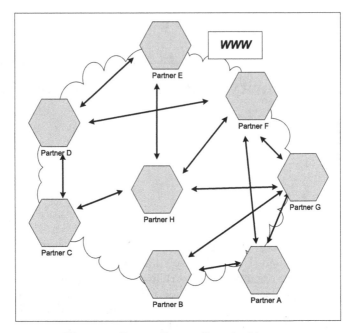

Fig. 7.1. Generic Peer-to-Peer Architecture

resources, which are managed, used and accessed in a completely decentralized way (Figure 7.1).

In the domain of SECTET, *Global* and *Local Workflows* represent two central concepts of the DSL.

7.1.2 Global Worklfow

We define a *Global Workflow* (GWf) as a network of partners cooperating in a controlled way by calling services and exchanging documents. The GWf is a workflow with no central instance of control. This means that there is no central *Workflow Management System* (WfMS) or document repository. One can think of it as a virtual process that emerges through peer-to-peer interaction of executable local processes, which, traditionally, are located in different domains. This guarantees a considerable degree of loose coupling and design autonomy at the local level without compromising interoperability.

Figure 7.2 exemplarily shows the UML- model instance of a GWf, which was presented in-depth in Chapter 5. Syntax and semantics of the GWf will be introduced in Section 7.2.1.

7.1.3 Local Worklfow

In contrast to the GWf, a *Local Workflow* (LWf) is executed on a WfMS. This kind of process accesses back-end functionality by calling local services

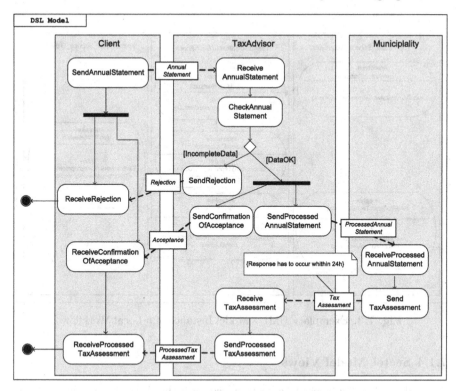

Fig. 7.2. Exemplary UML - Model Instance of a Global Workflow

and orchestrates these services according to some workflow logic. Through their collaboration as sub-systems of the GWf, LWfs – each one running on a WfMS of its own – realize the behavior as specified in the GWf. This kind of decentralized application is especially suited to scenarios where central management is not desirable, may it be for social, political or competitive reasons (e.g., public procurement, e-government).

Figure 7.3 shows the UML-model instance for a local workflow from the point of view of the service node TaxAdvisor. According to the model, the node specifies two interfaces to partners in the GWf (TaxAdivsor_Service _Requester and Municipality_Service_Provider), with services for receiving, forwarding and returning documents and one to the internal backend system (TaxAdisorInternalWebService1). It calls local services to process the document (e.g., processASDocument).

When realizing a GWf we assume that partners already have implemented the business functionality they agreed to contribute to the GWf. Seen that way the LWf simply represents a black box with interfaces specified. In later chapters, we nevertheless will consider the generation of code-stubs for interfaces to the LWfs from the GWf-model (cf. Chapter 9).

Syntax and semantics of the LWf will be covered in depth in Section 7.2.1.

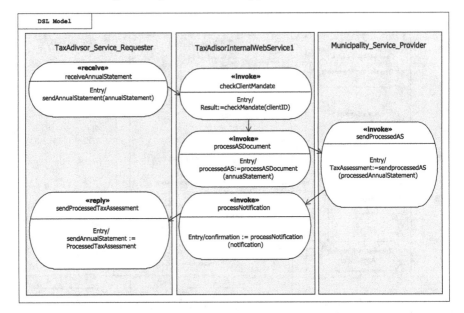

Fig. 7.3. Exemplary UML - Model Instance of a Local Workflow

7.1.4 Sectet Model Views

As explained in the preceding section, we base the definition of the DSL on two central concepts; the *Global* and the *Local Workflow*. We take these two concepts as a starting point for the identification of relevant views onto our modeled system. On one hand we have two concepts that complement each other to realize an inter-organizational workflow in peer-to-peer style. On the other hand we need to figure out how they are related to each other. Dependencies are captured in a cross-cutting (so-called "orthogonal") view onto the system.

Our DSL covers two orthogonal *Model Views*, necessary to cover all aspects needed for the design of inter-organizational peer-to-peer workflows (cf. Figure 7.4). Both views consist of sub-models, which either capture different aspects of the *Problem Space*, like the models of the *Interface View*, or, as do the models of the *Workflow View*, describe the domain at different levels of abstraction.

The application of orthogonal perspectives allows us to combine the design of the components that provide the services that may be part of various global workflows, each one realizing a particular usage scenario. In our scenario, the assumption id that partners have already implemented their local application logic and made it available as Web services. As the integration of widespread standards fosters interoperability, models can systematically be mapped to a choreography standard like the Web Services Choreography Description language (WS-CDL) (as shown in e.g., [141]). The actors of an

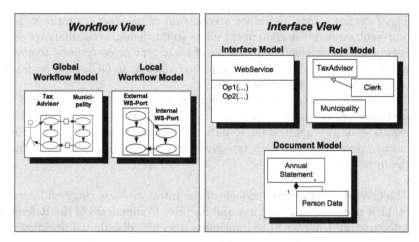

Fig. 7.4. SECTET Model Views and Related Sub-models

inter-organizational process can take the formal WS-CDL choreography defin-ition to check the compliance of their internal processes to the requirements of the choreography, to generate public interfaces or to control correct proceeding during run-time.

The Workflow View

The Workflow View is further divided into the *Global Workflow Model* (GWfM), which captures the interactions between cooperating partners in the Global Workflow by specifying the message they exchange, and the *Local Workflow Model* (LWfM) that describes an executable process, which is local to each partner and implements application logic.

The Interface View

The *Interface View* links the GWfM to the LWfM. It describes the interface of every partner independently of its usage scenario and represents a contrac-tual agreement between the parties to provide a set of services based on the minimum set of technical (operation signatures, invocation style (e.g., syn-chronous), formats etc.) and domain level constraints, thereby guaranteeing a considerable level of local design autonomy. According to the interaction paradigm of Web services, service invocation is modeled as a bilateral inter-action with a service calling and a service providing partner. This is modeled through an Object Flow between two roles.

The Interface View consists of three core sub-models:

- The *Role Model* – modeled as a UML class diagram – specifies the roles ac-cessing the services in the global application scenario and the relationship between them.

- The *Interface Model* describes a collection of abstract operations. They represent services the component offers to its clients, accessible over some network. The parameters are either of basic type or correspond to classes in the Document Model. Pre- and post-conditions in OCL-style [153] may set constraints on service behaviour.
- The *Document Model* specifies the application-level information and the structure of the documents that are exchanged by the partners in the workflow or the application scenario. We model it as a UML class diagram representing the data type view of those partners participating in the interaction.

The GWfM and the three models of the Interface View carry all information that is needed by the Services and Security Components of the Reference Architecture (cf. Chapter 8) to implement a secure, distributed workflow.

7.1.5 Security Policies

According to the definition of our *Problem Domain*, we relate *Security Objectives* primarily to the *Global Workflow*.

Security Objectives are realized through *Security Policies*. The latter are modeled at the design level and associated to models elements of either the Workflow- or the Interface View (Figure 7.5). Security Policies are translated into executable artifacts for the Reference Architecture. We differentiate between *Basic Security Policies* and *Advanced Security Policies*.

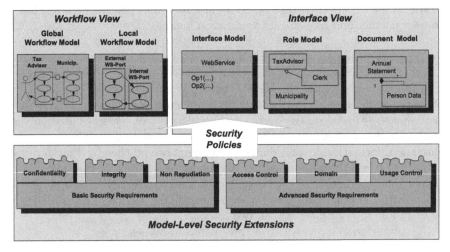

Fig. 7.5. Security Extensions to Model Views

Basic Security Policies

Basic Security Policies realize exactly one *Security Objective* in a straight-forward way. In the context of our running example, these policies should support the specification of a secure document exchange satisfying "end-to-end security" in a peer-to-peer process. This means that the requirements are to be satisfied even in case of being routed via intermediaries maybe even to originally unkown recipients – as opposed to point-to-point style security, where the sending and the receiving end communicate directly over a secure channel (e.g., SSL).

Confidentiality Policy. Documents or parts can be qualified as confidential, confining read rights to specific subjects or groups of subjects with specific attributes (e.g., Roles). This is usually implemented with the help of public key encryption. The cryptographic operations are directly applied to the XML-documents (XML-tags and elements), as specified in [119, 43] and then embedded into the SOAP message structure as defined in [37]. Thus, only the intended recipient, who is in possession of the corresponding private key, or in possession of the corresponding "Role Certificate" can read confidential information.

Integrity Policy. The receiver of a message can verify the Integrity of documents or parts of them, thereby making sure that an unauthorized third party did not modify information. Integrity is usually implemented with the help of public key encryption, requiring the sender to "sign" a hash of the message with his private key. The cryptographic operations are directly applied to the XML documents (XML-tags and elements), as specified in [43]. The result is embedded in a SOAP message structure, as specified in [119]. The *Qualified Signature* is an e-government specific *Security Policy* that extends the basic concept of the system signature, which is used to guarantee integrity, to a legal entity (e.g., a citizen, a chartered accountant, a senior clerk etc.). We will cover that advanced policy in Chapter 11.

Non-repudiation Policy. Non-repudiation protocols aim at preventing parties in a communication from falsely denying having taken part in that communication (as detailed in e.g., [134, 17, 122, 18]).

The challenging part of non-repudiation protocols is to prevent one of the implied entities to cheat (e.g., [128]). A fair protocol for non-repudiation guarantees that a sender of a message has no advantage over the receiver, or vice versa (e.g., [213]). Although we acknowledge the importance of the fairness property, we only consider the implementation of a naïve protocol with no special care for the fairness property at this place (like in e.g., [134, 17, 122, 18]). This assumption is justified, because the implementation of an advanced, fair non-repudiation protocol – like the gradual change (e.g., [187, 186]) or some probabilistic protocol (e.g., [48, 138]) – is exclusively a matter of implementation at the component level, leaving the modeling level untouched (for a detailed description on various protocol implementations for non-repudiation please refer to [201]).

In our context, this means that - based on the Objective of Non-repudiation - Securiy Policies come in two flavors. Non-repudiation of Reception requires the receiver to return a signed message carrying a time-stamp to the sender, optionally keeping a copy in his system log. Non-repudiation of Sending requires the receiver to keep a copy of the message. The message was previously complemented by a timestamp and signed by the sender. Messaging that has to comply to such a policy triggers signalling at the protocol layer through the exchange of signed messages with timestamps. This means that the security component takes care of producing and consuming the messages and initiating logging activities.

Advanced Security Policies

Many scenarios have to integrate advanced security concerns that satisfy complex legal or business-driven requirements. *Advanced Security Policies* cover various contextual aspects along three dimensions: system attributes (e.g, available resources, time, location), user attributes (e.g., prime member status), ressource attributes (e.g., consumable resource). These policies realize one or more Security Objectives. We differentiate between the following three categories of Advanced Security Policies. Each one is specialized into a set of one or more concrete Security Policies.

Access Control Policies specify a specific set of rules for accessing resources. Examples are Dynamic Access Control Policies, Delegation Policies, Break-Glass Policies, and the 4-Eyes-Principle.

Usage Control Policies complement Access Policies in that they specify a set of rules for the usage of resources onc access is granted. Examples are Privacy Policies, and Usage Policies.

Finally we have *Domain Policies*, policies that do not fall into either category. An example is the *Qualified Signature*.

We will cover these policies in extenso in Chapter 11.

7.2 The DSL Meta-models

In this section we define the SECTET Domain Specific Language (DSL). The DSL is structured into views. Every view has its own sub-models, whose syntax is defined through meta-models. We start with the meta-models of the workflow view in Section 7.2.1. They define the syntax for modeling inter-organizational workflows as a composition of Local and Global Worklfows. The sub-models of the Interface View are introduced in Section 7.2.2. We extend the basic meta-models to integrate Security Requirements into the DSL in Section 7.3.

In every section, we present the abstract syntax (represented as meta-models), the concrete syntax (expressed as a UML-profile), give examples in order to describe the semantics in context, and, where necessary, analyze important relations between the sub-models of the Interface View and the Workflow View.

In order to differentiate between terms used in various contexts we introduce the following notational conventions. Key concepts of the DSL are rendered in *italized fonts*, keywords describing workflow semantics are in **boldface Times**, UML 2.0 elements are in ***boldface, italicized Times*** and meta-model elements are in `Courier`.

7.2.1 The Workflow View

The Global Workflow Model

The *Global Workflow* represents a virtual, inter-organizational workflow with no central instance of control. The GWfM captures information required by a collaboration protocol standard like WS-CDL [126] or BPSS [71].

This approach offers a standardized but intuitive means to model collaboration protocols graphically. The meta-model is extensible, so that the models can be enriched with concepts for workflow security as will be shown in subsequent sections.

Defining the Language Structure

A vast body of research literature focuses on how to model various types of processes and workflows with UML Activity Diagrams (e.g., [124, 77, 46, 82, 20]). They essentially show that UML 2.0 Activity Diagrams with their Petri nets-style semantics are suited to the task (e.g.,[19, 22]). Our approach takes a subset of the meta-model of UML 2.0 Activity Diagrams (as specified in [195]) to model Global Workflows. We put some special constraints on the semantics as to fit our modeling requirements.

Figure 7.6 presents the meta-model that defines the abstract syntax of our language for modeling the GWf. In the following, we briefly describe the meta-classes according to their intended meaning for UML 2.0 activity diagrams and adapt the semantics to the context of inter-organizational workflows. We only describe those concepts relevant to our context. A comprehensive specification can be found in [195, 193].

- An ***Activity Node*** is an abstract class for elements in the flow of an activity connected by edges. ***Invocation Nodes, Control Nodes***, and ***Object Nodes*** inherit from this class. Being an abstract class it has no particular meaning in our context. An ***Action*** is of type ***Activity Node*** and is the fundamental unit of behavior specification. It takes a set of inputs and converts them into a set of outputs. According to UML 2.0, the execution of an ***Action*** represents some transformation or processing in the modeled system. In our case, an ***Action*** corresponds to a step in the execution of a workflow.

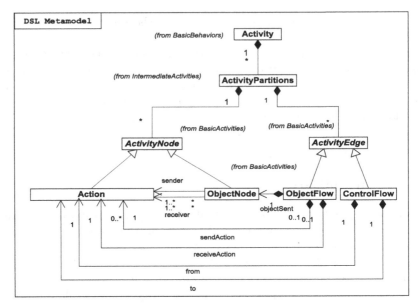

Fig. 7.6. Abstract Syntax for the Global Workflow

- An *Object Node* is of type *Activity Node* and acts as a logical container for an instance of a particular classifier. It is an element of a message flow definition. In our case, it is some kind of document flowing as a message between two interacting partners. *Activities* group *Actions* and provide control and data sequencing constraints among *Actions* as well as nested structuring mechanisms for control and scope. Each *Action* in an *Activity* may execute zero, one, or more times. *Activities* correspond to the *Global Workflow*.
- An *Activity Partition* is an activity group that identifies basic actions that have some characteristic in common. In our case, they represent the domain of an *Actor* taking part in a *Global Workflow*.
- An *ActivityEdge* is an abstract class for the connections along which tokens move between activity nodes. *Control Flow* and *Data Flow Edges* inherit from this class. Being an abstract class it has no particular meaning in our context.
- A *Control Flow* is of type *Activity Edge* and represents an edge that starts either an *Invocation Node*, or a *Control Node* after the previous *Activity Node* is finished. In the context of a Global Workflow, the *Control Flow* models the sequence of workflow steps in the Local Workflow of a partner. This means that *Control Flow*-edges are not allowed to cross *Activity Partitions*.
- An *Object Flow* is an *Activity Edge* that can have objects or data passing along it and models the flow of values to or from *Object Nodes*. In our context the *Object Flow* exclusively captures the message exchange

between two or more interacting Actors. This means, that an *Object Flow* can only link *Activity Nodes* from distinct *Activity Partitions*.

- A *Control Node* is an *Activity Node* that coordinates the flows between *Children*, *Fork Node*, *Join Node*, *Decision Node*, and *Merge Nodes*.

Modeling the Global Workflow

Figure 7.7 summarizes the type of UML elements from the UML 2.0 meta-model, its corresponding notation (concrete syntax), their meaning in the context of the Global Workflow Model and the constraints we put on the classifiers in order to achieve the task.

Figure 7.8 shows the document exchange between three roles, who participate in a GWf: a `Company`, a `Tax Advisor`, and a `Municipality`. Later, we will add Security Policies so that the exchange complies with the Security Objectives of Confidentiality, Integrity, and Non-repudiation. For the sake of readability we set elements of the language for modeling the Global Workflow in *plain italics* and those UML 2.0 elemens that represent them graphically in *bold italics*.

- The *Global Workflow Model* is modeled as an *Activity*.
- An actor in a GWf is modeled as a *Partner Role* and represented as a *Partition* in the GWfM.
- Steps in the GWf correspond to either *Interaction Activities* or to some kind of *Process Logic* at the partner node that is relevant to the specification of the GWf (e.g., further processing of information according to GWf requirements). The former act as Web services interfaces to the outside world or make calls to some partner's interface. Both are modeled as *Actions*.

UML 2.0 Based Notation for Global Workflow Modelling			
UML Classifier	**UML Notation**	**GWf Semantics**	**Constraints on UML Classifier**
Activity Partitions	Tax Advisor Municipality	Partners of a Global Workflow	
Object Flow (linking two Actions)	F orward AS → processed AS → Receive AS	Document Flow in an interaction	A document can only flow between Actions in two or more Partitions.
Activity Partitions linked by Object Flow	Tax Advisor Municipality F orward AS → processed AS → Receive AS	Interaction between two partners	Partners can only be linked through Object Flow, which corresponds to a document exchange.
Object Node	processed AS →	Document Instance	
Action	F orward AS	Workflow step	An Action correspondes to one of the following cases 1) one of two complementary parts of a bilateral interaction 2) a part of a one-to-many or many-to-one interaction 3) a step in the local workflow logic, which is relevant to the definition of the Global Workflow
Control Flow (linking two Actions, inside an Activity Partition)	Tax Advisor F orward AS ↓ Receive Notification	Local Workflow	Control flow can only link actions inside of a partition, which corresponds to the Local Workflow

Fig. 7.7. Modeling Elements for the Definition of a Global Workflow

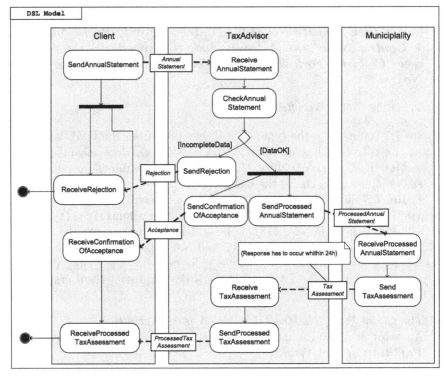

Fig. 7.8. Modeling an Example GWf with Three Roles

- The **Control Flow** orchestrates the sequence of **Actions** inside a **Partition** through **Control Flow Edges**. In the GWfM, this corresponds to a view on the public part of a Local Workflow implemented at a partner node. Internal processing steps of the Local Workflow at the partner nodes remain hidden. **Control Flow Edges** are not allowed to cross the ŞswimlanesŤ of a **Partition**.
- The **Object Flow** models an *Interaction Activity* between two or more *Partner Roles*. An **Object Flow** consists of two **Object Flow Edges** linking an **Object Node** and two or more **Actions**. In the GWfM, *Messages* travel as instances of XML-*Documents* through an **Object Node**, which acts as their logical container. An **Object Flow** represents a *Document* flowing from one *Partner Role* to the next and has always to cross the swimlanes from the party calling the service to the one offering it.
- In Web-services based environments, communication activities have the semantics of remote procedure calls, where one partner requests a service that another one may provide. An *Interaction Activity* starts on the calling partner's side with an action invoking a service and ends with an action receiving the *Message* on the provider's side.

- In case of a synchronous invocation, the **Control Flow** on the calling *Partner Role*'s side is blocked until he gets an answer from the service providing *Partner Role*, the workflow step on the caller's side is omitted. The providing role responds with a new *Message*. The **Object Flow** returns to the initial send action, which in turn is handed back the **Control Flow**.

The Local Workflow Model

We assume that the service component orchestrating business processes is a workflow management system implementing a Web services based process language like BPEL 1.1 or BEPL 2.0.[1]

Defining the Language Structure

Figure 7.9 shows the abstract syntax of a Local Workflow.

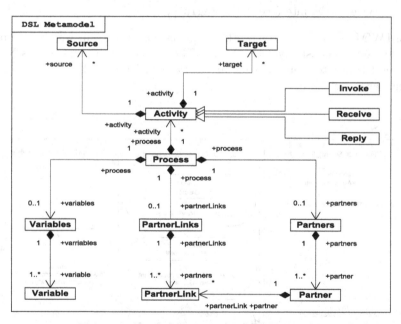

Fig. 7.9. Abstract Syntax for Local Workflows

---

[1] At the time of the SECTINO project we had to take BEPL4WS, the de-facto industry standard for Web services orchestration which was primarily still used by our partners from industry. Note that any other standard may do as well. It is just a matter of replacing or adjusting the meta-models for the language structure. Currently the Web Services Business Process Execution Language Version 2.0 [36] replaced BEPL4WS (aka BPEL 1.1) as the de-facto standard.

Modeling the Local Workflow

Figure 7.10 shows an **Activity Diagram** describing the LWfM of the *Partner Role* TaxAdvisor. It shows the **Control Flow** between **Actions** which are stereotyped with either «receive>> (and optionally «reply>>), in case the workflow provides a Web service interface or «invoke>> in case of a service call. We show the most relevant concepts through an example in the next section. For a detailed description of the concept, please refer to the specification for BPEL 1.1 [34].

- Web services calls and Web services interfaces are modeled as procedure calls with parameters in entry conditions to **Actions**, which are logically grouped to Web services ports by means of **Swimlanes**.
- Ports either provide interfaces to clients (e.g., TaxAdvisor_Service_Requester offers a service to the Client) or request services from the internal business logic (e.g., InternalWebService1 is a service port to internal services) or from external partners (e.g., Municipality_AS_Provider invokes a service on the interface of the Municipality).

The LWfM is an input to a workflow management system, which is implemented autonomously by each partner. The models can be exported as XMI-files and translated into runtime artefacts (e.g., BPEL4WS) for a workflow engine as described in [137].

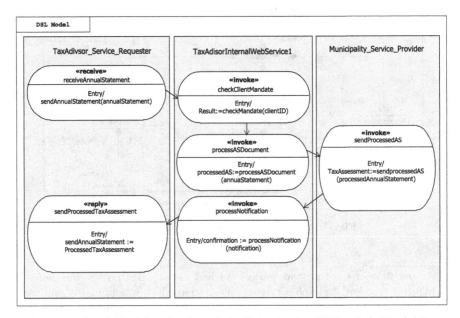

Fig. 7.10. Local Workflow for One of the Roles in the GWF – Role TaxAdvisor

7.2.2 The Interface View

The *Interface View* describes the partner nodes as components offering a set of services with given properties and permissions. Its three sub-models – the *Interface Model*, the *Document Model*, and the *Role Model* – correspond to the public part of the local application logic in terms of the *Local Workflow*, which is accessible to the inter-organizational workflow. The names of the model elements conform to the uniform technical and syntactical specifications the partners agreed upon when designing the *Global Workflow* (e.g., parameter format, interaction protocol, role names, service interfaces and parameters, operation semantics etc.).

The Document Model

According to our definition, a *Global Workflow* is a network of partners co-operating in a controlled way by calling services and exchanging documents. Thus, the *Document Model* is one of the central concepts on which all other model rely upon, either by referencing its elements directly or through other models via proxy classes.

Defining the Language Structure

Figure 7.11 shows the meta-model of the *Document Model*. It consists of three conceptual layers.

The *Data Layer* and the *Document Layer* model business data relevant to the domain modeler. *The Data Layer* specifies simple and complex data types (e.g., client ID), that are the building blocks for the document layer. This information is produced and consumed by applications at the back end. The *Message Layer* adds technical information to the message that is used by the infrastructure (e.g. routing information, encryption algorithms, security tokens etc.). Related meta-information is put into a class of type

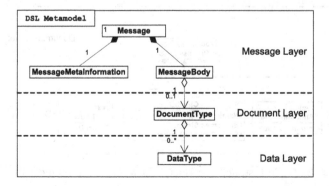

Fig. 7.11. Abstract Syntax of Document Model

`MessageMetaInformation`. The framework translates the meta-information according to its configuration to protocol-specific information (e.g., SOAP) and places it in a conforming message structure (e.g., the security token is placed in a SOAP Header information). *Message Layer* information is usually generated and added during the transformation process and remains hidden to the business analyst and the domain modeler. Instances of the *Document Model* correspond to the *Messages* traveling between the actors in the Global Workflow.

As will be described in Section 7.3, Security Policies can be associated to an ***ObjectNode*** acting as the logical container for a *Message* flowing during an interaction.

Modeling Documents

Figure 7.12 shows an example of an instance of a *Message* flowing between two *Partner Roles*. The *Message* is stereotyped accordingly and named `ProcessedAS`, the `documentType` is set to `XML`, which is also its default-type, and is composed of the simple and complex data types.

The Role Model

The *Role Model* specifies roles necessary in a Global Workflow-scenario. A user can be associated to one or more roles and has to guarantee the implementation of the Interfaces as specified in the GWfM and the Interface Model.

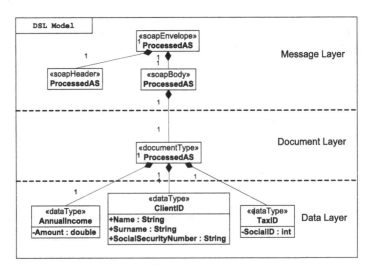

Fig. 7.12. Example Instance of a Document Model for Document `ProcessedAS`

Defining the Language Structure

Figure 7.13 shows the meta-model of the *Role Model*. A `Partner_Role` inherits from the abstract class `GWf_Role` and represents the actors in a *Global Workflow*-scenario. Usually, the role hierarchy of a `Partner_Role`'s domain remains hidden to his partners in the *Global Workflow*, but there may be cases, where security requirements require an explicit association to roles of his internal hierarchy (e.g., for the Qualified Signature or the 4-Eyes-Principle, cf. Chapter 11). These roles are represented through the element `Domain_RoleRef` in the GWfM.

Modeling Role Hierarchies

Figure 7.14 shows an example role hierarchy for a Global Workflow. The three actors taking part in the GWf are modeled as classes stereotyped «Partner_Role>>. The `Partner_Role` TaxAdvisor additionally is associated to two `Domain_RoleRefs`, which have to be mapped to roles in his internal hierarchy. The role associated to `CharteredAccountant` will have to be senior to the one associated to the role `JuniorAccountant`.

Mapping a Role from the GWfM to the LWfM

Figure 7.15 shows how the element `Partner_Role` maps to corresponding elements in the GWfM and the LWfM. A `Partner_Role` maps to an

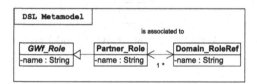

Fig. 7.13. Abstract Syntax of Role Model

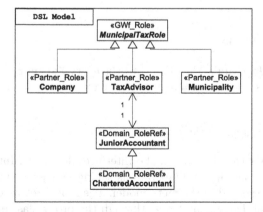

Fig. 7.14. Example Instance of Role Hierarchy for Role `TaxAdvisor`

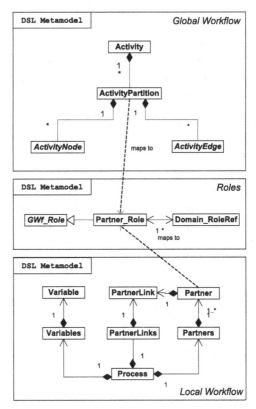

Fig. 7.15. Mapping of ActivityPartition (GWfM) and Partner (LWfM) to Part-ner_Roles

ActivityPartition in the GWfM according to the meta-model for *Activities* in the UML Superstructure [195] and to a `Partner` in the LWfM according to the BPEL syntax.

The Interface Model

The *Interface Model* links the GWfM to the every `Partner_Role`'s LWfM. It specifies *Services* and *Operations* that role have to provide or are required to use.

Defining the Language Structure

Figure 7.16 shows the elements of the Interface Model. An Interface consists of a Service with one or more Operations taking and/or returning Messages. All four are represented in the meta-model. The model references the element `Message` from the Document Model through the proxy-class `MessageRef`.

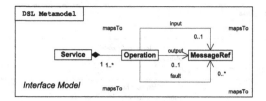

Fig. 7.16. Abstract Syntax of Interface Model

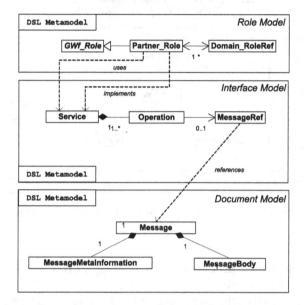

Fig. 7.17. Dependencies between Sub-models of the Interface View

Analysing Dependencies to the Role and the Document Model

The *Interface Model* depends on elements of the *Role Model* and the *Document Model* (Figure 7.17).

A `Partner_Role` implements `Services` or uses another `Partner_Role`'s Services. A `Partner_Role` provides and/or calls `Operations`. An `Operation` takes a `Message` as input and returns a `Message` as a response. `Messages` are defined as elements of the Document Model and are thus referenced by the class `MessageRef`.

Modeling Interfaces

Figure 7.18 shows an interface specification for an asynchronous interaction between two `Partner_Roles` in a GWf. Each `Partner_Role` implements and/or uses an `Interface` by calling and providing `Operations`. The element stereotyped «interface>> refers to a process activity in the GWfM. This case specifies a synchronous interaction. The role `Municipality` is waiting

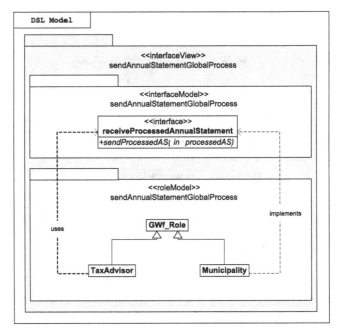

Fig. 7.18. Example Interface Specification for an Asynchronous Interaction

for a document named `processedAS` by offering a (Web service-) operation named `sendProcessedAS`.

Figure 7.19 specifies the same interaction as an asynchronous process. The `TaxAdvsior` as a caller would have to specify a call-back operation to get the result in the form of a response message `TaxAssessment`, which is passed as a return parameter to the operation `sendTA`. The latter is part of the `Interface sendProcessAnnualStatement` which maps to the process activity which had originally triggered the interaction (cf. p. 103 Figure 7.8).

Mapping an Operation from the GWfM to the LWfM

An element stereotyped «`interface`>> in the *Interface Model* maps to an UML 2.0 ***Action*** in the GWfM and an UML 1.4 ***Activity*** in the LWfM.[2] The `Message` that is passed along from one `Partner_Role` to the next and referenced through the proxy-class `MessageRef` maps to an ***ObjectNode*** in the GWfM and a ***Variable*** in a LWfM modeled in WSBPEL (Figure 7.20). The `Operation` maps to the specific service as declared in the WSDL file.

---

[2] There was a pragmatic reason for the use of UML 1.4 for the concrete syntax of the LWfM: the UML profile for modeling BPEL processes was only defined for the version 1.4 [137]. It has not been updated yet.

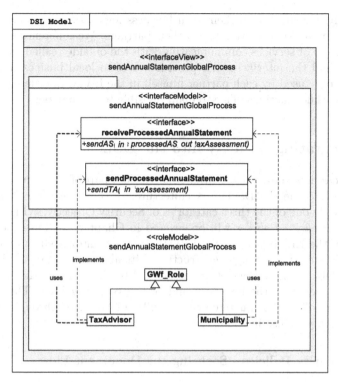

Fig. 7.19. Example Interface Specification for a Synchronous Interaction

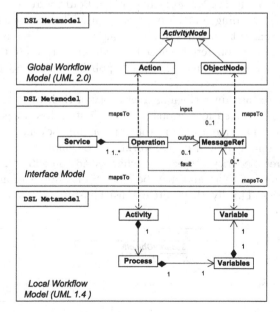

Fig. 7.20. Mapping of Operation Elements from Interface Model to LWfM and GWfM

Usually, partners wrap their local business logic in a Web services interface, thereby making it available to their partners. We differentiate between the interfaces of services communicating with the outside (called external interfaces), and the interfaces that provide access to local business logic. The latter are only used by each partner himself in the LWfM in order to perform internal workflow actions. They remain invisible to the partners.

7.3 Integrating Security into the DSL

In this section, we integrate security concerns as a part of the Domain Specific Language into the the Domain Architecture. A *Basic Security Policies* enforces exactly one of the three categories of Security Objectives (Figure 7.21). *Advanced Security Policies* will be covered in Chapter 11. Subsequently, we show how the three types of Security Policies are integrated into the DSL. As already stated, the language structure – its abstract syntax – is based on meta-models. Security Policies are associated to elements of other models of the DSL, specifically the Interface- and/or the Workflow View. The way how to model a policy, the concrete syntax, will be introduced through examples that exemplify its use in context.

Basic Security Policies - Securing the Document Flow

In this section, we consider three concrete policies specializing the abstract category `Basic SecurityPolicy`: `Integrity`, `Confidentiality`, and `Non-repudiation` (of sending and/or of Reception). These policies qualify the instance of a `Document` (or parts of it) flowing in the specific interaction. We label these policies as concrete because they can be instantiated during policy modeling and are translated into executable policies configuring the Reference Architecture.

We decided to introduce them as a category of their own and qualified as `BasicSecurityPolicies` for various reasons. Firstly, they are generic enough to be applicable to a wide array of problem domains beyond the actual challenge of securing inter-organizational workflows. Secondly they enforce exactly one of the three Security Objectives whereas `AdvancedSecurityPolicies` may refer to more of them and may be loaded with application- or industry specific semantics. Thirdly, they were extensively subject to scientific research

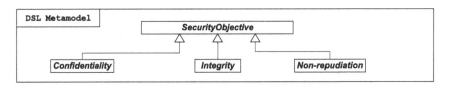

Fig. 7.21. Categories of Security Objectives

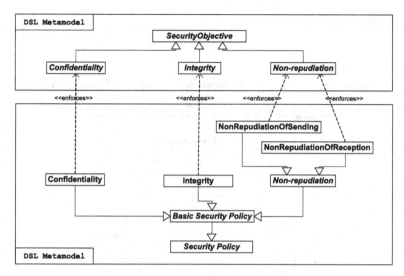

Fig. 7.22. Policies Realizing the Three Types of BasicSecurityRequirement

and industry application alike, and can be mapped to a proven implementation mechanism in a straightforward way (e.g., cryptographic functions enforcing a Confidentiality and/or an Integrity policy, protocols and a combination of cryptographic functions for a Non-repudiation policy).

Every Security Objective is realized by a specific *Security Policy* (Figure 7.22). These policies are associated to elements of the *GWfM* or the *LWfM* when the domain expert or a security administrator defines the policies for a specific scenario. But before moving on we have to make explicit the relation of these abstract security concepts to other parts of the DSL at the meta-level.

In general, a Confidentiality-policy is associated with one or more document nodes. It carries information about permissions to view the information, as the security gateway – a single point of entry into and exit from from the domain – encrypts the document with the corresponding public key of the recipient. Accordingly, an Integrity-policy demands that the gateway signs the document at the domain boundaries, whereas a Non-repudiation policy triggers a protocol to ensure that proof of reception and/or sending are exchanged. The policy requires the gateways at the Partner_Role's domain boundaries to exchange signed message receipts that carry timestamps or log message copies.

Defining the Language Structure

The abstract class *BasicSecurityPolicy* (Figure 7.23) inherits from the abstract class *SecurityPolicy* and is specialized into three concrete policies:

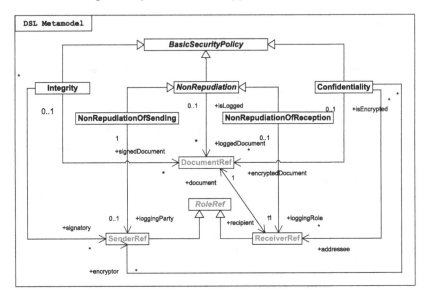

Fig. 7.23. Policies of Type *BasicSecurityPolicy*

- A `Confidentiality`-policy associates the proxy-element `DocumentRef`, referencing the elements of the Document and Data Layer of the Message, to a `ReceiverRef`, the intended reader of confidential information.
- An `Integrity`-policy associates the proxy-element `DocumentRef` to the `Sender` of a message. He is supposed to sign the document with his public key. Both types, `Sender` and `Receiver` inherit from the supertype `RoleRef`, a proxy-element referencing a `Partner_Role` in the Role Model.
- A specialized form of a `NonRepudiation`-policy – a `NonRepudiation OfRe-ception`-policy – associates the `Sender` and the `Receiver` with the `Doc-umentRef`.

Modeling a Basic Security Policy

Any of the three policies of the category *BasicSecurityPolicy* is specified by assigning a stereotyped constraint to an `ObjectNode` in the GWfM. The constraint's value specification consists of attributes assigned to a document node corresponding to the document parts to be encrypted and signed. Document nodes are referenced with the help of "OCL-style" [153] expression for navigation through an associated Document Model (cf. Chapter 11 for the exact syntax of SECTET-PL).

Referring to Figure 7.24, the **Object Node** processedAS is the logical container for an instance of the *Message* ProcessedAS. The node is associated with a constraint box stereotyped «BasicSecurityPolicy», setting the context to the message instance.

The policy `Confidentiality` declares that only the `Municipality` should be able to read the nodes `annualIncome` and `clientID`. `Integrity` requires

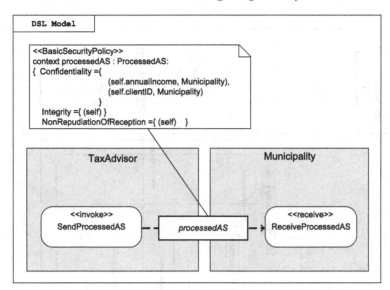

Fig. 7.24. Example Interaction with Basic Security Policies

```
 1  security_policy = stereotype , context_declaration , sec_policy_body;
 2
 3  stereotype = '<<' , 'BasicSecurityPolicy' , '>>';
 4
 5  context_declaration = 'context' , document_instance , ':' , document_type , ':' ;
 6  document_instance = instance_name ;
 7  document_type = class_name ;
 8
 9  sec_policy_body = security_policy+;
10  security_policy= policy_declaration , '=' , node_receiver_pair_list;
11  policy_declaration = 'confidentiality' | 'integrity' | 'nr_Sending'| 'nr_Reception';
12  node_receiver_sender_tripple_list = '{' , node_receiver_sender_tripple* , '}';
13  node_receiver_sender_tripple = '(' , node , (',' , receiver)* , [(',' , sender)] ')';
14  node = 'self' , ( '.' , name)* ;
15
16  receiver = name;
17  sender = name;
18  name = lowercase , ( lowercase | digit | uppercase | '_' )*;
19  instance_name = lowercase , ( lowercase | digit | uppercase | '_' )*;
20  class_name = uppercase , ( lowercase | digit | uppercase | '_' )*;
21
22  uppercase = ['A' .. 'Z'];
23  lowercase = ['a' .. 'z'];
24  digit = ['0' .. '9'];
```

Fig. 7.25. Production Rules for Category *BasicSecurityPolicies*

the security gateway at the TaxAdvisor's domain boundary to provide a system signature in order to provide means to identify possible unauthorized changes to the message content. nr_Reception requires the Municipality's security gateway to return a signed receipt with a time-stamp.

Figure 7.25 shows the production rules for security policies of category *BasicSecurityPolicies*.

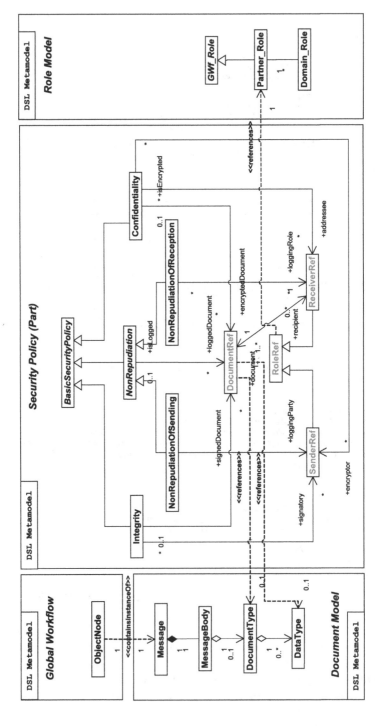

Fig. 7.26. Dependencies between Security and Elements of Model View at the Meta-model Level

Model Dependencies

Figure 7.26 shows the main dependencies between the meta-model for the abstract type `BasicSecurityPolicy` and the GWfM, the Role Model, and the Document Model. The `ObjectNode` in GWfM acts as the logical container for an instance of the `Message` travelling between two `Partner_Roles`. A `Message` carries information in the form of `DataTypes`, that are grouped into a `DocumentType`. Both can be referenced through the proxy-class `DocumentRef` from the `Security Policy` meta-model. In this meta-model the class `RoleRef` acts as a proxy-class to a `Partner_Role`.

8

Enforcing Security with the Sectet Reference Architecture

This chapter introduces the target Reference Architecture (RA) of the SECTET-Domain Architecture. The RA specifies a component infrastructure based on Web services technology and specifications. It acts as a runtime environment for services provided by *Partners* in a *Global Workflow (GWf)*. A *Partner* implements a portion of a GWf as specified for the specific *Partner_Role* he is holding (cf. Chapter 7).

We start with the introduction of the XACML-data-flow model, which is the architectural blueprint for the RA in Section 8.1. We then specify Service and Security Components in Section 8.2. These components extend the XACML Data-flow Model to a full-blown *Reference Architecture* as a target infrastructure for the SECTET-framework. We move on to describe the working of enforcement mechanisms and services by specifying the messaging protocols between security components through UML Sequence Diagrams in Section 8.3. In Section 8.4 we finally show how the components are configured with the help of executable XML-artifacts called *Executable Policy Files* based on Web services security standards.

8.1 Architectural Blueprint

Designed for deployment in SOA based scenarios, the implementation of the SECTET-Reference Architecture is primarily based on Web services standards and technologies. We will reference respective standards along with the specification of the components. The implementation specifically relies on the XACML Standard [147] for the following purposes:

1. the XACML data-flow model represents the core of the architectural blueprint. The SECTET-RA adds security components to the model.
2. *Security Policies* for inbound and outbound communication flow are translated to executable policies based on the XACML syntax.

3. we use XACML's standard request/response protocol for communication between the security components. Specifically, the single point of access and the component that performs the compliance checks work as specified in the XACML specification for decision on authorization requests.
4. Sun's XACML reference implementation [184] was used as the core component for our security infrastructure. It is important to acknowledge, that we use it not only for its intended purpose (according to which the Policy Decision Point evaluates access requests) but also for the evaluation of requests for security compliance check by the Policy Configuration Engine.

8.2 Components

In the following we introduce those components of the *Reference Architecture*, necessary to realize basic scenarios demanding *Basic Security Policies* (cf. Chapter 7). Extensions to the Reference Architecture needed for the enforcement of *Advanced Security Policies* will be discussed in Chapter 11.

Figure 8.1 shows the SECTET-Reference Architecture for a partner who implements his portion of the Global Workflow. He does so by offering an interface to specific services of his Local Workflow to his partners.

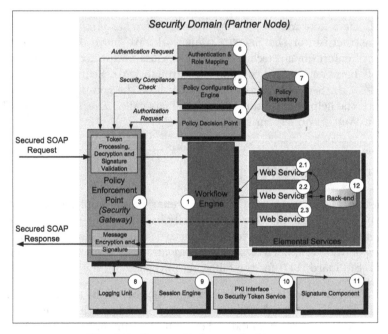

Fig. 8.1. SECTET-Reference Architecture

8.2.1 Service Components

Services

Services represent elemental units of functionality. They may call other services (internal and/or external) or may be called by services (2.1, 2.2, and 2.3), forming composite services. Wrapper services (2.2) wrap back-end functionality (e.g., databases, enterprise ressource planning systems etc.) in order to make it accessible via Web services. Services can also directly be called by partners from the outside (2.3), thus bypassing the workflow engine, but intercepted by the security gateway.

Workflow Engine

The core component is the workflow engine (1)(e.g., Oracle BPEL Process Manager [7] or ActiveBPEL [80]) which implements an orchestration language such as BPEL4WS [36] or BPML ([35]) and aggregates and controls the sequence of existing Web services (2.1) and (2.2) to a composition that may be offered as a Web service of its own to external business partners.

8.2.2 Security Components

In order to provide a trusted domain, elemental and composite services are wrapped by *Security Components*.

External Policy Enforcement Point

The external Policy Enforcement Point (PEP) represents a single point of entry and acts as a security gateway. It intercepts incoming SOAP messages and applies basic security processing to the message structure. It extracts tokens from the inbound SOAP messages, decrypts elements and checks the validity of signatures. Accordingly, the PEP adds tokens to, encrypts and signs elements in outbound messages. This basic functionality for processing the security-structure of messages leverages standards like XML-Encryption [119], XML-Digital signature [43] and WS-Security [37]. The PEP reference implementation is based on Apache's WSS4J – a Java library for signing and verifying SOAP Messages with WS-Security information [89].

Figure 8.2 shows an example WS-Security compliant SOAP message, that may be intercepted by the PEP. The SOAP message consist of two parts, a header-block and a body. The header-block contains security-relevant information in the wsse:security section consisting of:

1. The timestamp information (lines 6-9).
2. The X.509 certificate as a security token associated with the message (lines 9-12).

```
1   <?xml version="1.0" encoding="utf-8"?>
2     <S11:Envelope xmlns:S11="..." xmlns:wsse="..." xmlns:wsu="..." xmlns:xenc="..."
3                   xmlns:ds="...">
4       <S11:Header>
5         <wsse:Security>
6           <wsu:Timestamp wsu:Id="T0">                                              (1)
7             <wsu:Created>2006-09-13T08:42:00Z</wsu:Created>
8           </wsu:Timestamp>
9           <wsse:BinarySecurityToken ValueType="...#X509v3" wsu:Id="X509Token"
10                            EncodingType="...#Base64Binary">                        (2)
11            MIIEZzCCA9CgAwIBAgIQEmtJZcOrqrKh5i...
12          </wsse:BinarySecurityToken>
13          <xenc:EncryptedKey>
14            <xenc:EncryptionMethod Algorithm= "http://www.w3.org/2001/04/xmlenc#rsa-1_5"/>
15            <ds:KeyInfo>
16              <wsse:KeyIdentifier   EncodingType="...#Base64Binary"                (3)
17                              ValueType="...#X509v3">MIGfMa0GCSq...
18              </wsse:KeyIdentifier>
19            </ds:KeyInfo>
20            <xenc:CipherData>
21              <xenc:CipherValue>d2FpbmdvbGRfE0lm4byV0...
22              </xenc:CipherValue>
23            </xenc:CipherData>
24            <xenc:ReferenceList>
25              <xenc:DataReference URI="#enc1"/>
26            </xenc:ReferenceList>
27          </xenc:EncryptedKey>
28          <ds:Signature>                                                           (4)
29            <ds:SignedInfo>
30              <ds:CanonicalizationMethod
31                Algorithm="http://www.w3.org/2001/10/xml-exc-c14n#"/>
32              <ds:SignatureMethod
33                Algorithm="http://www.w3.org/2000/09/xmldsig#rsa-sha1"/>
34              <ds:Reference URI="#T0">
35                <ds:Transforms>
36                  <ds:Transform Algorithm="http://www.w3.org/2001/10/xml-exc-c14n#"/>
37                </ds:Transforms>
38                <ds:DigestMethod Algorithm="http://www.w3.org/2000/09/xmldsig#sha1"/>
39                <ds:DigestValue>LyLsF094hPi4wPU… </ds:DigestValue>
40              </ds:Reference>
41              <ds:Reference URI="#body">
42                <ds:Transforms>
43                  <ds:Transform Algorithm="http://www.w3.org/2001/10/xml-exc-c14n#"/>
44                </ds:Transforms>
45                <ds:DigestMethod Algorithm="http://www.w3.org/2000/09/xmldsig#sha1"/>
46                <ds:DigestValue>LyLsF094hPi4wPU...</ds:DigestValue>
47              </ds:Reference>
48            </ds:SignedInfo>
49            <ds:SignatureValue>Hp1ZkmFZ/2kQLXDJbchm5gK...</ds:SignatureValue>
50            <ds:KeyInfo>
51              <wsse:SecurityTokenReference>
52                <wsse:Reference URI="#X509Token"/>
53              </wsse:SecurityTokenReference>
54            </ds:KeyInfo>
55          </ds:Signature>
56        </wsse:Security>
57      </S11:Header>
58      <S11:Body wsu:Id="body">
59        <xenc:EncryptedData Type="http://www.w3.org/2001/04/xmlenc#Element" wsu:Id="enc1">
60          <xenc:EncryptionMethod
61            Algorithm="http://www.w3.org/2001/04/xmlenc#tripledes1450cbc"/>
62          <xenc:CipherData>
63            <xenc:CipherValue>d2FpbmdvbGRfE0lm4byV0...</xenc:CipherValue>
64          </xenc:CipherData>
65        </xenc:EncryptedData>                                                      (5)
66      </S11:Body>
67    </S11:Envelope>
```

Fig. 8.2. Exemplary WS-Security Compliant SOAP Message

3. The key that is used to encrypt the body of the message. Since this is a symmetric key, it is passed in an encrypted form (lines 13-27). The algorithm used to encrypt the key is specified to RSA (line 14). Lines 15-19 specify the identifier of the key that was used to encrypt the symmetric key. Lines 20-23 specify the encrypted form of the symmetric key.
4. The encryption block in the message that uses this symmetric key (lines 24-26). In this case it is only used to encrypt the whole body (`Id="enc1"`).
5. The digital signature based on the X.509 certificate, with the content to be signed indicated in lines 29-48 being signed. Line 41 references the message body.
6. The actual signature value (line 49).
7. The key that was used for the signature. In this case, it is the X.509 certificate included in the message (lines 50-54).

The actual business relevant payload is part of the body of the message (lines 58-66) with encrypted meta-data and consist of:

1. The element value being replaced line 59).
2. The encryption algorithm – Triple-DES in this case (lines 60-61).
3. The cipher text (lines 62-64).

For more information, on syntax and semantics, please refer to related specifications, e.g., [119, 43, 37].

In case Non-repudiation-of-reception was specified as a security requirement, the PEP returns a time-stamped and signed notification of receipt to the sender. In case of a specified Non-repudiation-of-sending, the PEP forwards a time-stamped copy of the signed message he received from the sender to the logging unit. The PEP interacts with other security components before forwarding an inbound message to the end-recipient (e.g., back-end application).

Authentication and Role Mapping Unit

The PEP first makes an authentication request to the Role Mapping Unit (6), which assigns a role to the caller. The request/response protocol is based on XACML 2.0.

Policy Configuration Engine

In a second step, the PEP checks the inbound message for compliance with security policies by querying the Policy Configuration Engine (PCE) (5). Alternatively, for outbound messages, the PEP queries the Policy Configuration Engine for security requirements to integrate into the message structure. The requirements for inbound and outbound messages are specified in a policy file based on the standards WS-Policy, XACML and WS-Security. The security policies, which were specified in the Global Workflow Model, are directly translated into policy files for inbound- as well as outbound messaging for the Policy Configuration Engine.

Policy Decision Point

The PEP finally queries the Policy Decision Point (4) for Authorization. It checks invocation requests from workflow partners to exposed services and forwards requests to the Policy Decision Points (4) - which check the requests according to some policy stored in the Policy Repository (PR) (7). The query protocol is based on XACML, whereas the policy files are based on WS-Policy, XACML and WS-Security.

Internal Policy Enforcement Point

The external PEP implements security objectives like user authentication, confidentiality and integrity regarding data exchange with external partners, whereas the internal PEP maps and enforces access rights to the local environment.

8.2.3 Supporting Security Components

Logging Unit

The Logging Unit (8) provides application level tracing and error logging and basically supports the realization the security requirements of Non-repudiation (Non-repudiation-of-reception and Non-repudiation-of-sending).

The Session Engine

The Session Engine (9) implements a security context engine for handling sessions. It works at the application layer and relies on WS-Trust [33] and WS-Secure Conversation [32].

Public Key Infrastructure

The PKI Interface (10) is based on WS-Trust and provides access to external Security Token Services for token issuance, validation or mapping.

8.3 Communication Protocols

This section describes the interplay between the security components PEP, PDP, PCE, and PR when enforcing Basic Security Policies on inbound and outbound messages. We first describe how *Confidentiality* and *Integrity* policies are enforced by the Security Components (Section 8.3.1) and then move on to *Non-repudiation-of-sending* and *Non-repudiation-of-reception* (Section 8.3.2).

8.3.1 Enforcing Confidentiality and Integrity

Inbound Messages

Figure 8.3 describes the sequence of messages between the security components for incoming messages that have to comply with the security requirements of confidentiality or integrity. The PEP acts as a single point of entry
into the secured domain and intercepts every application bound SOAP message. In a first step, basic SOAP message processing is performed. The PEP
extracts the SOAP message security-structure and retrieves the keys embedded in the message, decrypts encrypted parts and verifies signatures. It caches
those elements targeted to other recipients in order to reinsert them, when forwarding or relaying parts of the message. In a second step, the PEP builds a
message Request for Compliance Check with information on those elements
that were encrypted and/or signed and sends it to the Policy Configuration
Engine (PCE). The PCE loads the corresponding policy file from the Policy
Repository, performs a compliance check, and compares the information of
the request with the security requirements specified in the policy file. In case
the message was correctly encrypted and signed it signals a positive result
to the PEP, which in his turn forwards the plain SOAP message to the local
service. Alternatively, the PEP discards the message and optionally returns a
fault message to the sender.

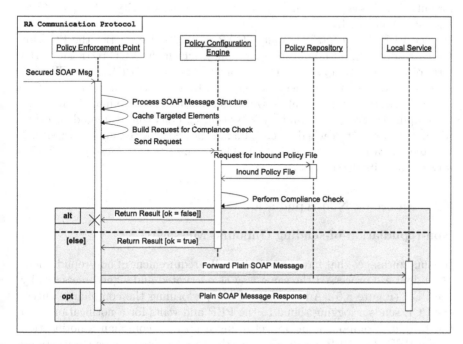

Fig. 8.3. Components Communication Protocol for Inbound Messages (Confidentiality and Integrity)

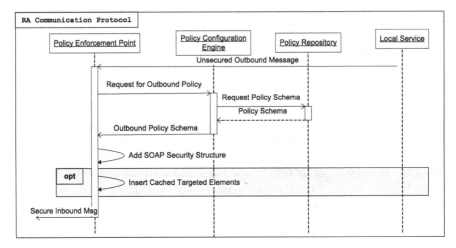

Fig. 8.4. Components Communication Protocol for Outbound Messages (Confidentiality and Integrity)

Outbound Messages

Figure 8.4 describes the sequence of messages between security components for outgoing messages that have to comply with the security policies for Confidentiality and/or Integrity.

The PEP "intercepts" outgoing SOAP messages. He queries the PCE for the corresponding outbound message policy, which the PCE retrieves in the form of a Policy Template from the Policy Repository (PR). The PEP then encrypts and signs the elements as required by the outbound policy schema, and embeds security information within a security structure into the message in compliance with the standard WS-Security (Elements targeted to other recipients that were cached when inbound message processing occurred, are inserted in case they are available). The secured SOAP Message is finally forwarded to its destination.

8.3.2 Enforcing Non-repudiation

Non-repudiation-of-sending (Inbound Message)

Inbound messages that have to comply to the requirement of non-repudiation-of-sending are processed the same way as encrypted and signed messages by the PEP (Figure 8.5). Additionally, when performing the compliance check, the PCE sends a logging signal to the PEP and waits for a notification from the Logging Component before returning a positive compliance notification to the PEP. The PEP, when receiving the logging signal, adds a timestamp

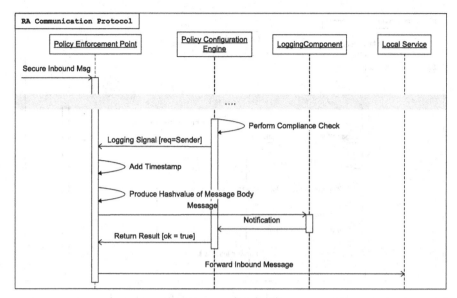

Fig. 8.5. Components Communication Protocol for Inbound Messages (Non-repudiation-of-sending)

to the message structure produces a hash value over the message and sends it for logging to the Logging Component.

Non-repudiation-of-reception (Inbound Message)

Non-Repudiation-of-Reception for inbound messages works almost similar as non-repudiation of sending, but the PEP, when receiving the logging signal from the PCE, returns a signed proof of reception with timestamp to the sender (Figure 8.6). It notifies the PCE, which acknowledges full compliance to specified security requirements with a positive message.

Non-repudiation-of-reception (Outbound Message)

When sending messages, only the case of non-repudiation of reception is relevant (Figure 8.7). After intercepting the plain SOAP Message, the PEP retrieves the outbound policy schema and applies encryption and signature as specified and forwards the message to the ultimate recipient. The PEP waits for a Proof of Reception and logs the acknowledgement, when received or in case of a specified timeout throws an error and notifies the sending service.

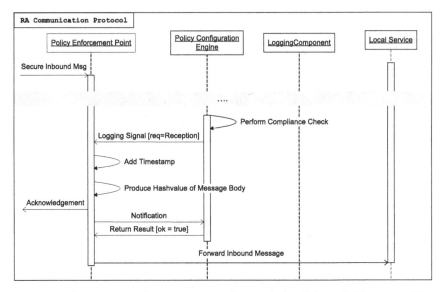

Fig. 8.6. Components Communication Protocol for Inbound Messages (Non-repudiation-of-reception)

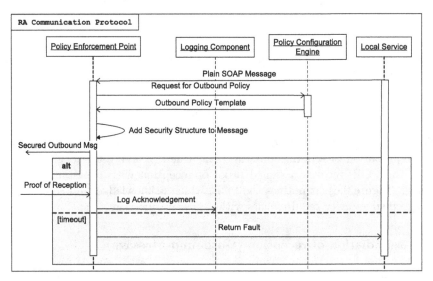

Fig. 8.7. Components Communication Protocol for Outbound Messages (Non-repudiation-of-reception)

8.4 Component Configuration

This section describes the syntax and semantics for Policy Files, specifying inbound message security (Section 8.4.1) and outbound message security (Section 8.4.2).

8.4.1 Inbound Messaging - (Executable Security Policy File)

We use an XACML reference implementation [184] for the evaluation of requests for compliance check coming from the PEP to the PCE. The component is actually called Policy Decision Point and also implements the logic for the evaluation of decision requests for access control. Although we rely on the same technology for the PCE and use the same syntactical elements of the XACML language the semantics are different. This is why we decided to call the component Policy Configuration Engine.

In order to be processable by the PCE, Policy Files need to integrate all XACML elements whose usage is required according to the specification even those who are irrelevant to the specification of the Inbound Policy File. The syntax will be marked correspondingly.

The syntax for the specification of executable security policies for inbound messages in the Policy File basically relies on a subset of the of XACML 2.0 core specification. Although the figures of this section and associated schemas in the appendix, show all XACML language elements necessary to comply to the schemas as defined in [147], we only describe those syntactical elements of the XACML 2.0 core syntax used in an Inbound Policy File. Those elements, which are relevant to the specification of a Policy File are highlighted in bold face.

For every element, we will proceed as follows: we will first describe its syntax inclusive of sub-elements in the context of the XACML specification. We then explain its meaning it the context of a Policy File. For a full specification of the XACML syntax, please refer to [147].

For the sake of readability we do not include namespaces and standard XML syntax (e.g., `<?xml version="1.0" encoding="UTF-8"?>`). The only exception being schemas, where the prefix `xs:` stands for the W3C XML Schema namespace.

Figure 8.8 shows the all relevant elements of a Policy File. Attributes of XACML syntax elements are shown as class attributes. The main elements are the `PolicySet`, the `Target`, the `Policy` and the `Rule` element. They are described subsequently.

The `Rule` element

A rule is the most elementary unit of an *Executable Policy File*. A rule is evaluated on the basis of its contents. According to [147], the main components of a rule are:

1. the `target` element that defines the set of `resources`, `subjects`, `actions` and `environments` to which the rule is intended to apply. It is included as an empty element into the Policy File, because its presence is irrelevant in the security context. In that case, according to [147]), the target of the `Rule` is the same as that of the parent `Policy` element.

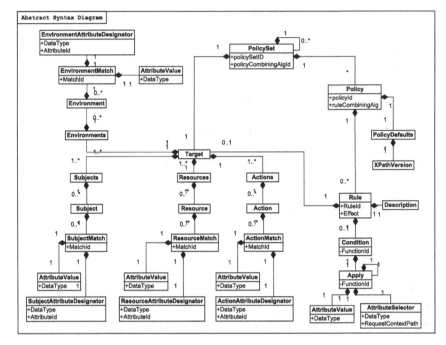

Fig. 8.8. Abstract Syntax of XACML 2.0

2. the `effect` attribute of the rule indicates the rule-writer's intended consequence of a `True` evaluation for the rule. Two values are allowed: `Permit`
and `Deny`.

3. The `Condition` element is the core of every rule. It represents a boolean
expression that defines the applicability of a rule to an incoming message.
Every security requirement is captured within two nested `Apply` elements.
The first `Apply` element additionally contains an `AttributeValue` element
of data-type String, whose value specifies either a sending role or a receiving role, depending on the security requirement. The nested `Apply` element
contains an `AttributeSelector` element of data-type `String` specifying
the document node and the security requirement. This is placed in the
element's `RequestContextPath` attribute.

Listing 8.9 shows an example rule for two nodes of a document called
`ProcessedAS`, set through the `RuleId` attribute [line 1]. The `Effect` attribute
should be a `Permit`, once all conditions are met by the inbound document [line
1]. The `Target` section remains empty [lines 3-7], as this element is specified
by the parent `Policy` element.

The `Condition` section [lines 8-27] defines two security requirements to
be met by specific nodes in the document `ProcessedAS`. Every requirement
for a specific node is defined within two nested `Apply` elements. The syntactical structure remains the same for every requirement. The `Apply` element,

```
1  <Rule RuleId="processedAS" Effect="Permit">
2      <Description>Rule for sending documents of type ProcessedAS  </Description>
3      <Target>
4          <Subjects> <AnySubject/> </Subjects>
5          <Resources><AnyResource/></Resources>
6          <Actions>  <AnyAction/>  </Actions>
7      </Target>
8      <Condition FunctionId="and">
9      <Apply FunctionId="string-equal">
10         <AttributeValue DataType="XMLSchema#string">Municipality</AttributeValue>
11         <Apply FunctionId="string-one-and-only">
12             <AttributeSelector DataType="XMLSchema#string"
13             RequestContextPath="//Environment/Attribute
14             [@AttributeId='Confidentiality/body.processedAS.annualIncome']
15             /AttributeValue/text()"/>
16         </Apply>
17     </Apply>
18     <Apply FunctionId="string-equal">
19         <AttributeValue DataType="XMLSchema#string">TaxAdvisor</AttributeValue>
20         <Apply FunctionId="string-one-and-only">
21             <AttributeSelector DataType="http://www.w3.org/2001/XMLSchema#string"
22             RequestContextPath="//Environment/Attribute
23             [@AttributeId='Integrity/body.processedAS']
24             /AttributeValue/text()"/>
25         </Apply>
26     </Apply>
27     </Condition>
28 </Rule>
```

Fig. 8.9. Example Rule for Two Nodes of a Document of Type ProcessedAS

whose FunctionId attribute is set to string-equal contains two elements. An AttributeValue element indicating the role which is involved and an AttributeSelector element indicating in it RequestContextPath attribute the documents and the security requirement that has to be complied with.

The first Apply section [lines 9-17] indicates that the node annualIncome [line 14] should only be readable to the Municipality [line 10], implying encryption with its public key. The RequestContextPath attribute [lines 13-15] references the location of security information within the request for compliance check message coming from the PEP. The XPath expression indicates that the information will be stored as an Attribute value within the Environment section [line 13]. The information coming with the request (a node-requirement pair) will be compared with the information in the policy (line 14). In case of an exact match of the two string expressions the message is considered to be compliant to the requirement. Please, refer to Section 8.4.3 for the syntax of the Request for Compliance Check.

The second Apply section [lines 18-26] indicates that the node processedAS [line 19] – actually corresponding to the whole message payload (documents root node) – should be signed by the role TaxAdvisor [line 23]. This necessitates the application of a system signature with the role's private key. The condition's FunctionId attribute [line 8] is set to and thereby indicates that both Apply sections have to be met.

The Policy element

The Policy element combines rules into a policy. A Policy element comprises four main components:

1. a set of Rule elements defining node-requirements pairs (as described in the section The Rule Element).
2. an attribute RuleCombiningAlgId, corresponding to a rule-combining algorithm-identifier. It defines a procedure for reaching a decision given the individual results of evaluation of a set of rules. In the case of the Permit-overrides algorithm, if a single result yielding a Permit is returned, then the combined result is Permit.
3. a target element that specifies the roles taking part in an interaction. The Subject element's value defines the service caller, whereas the Resource element defines the service provider.
4. a PolicyDefault element specifying the X-Path version through the value of a nested XPathVersion element.

Listing 8.10 shows the structure of policy nesting the rules of Listing 8-1 [line 28]. The PolicyId attribute [line 1] identifies the name of the interaction, sendProcessedAS corresponding to a specific operation on a service provider's Web services port. The attribute RuleCombiningAlgId [line 1] is by default set to permit-overrides, saying that any call who matches one of the rules will be seen as compliant to security requirements as specified. The Target element

```
1  <Policy PolicyId="sendProcessedAS" RuleCombiningAlgId="permit-overrides">
2      <PolicyDefaults>
3          <XPathVersion>Rec-xpath-19991116 </XPathVersion>
4      </PolicyDefaults>
5      <Target>
6        <Subjects>
7          <Subject>
8            <SubjectMatch MatchId="string-equal">
9              <AttributeValue DataType="XMLSchema#string">TaxAdvisor</AttributeValue>
10             <SubjectAttributeDesignator DataType="XMLSchema#string"
11                                     AttributeId="subject-id"/>
12            </SubjectMatch>
13          </Subject>
14        </Subjects>
15        <Resources>
16          <Resource>
17          <ResourceMatch MatchId="string-equal">
18             <AttributeValue DataType="XMLSchema#string">Municipality</AttributeValue>
19             <ResourceAttributeDesignator DataType="XMLSchema#string"
20                                     AttributeId="resource-id"/>
21          </ResourceMatch>
22          </Resource>
23        </Resources>
24        <Actions>
25          <AnyAction/>
26        </Actions>
27      </Target>
28      <Rule RuleId="ProcessedAS" Effect="Permit">  …   </Rule>
29  </Policy>
```

Fig. 8.10. Example Policy Nesting a Set of Rules

section [lines 5-27] defines the two interacting roles. The Subject element [lines 7-13] specifies the role TaxAdvisor as the invoking party, whereas the Resource element specifies the role Municipality as the providing party.

The PolicySet element

Policies define interactions. Every Interaction is associated to a specific document instance. A particular type of a document (as defined in the Document Model) may be used in several interactions, every time as a specific instance of the document type.

A PolicySet groups all policies involving a specific document type, specified within the Resource element of the Target section. All policy sets referring to documents of a GWf are grouped into an additional PolicySet element which is associated to the GWf, specified within the Resource element of the Target section.

Listing 8.11 shows the two nested PolicySet elements. The first PolicySet element refers to the GWF AnnualStatement as stated through its attribute PolicySetId. The actual specification occurs within the Target sec-

```
1  <PolicySet  PolicySetId="AnnualStatement"
2                 PolicyCombiningAlgId="deny-overrides">
3    <Description>Policy Setfor the Role Municipality</Description>
4    <Target>
5      <Resources>
6        <Resource>
7          <ResourceMatch MatchId="string-equal">
8            <AttributeValue DataType="XMLSchema#string">
9            AnnualStatement</AttributeValue>
10           <ResourceAttributeDesignator   DataType="XMLSchema#string"
11                                  AttributeId="resource-id"/>
12         </ResourceMatch>
13       </Resource>
14     </Resources>
15   </Target>
16   <PolicySet  PolicySetId="ProcessedAS"
17                 PolicyCombiningAlgId="deny-overrides">
18     <Description>Policy Set for the document ProcessedAS</Description>
19     <Target>
20       <Resources>
21         <Resource>
22           <ResourceMatch MatchId="string-equal">
23             <AttributeValue DataType="XMLSchema#string">
24             ProcessedAS</AttributeValue>
25             <ResourceAttributeDesignator   DataType="XMLSchema#string"
26                                  AttributeId="resource-id"/>
27           </ResourceMatch>
28         </Resource>
29       </Resources>
30     </Target>
31     <Policy PolicyId="sendProcessedAS" RuleCombiningAlgId="permit-overrides">
32       <Rule RuleId="ProcessedAS" Effect="Permit">  ...    </Rule>
33     </Policy>
34   </PolicySet>
35 </PolicySet>
```

Fig. 8.11. Example of Nested PolicySet Element Targeting the GWf and a Document

tion [lines 4-15], where the `Resource` element's value is set to AnnualStatement. The second `PolicySet` element [lines 16-34] groups all policies related to instances of a `ProcessedAS` document, as indicated through the `PolicySet` element's attribute [line 16] and the corresponding `Resource` element's value [line 24] in the `Target` section [lines 16-34].

8.4.2 Outbound Messaging - (Executable Security Policy Files)

Figure 8.12 shows the abstract syntax for the composition of an Executable Security Policy File for policy enforcement on outbound messaging.

An `xsd:element` can be of complex type or simple type, specified through an attribute, as is the name of the element. A Policy File for outbound messaging starts with an element of type `ComplexType` that contains a sequence of elements structured according to the document type defined in the Document Model.

The security policies are specified within an `xsd:annotation` element. This container nest an `xsd:appinfo` element, indicating that the information is meant for machine processing. The latter nests all elements necessary to specify the security requirements (`sectet:Confidentiality`, `sectet:Integrity`, `sectet:NonRepudiationOfSending`, `sectet:NonRepudiationOfReception`).

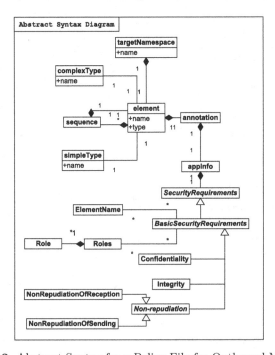

Fig. 8.12. Abstract Syntax for a Policy File for Outbound Messaging

```
1  <xsd:schema xmlns:xsd="http://www.w3.org/2001/XMLSchema"
2              targetNamespace="Municipality/sendNotification/Notification">
3    <xsd:element name="Notification" type="NotificationType"/>
4      <xsd:complexType name="NotificationType">
5          <xsd:annotation>
6              <xsd:appinfo>
7                  <BasicSecurityPolicy>
8                      <Confidentiality>
9                          <ElementName>Notification</ElementName>
10                         <Roles>
11                             <Role>TaxAdvisor</Role>
12                         </Roles>
13                     </Confidentiality>
14                     <Integrity>
15                         <ElementName>Notification</ElementName>
16                         <Roles>
17                             <Role>TaxAdvisor</Role>
18                         </Roles>
19                     </Integrity>
20                     <NonRepudiationOfReception>
21                         <ElementName>Notification</ElementName>
22                         <Roles>
23                             <Role>TaxAdvisor</Role>
24                         </Roles>
25                     </NonRepudiationOfReception>
26                 </BasicSecurityPolicy>
27             </xsd:appinfo>
28         </xsd:annotation>
29         <xsd:sequence>
30             <xsd:element name="ResponseComment"
31               type="ntf:ResponseCommentType"/>
32             <xsd:element name="ClientID" type="ntf:ClientIDType"/>
33             <xsd:element name="ClerkID" type="ntf:ClerkIDType"/>
34         </xsd:sequence>
35     </xsd:complexType>
36     <xsd:simpleType name="ResponseCommentType">
37         <xsd:restriction base="xsd:string"/>
38     </xsd:simpleType>
39     <xsd:simpleType name="ClientIDType">
40         <xsd:restriction base="xsd:string"/>
41     </xsd:simpleType>
42     <xsd:simpleType name="ClerkIDType">
43         <xsd:restriction base="xsd:string"/>
44     </xsd:simpleType>
45 </xsd:schema>
```

Fig. 8.13. Example Policy File for Document of Type Notification

Figure 8.13 shows an example file for a document of type Notification, which is sent – as indicated through the TargetNamespace attribute [line 2] – by the role Municipality by invoking the operation sendNotification. The policy file applies to the document specified within the xsd:complexType declaration, which in our case is of type NotificationType. The section BasicSecurityPolicy [lines 7-26] contains the three sections for the specification of policies, one for each type. All of them specify that the policy applies to the whole document – one single ElementName element referencing the document root element [lines 9, 15, and 21].

The role element defines either the sending or receiving party, depending on the security policies. Confidentiality requires a reference to the public key of a receiver role for the encryption. Integrity requires the signature of the sending role. NonRepudiationOfReception waits for an acknowledgement by a receiver role.

The mapping of a role to a particular user, playing the receiving end in the interaction is done through the Role Mapping Unit of the RA (cf. Figure 8.1 on p. 122), before the PEP applies the processing steps to the SOAP message. In case there is more then one user holding the specific role, the first match is taken by default. Other algorithms may be applied as well.

8.4.3 Request for Compliance Check

Figure 8.14 shows the syntax elements of a Request for Compliance Check. A Request consists of a Subject, who is the service requester, a Resource, being the service Provider, an Action being the operation called, and the Environment section which will be accessed by the Policy Configuration Engine (PCE) when evaluating the request against the Policy (Component Nr5 in Figure 8.1 on p. 122).

The Environment section captures two units of information. It specifies the policy/node pairs as identified in the inbound message as an AttributeId attribute of an Attribute element and it specifies the role holding the key for encryption (sender) or signature (receiver) through an AttributeValue element, respectively.

Figure 8.15 shows an example Request for Compliance Check which was constructed by the PEP at the boundaries of the domain of a holder of the role Municipality and forwarded to the PCE for evaluation. As can easily be seen the document was sent by the TaxAdvsior (line 4) to the Municipality (line 9) by invoking the operation sendProcessedAS (line 14). After processing the security information the PEP added the following information: the element ClientID was encrypted with the Municipality's public key (lines 18-20), and the TaxAdvisor signed the whole document (lines 22-24).

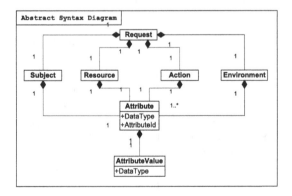

Fig. 8.14. Abstract Syntax for Request for Compliance Check

```
1  <Request>
2      <Subject>
3          <Attribute AttributeId="subject-id" DataType="XMLSchema#string">
4              <AttributeValue>TaxAdvisor</AttributeValue>
5          </Attribute>
6      </Subject>
7      <Resource>
8          <Attribute AttributeId="resource-id" DataType="XMLSchema#string">
9              <AttributeValue>Municipality</AttributeValue>
10         </Attribute>
11     </Resource>
12     <Action>
13         <Attribute AttributeId="action-id" DataType="XMLSchema#string">
14             <AttributeValue>sendProcessedAS</AttributeValue>
15         </Attribute>
16     </Action>
17     <Environment>
18         <Attribute AttributeId="_SEC_POL_CONFIDENTIALITY_/body.processedAS.clientID"
19             DataType="XMLSchema#string">
20             <AttributeValue>Municipality</AttributeValue>
21         </Attribute>
22         <Attribute AttributeId="_SEC_POL_INTEGRITY_/body.processedAS"
23             DataType="XMLSchema#string">
24             <AttributeValue>TaxAdvisor</AttributeValue>
25         </Attribute>
26     </Environment>
27 </Request>
```

Fig. 8.15. Example Request for Compliance Check

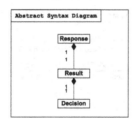

Fig. 8.16. Abstract Syntax for PCE Response Message

```
1  <Response>
2      <Result>
3          <Decision>Permit</Decision>
4      </Result>
5  </Response>
```

Fig. 8.17. Example Positive Response

8.4.4 Response Request for Compliance Check

After evaluation, the PCE sends back a response message, whose root element is a `Response` containing a `Result`, which nests the `Decision`. The answer could be either a `Permit` after positive Evaluation, a `Deny` after negative evaluation or in case of default.

Figure 8.16 shows the abstract syntax for a response, and Figure 8.17 shows an example positive response.

Security Requirement	Security Component	Provided Functionality	Technologies & Standards
Authentication	Policy Enforcement Point	Process SOAP Message Structure	XML, XML-Encr.,XML-Sign WS-Sec, SAML
	Role Mapping Unit	Assign User to Role	XACML, XML
	Policy Repository	Access to User-Role Database	XACML, XML
Authorization	Policy Enforcement Point	Process SOAP Message Structure	XML, XML-Encr.,XML-Sign WS-Sec, SAML
	Policy Decision Point	Check Dynamic Constraint Policies Check Static Constraint Policies	XACML, XML XACML, XML
	Policy Repository	Access to Permission-Role Database	XACML, XML
Confidentiality	Policy Enforcement Point	Process SOAP Security Structure (Inbound)	XML, XML-Encr.,XML-Sign WS-Sec, SAML
		Build SOAP Security Structure (Outbound)	XML, XML-Encr.,XML-Sign WS-Sec, SAML
	PEP Configuration Engine	Security Compliance Check (Inbound) Provide Security Requirements (Outbound)	PKI, WSS4J, XML PKI, WSS4J, XML
	PEP Configuration Engine	Check of Complimnace to Security Requirements	PKI, WSS4J, XML
Integrity	Policy Enforcement Point	Process SOAP Security Structure (Inbound)	XML, XML-Encr.,XML-Sign WS-Sec, SAML
		Build SOAP Security Structure (Outbound)	XML, XML-Encr.,XML-Sign WS-Sec, SAML
	PEP Configuration Engine	Security Compliance Check (Inbound) Provide Security Requirements (Outbound)	PKI, WSS4J, XML PKI, WSS4J, XML
	PEP Configuration Engine	Check of Complimnace to Security Requirements	PKI, WSS4J, XML
Non Repudiation of Reception	Policy Enforcement Point	Process SOAP Security Structure (Inbound)	XML, XML-Encr.,XML-Sign WS-Sec, SAML
		Return Signed Receipt (Inbound)	XML, XML-Encr.,XML-Sign WS-Sec, SAML
		Wait for Signed Recept (Outbound)	XML, XML-Encr.,XML-Sign WS-Sec, SAML
	PEP Configuration Engine	Security Compliance Check (Inbound) Provide Security Requirements (Outbound)	PKI, WSS4J, XML PKI, WSS4J, XML
	Logging Unit	Log Signed Receipt (Outbound)	PKI, WSS4J, XML
Non Repudiation of Sending	Policy Enforcement Point	Process SOAP Security Structure (Inbound)	XML, XML-Encr.,XML-Sign WS-Sec, SAML
		Ask for Signed Receipt (Inbound)	XML, XML-Encr.,XML-Sign WS-Sec, SAML
		Wait for Request for Signed Recept (Outbound)	XML, XML-Encr.,XML-Sign WS-Sec, SAML
	PEP Configuration Engine	Security Compliance Check (Inbound) Provide Security Requirements (Outbound)	PKI, WSS4J, XML
	Logging Unit	Log Signed Receipt (Inbound)	PKI, WSS4J, XML

SAML	Security Assertion Markup Language (SAML)
XACML	Extensible Access Control Markup Language (XACML)
Sign	XML Digital Signature
Encr	XML Encryption
WS-Sec	Web-Services Security Specification
XSD	XML Schema Definition
WSS4J	Web-Services Security for Java
XML	Extensible Mark up Language
PKI	Public Key Infrastructure

Fig. 8.18. XML-, Web Services and Security Standards in the Reference Architecture

8.4.5 Technology and Standards

Figure 8.18 gives an overview over which security component enforces which security policy by providing a specific service, implemented through a specific standard.

9

Model Transformation & Code Generation

In this chapter, we complete the Domain Architecture by presenting the *Model Transformations*. Model Transformations link the Domain Specific Language (DSL) (introduced in Chapter 8) to the Reference Architecture (RA) (specified in Chapter 7). As the specific implementation of these Transformations is not necessary when applying the SECTET-framework, we confine ourselves to a sketch of the conceptual mapping (a rough description of how model elements map to specific syntactical blocks or patterns of code) and refer the reader interested in the implementation of these Transformation to a broad array of literature on resective tools and approaches (e.g., [180, 135, 157])

This Chapter is structured as follows. Section 9.1 gives a general overview of transformation types in the SECTET-framework. Section 9.2 introduces the conceptual mapping of meta-model elements defining a GWf and related security requirements (as identified in Chapter 6 and modeled in Chapter 7) to syntactical elements for executable artefacts configuring the security components of the RA. Section 9.3 introduces the mapping of meta-model elements of the GWfM to elements of the abstract syntax for service components of the RA. Having defined the mapping conceptually with the tables, we close this Chapter with Section 9.4 giving an overview on apporaches on how to implement Transformations and actually generate the artefacts.

9.1 Transformations in the Sectet-Framework

The platform independent models of the DSL represent the means to configure the security components and (in parts) the service components of the RA with the help of XACML-files. The SECTET-framework differentiates between two types of model transformations.

9.1.1 The Generation of Security Artefacts

The first type of transformation – depicted as box Nr.1 in Figure 9.1 – covers the transformation of security relevant information captured at the *Model Level* (as *Platform Independent Models*) into configuration files for the RA.

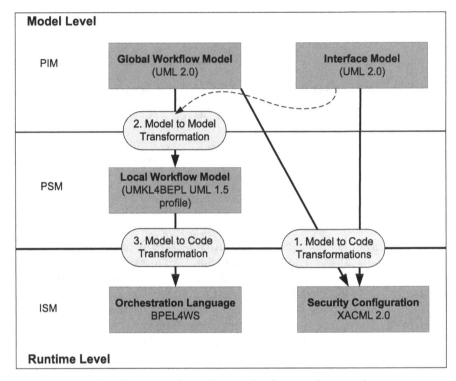

Fig. 9.1. Transformations in the SECTET-framework

The configuration files are conceptually defined as *Implementation Specific Models* located at the *Component Level*. A transformation process taking UML 2.0 models as input and generating code is called *Model-to-Code Transformation*. We will follow that apporach to generate security Artefacts in Section 9.2.

9.1.2 The Generation of Services Artefacts

The second type of transformation - depicted as boxes Nr. 2 and Nr. 3 in Figure 9.1 - refers to the generation of code skeletons for service components at local partner nodes (e.g., BPEL- worklfow engine). Generated code is confined by the information available in the GWfM. This corresponds to the interface of a Local Workflow (LWf) to the "outside". The "outside" refers to all partner roles in the Global Workflow.

There are many ways to represent a GWf in a machine readable format for further processing by transformation functions of the framework. One possibility would be to describe a GWf as a chorography specified in the XML-based WS-CDL language and map WS-CDL-elements to their syntactical counter-parts in an orchestration language (e.g., BPEL). This can be repeated for all partners in a peer-to-peer process. The approach is extensively presented in [141].

In the present work, we took an alternative approach for the modeling of a GWf. We take the much more intuitive UML 2.0 Activity Diagrams for the representation of a GWf (cf. Chapter 7). UML 2.0 Actions define interactions with partners in the GWfM (invoking or providing a service) and are transformed into platform specific models for further transformation *Model-to-Model Transformation* or, alternatively, into code, which corresponds to *Model-to-Code Transformation.*

The target for generated services artefacts could either be a worklfow engine with a workflow language like BPEL or plain Web services wrapping back-end functionality (cf. Chapter 8). In the latter case, the control flow of the LWf is left over to the wrapped application. In case the target is a worflow engine, calls to local services would have to be inserted manually, as this kind of information would not show up in the GWfM.

9.2 Security Transformations

Security Transformations define how model instances capturing a GWf are translated into artefacts configuring the security components of the RA. The transformations are specified at the level of the meta-models. This means, that we define a conceptual mapping from elements of the platform independent meta-models of the DSL (Chapter 7 pp. 100) to elements of the abstract syntax of the platform specific target artifact (Chapter 8 pp. 130).

The mapping is defined through rules listed in tables which can be found in Appendix A. The tables map elements, attributes and functions of the target artefact on the left hand side to the corresponding source element at the platform independent level. By default, elements of the source meta-models refer to the security meta-model (Section 7.3 pp. 114), in case they do not, they are prefixed by the name of the meta-model in the corresponding model view (Chapter 7 pp. 100).

Abstract and concrete syntax of *Inbound-* as well as *Outbound Policy Files* fully comply to the XACML 2.0 specification [147]. All XACML elements, attributes and functions needed by the component are listed in the table.

Section 9.2.1 defines the rules for the generation of the Inbound Policy File, and section 9.2.2 defines the rules for the generation of the Outbound Policy File.

9.2.1 Inbound Policy File

Figure A.1 in the Appendix on page 226 contains the rules for the generation of *Inbound Policy Files*. These artefacts configure the security components for inbound messaging.

The relationships between elements of the target model are expressed either through nesting of sub-elements within parent-element or by associating attributes to elements. These elements are prefixed with a path expression defining their location with respect to the root element realizing a particular concept of the language as defined in Chapter 8 on pp. 8.4.1. There are four main concepts:

1. `Rules` capture security policies as defined in the models. They are associated to document instances travelling through object nodes in an interaction between two partners.
2. `Policies` group rules into a set. They are associated the document classes, thus referring to all instances of the respective document.
3. `PolicySet` elements group policies into sets. We use a `PolicySet` element as root element, associating a policy with a specific GWf. The root `PolicySet` nests one or more additional `PolicySet` elements, one for every document class in the Document Model (cf. p. 107 in Section 7.2.2).
4. `Target` elements are syntactical XACML constructs that set a context in terms subject, resource and action referring to a `Rule`, a `Policy` or a `PolicySet`. The sub-elements of a `Target` nested within a `Rule` are empty. The reason being that the context is established through the `RuleId` attribute. Its presence is mandatory in order to comply with the specification. Nested within a `Policy` element the `Target` defines the sender (`Subject` element) and receiver (`Resource` element) in an interaction. Nested within a `PolicySet` element it either refers to the document class or a Global Workflow (`Resource` element).

The transformation algorithm performs a depth-first search through the object tree holding the document nodes represented as an XML tree in the XMI-file. In the example, the order of the sequence's children is kept, each one translated according to the defined order.

The attribute `RequestContextPath` of the element `Rule` defines two of the four core pieces of information: it specifies a pair consisting of a document node and an associated Security Policy (e.g., Confidentiality, Integrity or Non-repudiation). The value is produced according to the production rules specified in Figure 9.2. The other two information parts correspond to the `Sender` and the `Receiver`. The invoking party (`Sender`) is referenced in the `Resource` section of the policy's `Target`.

The result of the transformation process is a policy file specifying the Security Policy for inbound messaging. For an example please, refer to Figure 8.11 in Chapter 8 on p. 131.

9.2.2 Outbound Policy Files

Figure A.2 in the Appendix on page 227 contains the rules for the model-to-code generation of *Outbound Policy Files*. All XACML elements, attributes

```
 1  RequestContextPathValue = PathExpression, AttributeExpression, TextNodeFunction;
 2
 3  PathExpression = '//Environment/Attribute'
 4  AttributeExpression = '[@AttributeId=', "", SecurityRequirementNodePair, "", ']';
 5  TextNodeFunction = '/AttributeValue/text()';
 6
 7  SecurityRequirementNodePair = SecurityRequirement, Node;
 8  SecurityRequirement = (Integrity | Confidentiality | NRS | NRR);
 9  Node = '/body.', ElementPathExpression, Element;
10  ElementPathExpression = Element, ('.', Element;
11  Element = ( lowercase | digit | uppercase | '_' )*;
12
13  uppercase = ['A' .. 'Z'];
14
15  lowercase = ['a' .. 'z'];
16
17  digit = ['0' .. '9'];
```

Fig. 9.2. Production Rules for RequestContextPath Attribute

and functions needed by the component are listed in the table. Abstract and concrete syntax of Outbound Policy templates comply to the abstract syntax specified on p. 136 in Chapter 8.

The result of the transformation process is a policy template for outbound messaging (cf. Figure 8.13 on p. 137).

9.3 Services Transformations

Services Transformations describe the rules for the generation of those files that will configure the service components of the target architecture so that their interface definitions realize the specifications of the interactions as defined in the Global Workflow Model and the Document Model. Here, we assume that the target service component is a process engine implementing a Web services based process language (e.g., Oracle BPEL Process Manager [7]). We chose the WSBPEL orchestration language, one of the de-facto industry standards. It may be any other process standard as well. The process of Services Transformation yields two categories of artefacts (for the sake of simplicity, we assume that a category corresponds to one file):

1. BPEL process description files (.bpel file extension) capture those parts of the process logic that specify interaction activities with partners and the messages that are exchanged. This corresponds to information contained in the Global Workflow Model and the Interface Model.
2. Calls to and from local service components are added manually after the generation process. WSDL files (.wsdl file extension) correspond to a technical description of interfaces and data types used and provided when interacting with partners.

3. XML Schema files are used to define the communication contract between Partner Roles in a Gwf. This means that the actual data format in which XML data is transmitted is described in XML Schema (for the basic specification please refer to [54]). We use XML Schema to define the structure of messages in an interaction.

Please refer to [86] for a detailed account on services transformation with SECTET.

9.3.1 Global Workflow to Local Workflow Translation

BPEL4WS depends on XML-based specifications like WSDL 1.1, XML Schema 1.0, XPath 1.0 and WS-Addressing. The BPEL4WS process model is layered on top of the service model defined by WSDL. The aim of this section is to cover transformations only for basic structures and concepts of the language needed to describe those process tasks representing endpoint of binary interactions. We do not discuss advanced data handling (e.g., assignment), message correlation, scopes and fault handling. As to structured activities we only use sequence indicating a sequential flow of control between interaction tasks. We cover the following interaction patterns:

1. In an asynchronous interaction, a task either invokes or provides an operation of an interface.
2. In a synchronous invocation, a task invokes an operation but also provides a call-back operation.

Figures A.3 and Figure A.4 in the Appendix on pages 228 and 229 show the translation rules for the BPEL file.

Figure 9.3 diagrammatically shows how the part of the GWfM relevant to the Municipality is mapped to BPEL Activities according to the UML Profile for Automated Business Processes [137]. Code generation out of the LWfM specified in UML is straightforward using the approach and the tools described in [137].

In our case, the binary interaction with the role TaxAdvisor is mapped to synchronous receive-reply BPEL interaction-pattern. In case the workflow engine makes additional calls to local services, the Municipality would have to insert respective activities manually (e.g., by inserting an additional partition for a port and changing the control flow by rearranging the graph depicting the control flow, as done in Figure 7.10 on p. 106 in Chapter 7).

9.3.2 Global Workflow to WSDL Description

A BPEL4WS process is generally defined "in the abstract" by referencing only the portTypes of the services involved in the process Ú corresponding to the abstract part of the WSDL file. The absence of bindings and service elements in the WSDL document aims the reuse of business process definitions

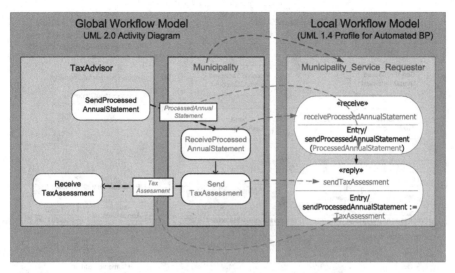

Fig. 9.3. Model-to-model Transformation Generating a BEPL File for Role `Municipality`

over multiple deployments of compatible services. For simplicity, all WSDL definitions required by the business process are included in the same WSDL document.

The main concepts are:

1. The `definitions` element acting as the root element
2. `type` definitions defining the complex data-types. The schemas of data-types correspond to the documents defined in the Document models. The classes of the Document Model are mapped in a standard way to xsd schemas, as described in [136]. Every document is imported through an import declaration.
3. `message` definitions describe the parameters for service invocations. They use data-types defined in the type definitions section and correspond to document classes.
4. `portType` definitions group operations into logical sets.
5. `partnerLinkType` definitions are BEPL specific WSDL extensions (indicated by the namespace `plnk`) that specify the pattern of interaction used by process tasks.

Figure A.5 in the Appendix on page 230 contains all the rules for translating WSDL elements out of respective elements in the Global Workflow Model and the Interface Model.

Figure 9.4 diagrammatically shows how the part of the GWfM and the Document Model relevant to the Municipality is mapped to Message Classes according to the UML Profile for Automated Business Processes [137]. Code generation out of the LWfM specified in UML is straightforward using the approach and the tools described in [137].

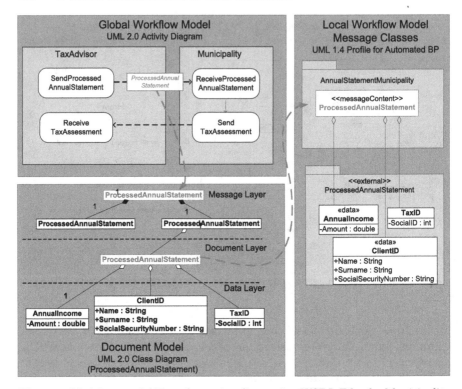

Fig. 9.4. Model-to-model Transformation Generating WSDL Files for Municipality

9.3.3 Global Workflow to XSD Schema Template

Elements of the Document Model are translated into the XML Schema data definitions which are referenced by the WSDL file of a process.

XML Schema has many predefined basic data types such as integer, string, or date. Basic data types are extended by introducing the simpleType tag. This allows to set constraints like, minimum length, character patterns or enumerations on a basic data type. With simple types one can describe the allowed content for attribute and the content of elements with character content. The nesting of XML elements and their attributes, is done with a complexType tag. Complex types support the description of the cardinalities and optional use of contained elements and attributes.

The generation process for the XML Schema files can be divided into the following steps (please refer to [86] for a detailed account on Services Transformation with SECTET):

1. For every Document Class in the Document Model a new XML Schema file and with the starting schema element and the respective the XML Schema namespace definition, and the definition of the target namespace of the process is created.

2. A top level **element** tag is added to the file with the name of the Schema, and a complex type is added.
3. **attribute** tags for all attributes of the schema that start with a @ are generated.
4. For all containment relationships **element** tags with the name of the relation as element name, and the name of the complex or simple type as associated type are added. Bounds are defined according to the cardinalities specified by the relation.
5. For each **element** tag that does not refer to a basic data type, a complex or simple type outside the previous element is created.
6. Repeat the creation of elements and attribute inside just created complex types.
7. Repeat the whole process for the outgoing message.

9.4 Implementing Transformation

The Transformation Component translates the models into executable configuration artifacts for the Reference Architecture. There are many approaches to implement transformation functions in order to generate executable or machine-readable policies. We sub-sequntyl briefly sketch these approaches.

9.4.1 Template Based Transformations

In a first project phase, the component was prototypically implemented with XSLT, a language for transforming XML documents into other XML documents. Transformations are expressed in XSLT rules that take a source tree and transform it into a result tree. The transformation is achieved by associating patterns with templates. A pattern is matched against elements in the source tree. In our case, the transformator worked the following way:

1. models are exported from UML tools as XMI files,
2. XMI files are parsed by the transformation component, an internal tree representation created,
3. template rules matching the nodes of the source document are identified
4. nodes of the source document are transformed according to the processing instructions in the XSLT stylesheet.

The opportunity to apply the approach to different scenarios (e.g., e-government and healthcare) gave rise to a set of requirements whose integration into the framework was essential to its usability in a real-life context. Most of these issues, like the problem on how to manage Role Based Access Control in a virtual process without a central instance of control (decentralized management of RBAC) were practical in nature and could be resolved by implementing additional modules for the framework. Nevertheless, some of them touched the conceptual foundations and questioned some of the early design decisions. Among them was the choice of XSLT for code generation from respective models. XSLT Ű a lightweight technology for the transformation of XML documents - perfectly fits the needs of a research project looking for an easy to use technology for the rapid development of a demonstrator tool as a proof-of-concept. Nevertheless, the technology showed its limitations. New requirements in the form of more complex security patterns were constantly emerging. The domain language had to be extended syntactically and the adaptation of XSLT templates to more complex transformation functions took a great deal of time. The handling of XSLT revealed as being too cumbersome. Consequently, the transformation component was redesigned from scratch using meta-model based transformation rules.

9.4.2 Meta-model Based Transformations

Based on OMG's transformation specification MOF Query/View/Transformation (QVT) [194], the component now supports an intuitive rule-based mapping between platform independent source and platform specific target models. Source and target models can easily be defined or adapted by importing the respective meta-models. This supports domain experts in rapidly developing and adapting a domain specific language in an agile way and visualizes the transformation process.

Figure 9.5 shows an excerpt from the scripts used to transform a Domain Model to the XACML policy meta-model.

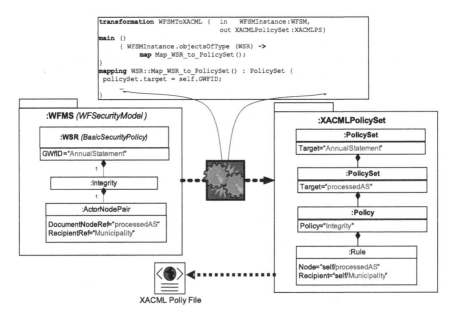

Fig. 9.5. Model-to-model Transformation Generating XACML Policy Files

The transformation defines two typed candidate models (as parameters): an input model WFSMInstance of type DomainModel and an output model XACMLPolicySet of type XACMLPolicy. Mappings are defined by refenrencing the source model elements to their counterparts in the target (e.g., the id of the Gwf GWfID to the destination element of the root policy set Target).

For details on MOF/QVT transformations in the SECTET-framework, please refer to [107].

10

Software & Security Management

For its successful application, Model Driven Security relies heavily on a series
of tools. We have implemented our approach as a proof-of-concept framework.
The framework consists of prototypical tools, we developed ourselves and integrates various third party components. It supports the development of all
models and the generation of systems for their implementation in local run-
time environments. We first introduce the set of tools the stakeholders planning the realization of a Global Workflow may need (Section 10.1) and give
an overview of how the deployment process may be managed (Section 10.2).

10.1 Tool Chain

10.1.1 Modeling

Modeling tools are at the core of every Model Driven Development initiative.
They are used to build the Models on the basis of the Domain Specific Language (DSL). Graphical DSLs provide a very intuitive way to build models,
and – if based on the UML – realizable with a reasonable amount of effort.
UML tools, like MagicDraw or Ecipse Omondo provide the features that are
absolutely necessary for the use of UML as a DSL in conjunction with other
tools. These features are:

1. Meta-modeling and profiling features. Ideally, the case tool supports the
   definition of meta-model types and allows for the specification of constraints on meta-models. In case this is not possible, the meta-model have
   to be expressed with a corresponding UML-Profile.
2. XMI-Export. The tools have at least to support the export of model instances in the XML Metadata Interchange format. Exporting models is
   a prerequisite for further processing by other tools e.g., Transformation
   Components. Its specification Version 2.0 XMI it represents an efficient
   and coherent way to define models that can be exchanged by different
   tools.

3. Stereotypes and Tagged Values. The tools have to support the annotation of model elements with stereotypes and/or tagged values and dependencies between them.

10.1.2 Code Generation

Once exported as XMI files, the models are parsed by a component that validates the models according to the meta-models and – in a second step translates the models into code or into another model.

An optimal design of the component realizes the following two principles. First, it would rely on Abstract Syntax: ideally, the model validation occurs independently of the concrete syntax of the model This allows for changes in the concrete syntax without affecting the component. A new parser for reading the changed syntax would be all that is needed. Validation rules would remain unaffected by the syntactical changes. Second it would work with explicit metamodel representations: by relying on representation of the meta-model the validation and transformations rules remain independent of their syntactical representation and vice versa. In this case models represent instances of the meta-model. The high level of abstraction allows for a more efficient specification of complex rules. Our code transformation component is a Java based tool that works according to the following steps (Figure 10.1):

1. It parses the source model in its XMI-format as exported from the UML tool.
2. It creates an instance of the source meta-model and populates the object structure (Document Object Model (DOM) tree), with values from the source model.
3. The source object structure is transformed in an object structure corresponding to the target meta-model.
4. The populated instance of the target meta-model is transformed into the concrete syntax of the target language.

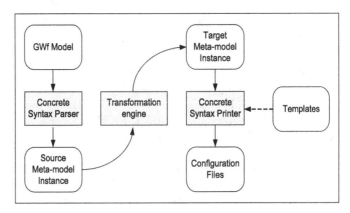

Fig. 10.1. Components and Artefacts in the Transformation Process

10.1.3 Build Tools and Integrated Development Environments

We use the Eclipse Integrated Development Environment as a framework for the integration of all the components [190]. The management of the source models and code artifacts requires a build tool that supports the compilation packaging and further processing. Ideally, the build process should also automate the deployment process on the Reference Architecture. We use the Java-based build tool Apache Ant [188].

10.1.4 The Realization Process

Roughly simplified, the realization process of an inter-organizational workflow actually consists of the three phases: analysis phase, design phase and the implementation phase. The analysis was presented in Chapter 6

The realization of an inter-organizational workflow usually starts with the requirements modeling phase. The stakeholders agree on the business goal, and the terms under which they want to realize through their collaboration, followed by the design phase and ends with the implementation. This first step leads to a common understanding of the structure of the "virtual" or the global workflow. The result is a semi-formal model called the Gloabl Workflow Model with asscoiated Security Policies. Ideally, this includes the format, the structure and the sequence of the messages that are exchanged, the interfaces to the "business" or workflow logic each partner agreed to contribute to the composition, to operation semantics and to run-time constraints specification, information that is typically published in WSDL files and technical Models of UDDI Registries.

From here on, the participants have all information necessary to implement "interface"-compliant functionality at their nodes. In practice it is almost impossible to impose a straight top-down realization process on the participants for various reasons. First, it is very improbable that the partners will implement their logic from scratch. Very often partners have already implemented some kind of application logic, maybe even made it accessible to customers as a Web service. They probably want to reuse functionality of existing components running on a working infrastructure. The components reuse and their integration is a matter of cost-efficiency and requires some in-depth expertise of the technical staff. Nor is it very likely that the partners will completely redesign the interfaces to their business logic to make them compliant to the naming conventions specified in the global workflow. Businesses and administrations can have organizational structures that may thwart a top-down approach from the very beginning (e.g., every business unit has its own technical infrastructure; administrative units may have different reporting hierarchies, etc.).

This is why the stakeholders will proceed according to a hybrid approach projecting some of the interfaces of their local business logic to operations in an Interface Model, which conforms to a uniform technical, syntactical and

semantic specification the partners agreed upon. In turn, they may wrap some
of their local applications in order to comply with operations signatures of the
Interface Model. If, for example, the partners agree to implement the global
workflow based on Web services, some partners will have to provide a Web
services wrapper for their application logic.

10.1.5 The Engineering Process

The realization of a scenario based on Model Driven Security needs two prerequisites: first, the existence of a comprehensive specification of functional
and security requirements, second, the existence of an MDS Framework consisting of tools supporting the Domain Architecture. The tools should support
the modeling in a Domain Specific Language and provide transformation functionality targeting a specific platform.

In case the Domain Architecture has to be adapted or even developed from
scratch, both strand of activity, the development of the domain architecture
as well as the requirements analysis for the solution to be realized, can occur
in parallel, possibly iteratively. They may partly dependent on artifacts from
the other activity, taking them as input, this supporting an incremental, agile
engineering methodology. For the sake of simplicity and readability, we depict this process without iterations in Figure 10.2. Once the DSL Framework

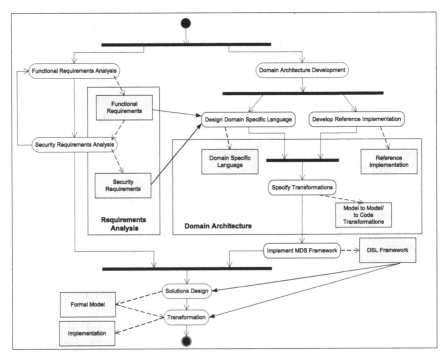

Fig. 10.2. The Process of Realizing a Domain Architecture

properly configured in order to support the Domain Architecture, the solution can be designed, and transformed into an implementation.

10.2 The Deployment Process

Figure 10.3 exemplarily shows the process of realizing a Global Workflow. The partitions represent the tools that are used for executing the actions. Tools used by all partners in a collaborative manner are rendered as grey partitions, whereas white boxes represent tools that have to be used by individually in order to configure their target architecture properly. Partners, having agreed on a Global Workflow scenario, model the scenario as a Global Workflow Model with all related models with the help of a UML tool. The files are exported as XMI files and imported into the SECTET framework, which translates them into configuration artifacts for the local environments. The files are placed in a shared workspace. Every partner picks his files and deploys them on his infrastructure. In case he uses a BPEL based workflow Management system, he loads the stubs into his design tool, completes them with calls of local services and finally deploy them.

Changes in the GWf (e.g., a reordering of the document flow or a change in Security Policies) necessitates a start of the deployment process from scratch. Changes in the LWf can be accommodated locally by Partner as long as the interfaces to his LWf as specified in the GWfM remain unchanged (the BPEL stubs generated out of the GWfM stay the same).

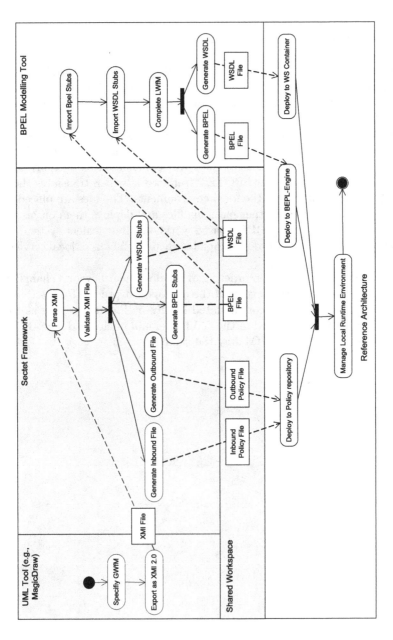

Fig. 10.3. The Deployment of a Global Workflow

11

Extending Sectet: Advanced Security Policy Modeling

In past chapters, we showed how to model Basic Security Policies based on the three Security Objectives Confidentiality, Integrity, and Non-repudiation. We specified a Reference Architecture based on Web services technologies and standards. Security Policies were mainly enforced through the integration of corresponding basic cryptographic primitives (e.g., encryption, digital signatures, and a combination of them orchestrated by a protocol). The gap between abstract policy models and technology was bridged by transformation rules for a Transformation Engine generating the artifacts for the configuration of architecural components enforcing the policies.

Nevertheless, in an industrial context, security concerns usually go way beyond what we cover with the category *Basic Security Policy*. This chapter shows how to extend the SECTET-framework to cope with complex security concerns. We introduce the category *Advanced Security Policy* which is of practical relevance to many contemporary scenarios in e-government and – as we will see in the next chapter – in healthcare. It covers policies like *Context Dependent Access Policies*, the *Qualified Signature*, the *Four-Eyes-Principle*, *Privacy Policies*, and *Usage Policies*. We show how the three building blocks of the SECTET-framework are extended to cope with this new categories of complex security concerns.

This chapter is organized as follows. We start with a brief motivation for the introduction of the category *Advanced Security Policy* in Section 11.1. We sketch the extensions to the existing structure of the *Domain Specific Language* (DSL) in Section 11.2. We show how to model *Advanced Security Policies* with SECTET-PL, a language for dynamic constraints modeling in Section 11.3. We will cover dynamic access control, rights delegation and privacy policies extensively. For these policies, we will show how to integrate the meta-model extension into the framework in Section 11.4, the extensions to the Target Architecture in Section 11.5, and SECTET-PL-Transformations in Section 11.6. We close with a brief sketch on how to model further *Advanced Security Policies* and how they may be enforced in the Reference Architecture.

11.1 Motivation

In almost any industry, the electronic realization of security-critical processes is tightly coupled with concerns about how to best realize security in compliance with the many provisions, regulations and laws imposed by regional, national, international and industry legislations.

In healthcare, access rights may have to dependent on dymanic, time- and context depend aspects. The so-called *Break-Glass Policy* is defined as an authorization scheme to allow access to a patient's medical record in case of an emergency (e.g., [173]). Another example from healthcare is the *4-Eyes-Principle*, a regulation for access control, stipulöating the patient's presence when a physician accesses her medical record (see e.g., [202, 182]).

E-procurement – the purchasing of goods via electronic media – can be carried out by either private-sector or public-sector actors. If the public sector calls for tenders, such as in the case of public utilities and telecoms, public sector regulations apply. Very often, this kind of scenario requires partial or full *Anonymity* of bidders to guarantee the execution of a fair procedure.

In all these cases, the notion of security obviously has to encompass much more advanced concepts. Compliance to the requirements of the legal environment is a major issue, but only one facet of the problem.

On the other hand, information-intensive industries, like e-government and healthcare usually have to cope with diverging interests of a scenario's stakeholders. For example, a patient may never be the producer of the data of his medical record. Nevertheless he retains exclusive legal rights over his medical records: he decides upon who accesses the records under which conditions. The organizations who store and process sensitive information are responsible for preserving data confidentiality at all cost, even if the records are distributed among various stakeholders (hospital, practitioners, insurances etc.) with different rights to read and process the information. The simple policy of end-to-end confidentiality becomes a complex privacy policy specifying fine-grained, revocable, time-, context- and history dependent access rights to heterogenous resources. This setting deserves to model and enforce *Dynamic Access-*, and *Ongoing Usage Policies* in a distributed environment where control over information has to be enforced even on untrusted hosts.

As a consequence, Security Objectives can only partially be realized with a *Basic Security Policy* or even a combination of them. Taking the *Qualified Signature* as an example: this is a policy which actually neither enforces the Objective of *Integrity* nor does it correspond to an *Integrity* policy. There is a different meaning in the context of the use of these two types of signatures in the Problem Domain: an Integrity policy is meant to identify unauthorized tampering with documents, whereas a policy stipulating a *Qualified Signature* is primarily a means to prove someone's identity by making respective information available as needed. Thus the primary function of the concept of *Qualified Signature* seems to cater for some kind of *Availability*. However, the

Qualified Signature may also be used to enforce *Non-repudiation* - so as to "seal" an adminsitrative act (e.g., the registration of your marriage).

Modeling Advanced Security Policies based on consistent Security Models and their enforcement with appropiate technology in the Reference Architecture obviously represents a major challenge.

11.2 Extending the DSL

11.2.1 A New Security Objective

Following our discussion in the previous Section, *Access Control-* and *Usage Control-* and *Domain Policies* represent types of policies that obviously do not directly enforce either of the three *Basic Security Requirements*, namely *Confidentiality, Integrity* or *Non-repudiation*.

Therefore, we introduce *Availability* as a new class of Security Objective (Figure 11.1) to cope with these policies. Availability refers to the ability to use an object when needed. But Availability is not only an important aspect of reliability, guaranteeing existence of a resource. In security, the aspect of availability is interpreted in the sense that someone may use a resource, access information, or call a service as needed under specific conditions. These conditions may be linked to various attributes of the system, its environment or the actors themselves in the past, the present or even the future. Note that in this sense this new type of policy introduced subsequently also caters to the Objective of Confidentiality: information should not only be available at any time but should almost certainly remain confidential in most cases. Nevertheless, we only show the policies' link to the most dominant aspect. And this is Availability.

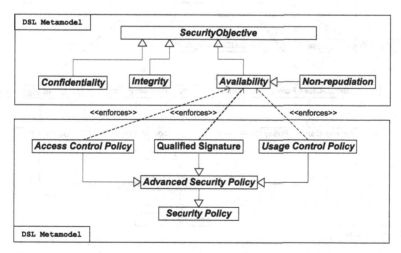

Fig. 11.1. Extending SECTET with Security Policies for Availability

We also note, that we sub-classed Non-repudiation as specializing Availability. We motivate that adaptation with the meaning of Non-repudiation as having information available when needed as a proof for dispute resolution.

11.2.2 Advanced Security Policies

Figure 11.2 shows some types of *Domain-*, *Access Control-* and *Usage Control Policies* enforcing the requirement of *Availablility*.

The *Four-Eyes-Principle*, the *Break-Glass-Policy*, and the *Authorization-Policy* and its "dynamic" specialization, *ContextDependentAP* represent policies realizing a specific aspect of *Access Control*, whereas a *Privacy Policy* specifies ongoing conditions under which a subject is granted access to some resource, thereby realizing *Usage Control*.

11.2.3 Introducing the RBAC Policy Model

We base our policies for the specification of access rights on Role Based Access Control (RBAC) [169]. RBAC is a security model for policies where *Users* are assigned *Roles*, holding *Permissions*, which in turn specify access rights to *Objects*. For example, a clerk holding the (local) role CharteredAccountant within a company holding the (global) role TaxAdvisor is allowed to send a

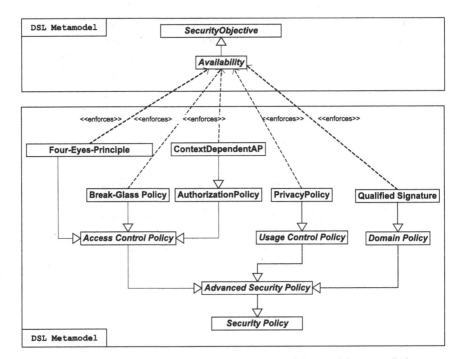

Fig. 11.2. Extending the Abstract Syntax with Advanced Security Policies

document of type `pocessedAS` to a service provider with role `Municipality` by calling a service `sendProcessedAS`.

So-called static constraints support the modeling of User-Role and Permission-Role Assignment. In our running example, in Chapter 7, static RBAC was modeled implicitly in the UML Activity Diagram by qualifying the document flow between the two roles as confidential (cf. Figure 7.24 on p. 117). It was modeled explicitely by associating roles to respective interfaces in the Interface Model (cf. Figure 7.19 on p. 113).

We integrate the RBAC model into the SECTET-DSL and enhance it by intoducing the concept of *Dynamic Constraints*. Figure 11.3 shows how the RBAC Policy Model (Box C) is related to Security Policies (Box B) and model elements of the Document- (Box D) and the Role Model (Box E): the policy model provides the conceptual structures to relate Security Policies to model elements of the Application Domain.

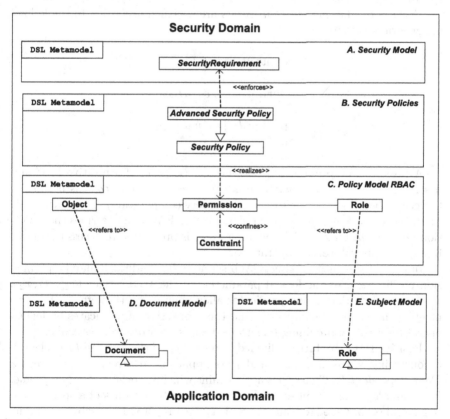

Fig. 11.3. RBAC Security Policy Model in SECTET

11.3 Modeling Policies with Dynamic Constraints

11.3.1 Sectet-PL

Dynamic Constraints define rules and conditions under which a given role is permitted (or prohibited) to access a specific ressource (e.g., to call a specific service). These rules are called *Permission Assignment Constraints* (PAC) and are expressed with SECTET-PL, a predicative language in the style of the Object Constraint Language (OCL) [41]. SECTET-PL allows the specification of fine-grained, context- and data dependent access permissions based on roles. Positive and negative permissions are specified based on predicates, and refer to any UML diagram. SECTET-PL [38] is tightly integrated into the modeling component of the SECTET-framework. Initially used for the specification of dynamic access control requirements, it has been extended to cope with attribute-based delegation of rights [15] and privacy-enhanced access control [14].

Permission Assignment Constraints are specified according to the following generic structure:

context Entity E

perm[$role_i$] : $condExp_i$

...

proh[$role_j$] : $nondExp_j$

...;

A positive rule **perm**[$role_i$] : $pcondExp_i$ (is part) of a positive PAC and describes the condition $pcondExp_i$ under which some role $role_i$ is permitted to access the ressource (or to call a web service operation). A negative rule **proh**[$role_j$] : $ncondExp_j$ (is part) of a negative PAC and describes the condition $ncondExp_j$ under which some role $role_j$ is prohibited to access the entity E (e.g., to call web service operation).

In case of the entitiy being a Web service, the conditions may be permission predicates over the formal parameters of the Web service ($x_1 : T_1, x_2 : T_2, ..., x_n : T_n$). Permission predicates allow navigation through XML documents, comparison of expressions and the connection of predicates by logical operators, thereby providing fine-grained access control over ressource.

Positive PACs are further divided into two types: the *General PAC* classify a constraint which is general and thus applicable to every role whereas a *Data Dependent PAC* classifies a constraint which is specific to a role profile. For example, a constraint dependent on the attribute values of a specific role (e.g., a role `CharteredAccountant` with a `Special_Skills`-attribute in public finance). These constraint types are used to refine the inheritable permissions in the presence of role hierarchies.

A PAC is attached with a UML stereotype named accordingly (cf. Figure 11.5).

11.3.2 Static RBAC

Figure 11.4 exemplarily shows how to model permission-role assignment based on static RBAC. The Role Model is used to aggregate the rights of a particular role. In our scenario, the `TaxAdvisor` represents a `Partner_Role` in a global workflow. According to the model the `Partner_Role` and hence all local `Domain_Roles` are allowed to access the `Municipality`'s `TaxFileService` in order to get a `TaxFile`. Note that access permissions are defined at the service-level, which means, that the requester is allowed to get any file (not only his client's) at any time and would have complete access to the document's content. This is where the *Permission Assignment Constraints* come into operation.

11.3.3 Dynamic RBAC

Figure 11.5 shows how Permission-Role assignment may be further confined through Permission Access Constraints. PACs are associated to Interfaces in the Interface Model, but actually refer to elements of the Role Model – enhanced by roles internal to the domain (cf. Figure 11.3 on p. 163) – and to elements of the Document Model, thereby achieving document level granularity of access rights.

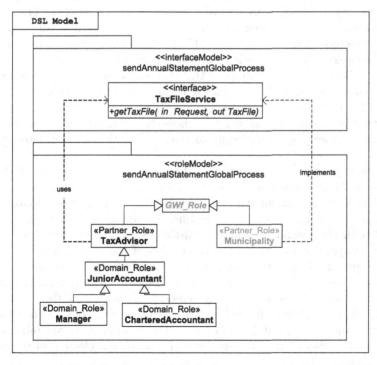

Fig. 11.4. Modeling Permission-Role Assignment with Static RBAC

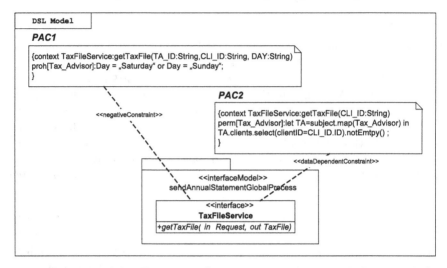

Fig. 11.5. Modeling Permission Assignment Constraints with SECTET-PL

Positive or Negative Constraints. PAC1 states that a requester holding the role TaxAdvisor, identified by his TA_ID, is not allowed to access the TaxFileService on weekends. A negative constraint (stereotyped **negative-Constraint**) is attached to the Web service TaxFileService. The service reroutes the call to the security infrastructure which verifies compliance to the parameters. Note that PAC1 could also have been formulated as a positive permission allowing access on working days only.

Data Dependent Constraints. PAC2 states that a requester holding the role TaxAdvisor can only read files of a client (identified through the parameter CLI_ID in the request) if he is mandating specifically that client. This constraint is a *Data Dependent PAC*, where the parameters of the service call refer to an underlying XML document representing the object of interest as a *Document Model*.

Data Dependent PACs depend on the "internal representation" of the requester in the *Document Model* of the provider (cf. Figure 11.6). The mapping is achieved by the function map() - an external library function supported by the Reference Architecture. The identification variables (e.g. subject) associated with these external functions distinguishes different types of callers. Hence, subject.map() makes the connection of the calling actor to his internal representation in the business logic, thereby enforcing data-dependent access control (e.g., the actor has access to his own data). External functions are stereotyped with **external**. This stereotype indicates that the corresponding interface is not transformed to XML schema but refers to the security infrastructure and that it is needed in order to verify a certain relationship between the caller of the Web service and a particular element of the *Document Model*.

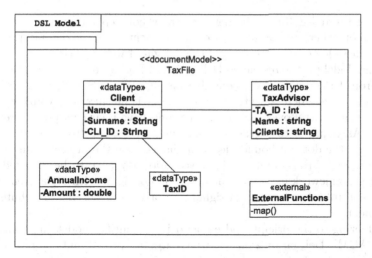

Fig. 11.6. Document Model for Data-dependent PAC

In PAC2, an association between the calling role `TaxAdvisor` and the `Client` is required. The latter's identity is passed as a parameter with the call (`CLI_ID`). The `subject.map` construct maps the caller to its internal representation in the *Document Model*, class `TaxAdvisor`. Notice the difference between the role `TaxAdvisor` in the *Role Model* standing for the service reuqester in the *Global Workflow* and the class `TaxAdvisor` in the *Document Model* standing for the internal representation of a tax advisor's data at the partner node.

11.3.4 Rights Delegation

Delegation of Rights in Distributed Environments

Conventionally, trust is enforced by a central authority that knows all actors and possibly all relationships between them. But the realization of the concept of trust through a central authority is not always a viable option. In distributed scenarios, where actors do not know all of their partners, where they cannot keep track of every relationship between all of them and do not want a central authority to enforce access rights to the resources in their domains, authorization remains a local responsibility and thus distributed by nature. The distributed delegation of rights is a concept that supports the notion of trust in distributed environments and thereby fosters cooperation of partners across domain boundaries.

Restricted Delegation of Rights & Privacy

The SECTET-framework supports the restricted delegation of rights in a Service Oriented Architecture (SOA). Restricted delegation of rights means that rights of the delegator or the delegatee may not depend only on their roles but also on other kind of information like credentials of the delegator, data of the business logic or parameters of the delegated web service.

Our Model for the restricted Delegation of Rights combines the concept of roles from RBAC with the predicative specification of SECTET-PL.

In scenarios where a centralized repository is not always a viable optione, peers retain control over their ressources and have their own privacy requirements. As requests to access personal data may come from within as well as outside the domain boundaries, compliance with the privacy requirements of other peers in an online business scenario may have to be enforced. The SECTET-Framework integrates the delegation of rights with privacy-enhanced access control i.e. delegation of rights in a privacy preserving distributed environment.

Adhering to the priciples od model driven security, models are translated into XACML Delegation Policies, which are interpreted and enforced by the security infsrtructure.

Modeling Delegation of Rights

Figure 11.7 shows an example delegation in a distributed environment. In the scenario the role `TaxAdvisor` delegates the right to access files of his clients to a subject holding the role `Lawyer`. The latter or may not be a sub-role of the former's domain (aka a `Domain_Role`). In our example the role `Lawyer` represents a security domain of its own (aka a `Partner_Role` in a Global Workflow).

In order to check the access rights of the service requester (SR) in our case holding the role `Lawyer`, the service provider (SP) – `Municipality` – clarifies the requester's attributes with a third party Ü- the attribute authority (AA), which in our case is the `TaxAdvisor`. In case the delegatee is a `Domain_Role` of the delegator, the attribute authority is the requester's home domain (e.g., `TaxAdvisor` for a `JuniorAccountant`). For security, privacy and management reasons, we assume that every `Partner_Role` maintains the attributes of the users associated to his domain.

Delegation Constraints are specified according to the following generic structure:

context webService : $op(x_1{:}T_1, \ldots, x_x{:}T_n)$

perm $[Delegator Delegator\_role_i, Delegator Delegator\_role_i] : condExp_i$
...
proh $[Delegator Delegator\_role_j, Delegator Delegator\_role_j] : ncondExp_j$
...;

A positive rule `pcondExp`$_i$ describes the condition under which a role `Delegator_role`$_i$ is permitted to delegate the right to execute an operation

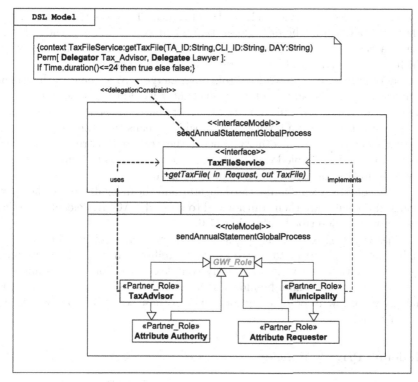

Fig. 11.7. Example Policy Specifying Delegation of Access Rights

op to a role Delegatee_role$_i$. A negative rule ncondExp$_j$ is to be interpreted accordingly. The conditions are permission predicates over the formal parameters of the Web service $(x_1 : T_1, x_2 : T_2, ..., x_n : T_n)$.

A Delegatee_role$_i$ can further delegate the right to execute a service to another role forming a delegation chain which is verified through a mechanism devised in XACML 3.0 called Chain Check (please refer to [24] for details).

Restricted delegation in distributed environments may require the declaration of *Identification Variables*. Associated with the external functions they help differentiating between different types of the caller e.g. the identification variable **delegator** classifies the individual who issues a delegation policy and the identification variable **delegatee** classifies the individual who was transfered the access right.

The special constructs **delegator.map(T)** and **delegatee.map(T)** authenticate the caller of the web service (where the way how authentication is done can be freely chosen), check if the participants (the delegator and the delegatee) are in the specified roles and map the participants to an internal representation (of type T) in the Document Model. In case if any of the participants in a delegation scenario belong to some other partner in an inter-organizational workflow, the function **map(T)** requests the attribute values that are not present locally from the corresponding domain through an attribute requesting service. The `delegator.map(T)` maps the issuer of the delegation policy and the `delegatee.map(T)` maps the caller of the web service to a class in the Document Model. The only difference is the context in which these special variables `delegator` and `delegatee` are used.

The functions map an external role (e.g., `Lawyer`) to element in the Document Model (e.g., `TaxAdvisor`). Such an element would have to be stereotyped `<d>` (d for distributed). This indicates that attribute values in the corresponding Document Model can be distributed, which means that the corresponding entity is located with some other partner in the workflow. Attributes and entities that are not available locally will be requested by an attribute requesting service from the corresponding attribute authority.

These constraints including the delegator and the delegatee roles, the operation and the rules are then transformed to trusted XACML delegation policy files. As will be described in Section 11.6.

Usually, the specification of restricted delegation is either limited to a single domain or subject to severe inter-operability issues. XACML provides a generic solution: it can express fairly complex delegation policies and can be deployed across domain boundaries. Nevertheless there remain substantial challenges on how to enforce authorization in these scenarios (please refer to [79] for details).

Modeling Privacy Policies

SECTET-PL also supports the specification of restricted Privacy Policies. This means that requests to access sensitive data may not depend only on the role of the data requestor but also on consent given by the subject.

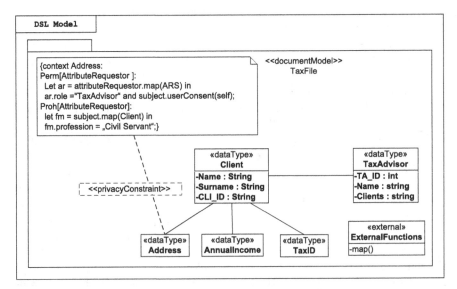

Fig. 11.8. Example Policy Specifying Privacy Requirements

Referring to our example an Attribute Authority may have a Privacy Policy restricting the release of information about its memebers, employees or users. Figure 11.8 shows an example Privacy Policy of an Attribute Authority permitting the release of the a client's address to a requester with role Tax-Advisor only in case the client is not employed in public services (attribute Profession) and explicitly gave his consent (method UserConsent(self)).

Privacy Policies are attached as constraints to the classes to be protected. This occurs with SECTET-PL. Constraints are specified according to the general structure of constraints as presented in Section 11.3.1.

11.4 Integrating Sectet-PL into the Sectet- Framework

11.4.1 Metamodel Extensions

The key extension at the meta level was the integration of the RBAC Security Policy Model (cf. Figure 11.3 on p. 163). Recalling our Security Domain Model we defined a Constraint as further confining a Permission by specifying a predicate referring to a Document or parts of it and one or more Roles.

Figure 11.9 shows how the basic Security Model is enriched with constraints to enforce specific model semantics. Each Permission can be either positive or negative depending on the isNegative attribute. The permissionType attribute categorizes a Permission (e.g., as either dataDependentPermission, generalPermission etc.). The Role element acts a proxy class and serves as a reference to a Domain_Role or a Partner_Role in the Role Model. In case of isDelegationPerm is true, two roles are associated with the corresponding Permission (this requirement is exemplarily

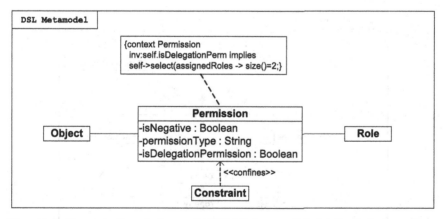

Fig. 11.9. Example Constraint on the RBAC Security Model for Expressing Delegation

described as an OCL constraint). The associated Object is also a proxy class and serves as a reference to a specific `Operation` of a Service within the Interface Model or a reference to a protected element in the DocumentModel.

So far, most conceptual elements needed for the integration of SECTET-PL were already defined in the meta-models of the Interface View. We subsequently give details on major meta-model level adaptations.

Role Model

The four roles for the delegation scenario, `Delegator_role`, `Delegatee_role`, `Attribute Authority`, and `Attribute Requester` are modeled as instances of type `Partner_Role`, the first two may be of type `Domain_Role`.

Document Model

The Document Model provides a data type view for the documents travelling between the partners in an inter-organizational workflow. However, in the context of dynamic constraints it also provides an abstract view of the attributes of the actors accessing the services, the resources and the corresponding relationship between them in the form of associations. This is the model that needs the most comprehensive extension compared to its use for basic Security Policies (cf. Chapter 7).

Each `DataType` in the Document metamodel is categorized as either `PrimitiveType`, `ComplexType`, or `Enumeration` (Figure 11.10). An `ActorClass` specialises `ComplexType` and corresponds to the representation of a caller's role in the Document Model. This is why it is not of type role. Its associated

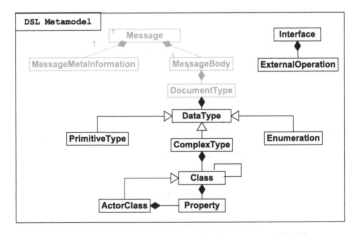

Fig. 11.10. Extensions to the Document Model

attributes are of type `Properties`. The `Interface` with the stereotype **external** contains external functions (`externalOperations`). This stereotype indicates that the corresponding entity is not transformed to XML schema but verifies the relationship between the caller of the service and a particular entity in the Document Model. However we do not consider it a conceptual element at the meta-model level, because it does not represent a modeling entity representing an artefact of the application or the security domain.

11.4.2 Sectet-PL - Abstract Syntax

A *Constraint* is represented using SECTET-PL, a language defined according to the EBNF grammar in Figure 11.11.

This grammar file is parsed by the transformation engine, and, upon instantiation, creates an abstract syntax tree of the expressions. The mapping expression (line 7) is optional. Nevertheless, more than object references could be defined within one mapping expression (lines 9-10). A mapping variable (line 11) could be a SUBJECT (representing the caller of the web service), a

```
1  DynamicConstraintExp : ContextDefinition (ConstraintType RoleDefinition SectetPLExp)*
   (OBLIG RoleDefinition ActionExp)*;
2  RoleDefinition : LBRACK (IDENT|("Delegator" IDENT COMMA "Delegatee" IDENT) ) RBRACK COLON;
3  ContextDefinition : CONTEXT IDENT COLON IDENT (LPAREN (FormalParameterList)* RPAREN)?;
4  FormalParameterList : Parameter (COMMA Parameter)*;
5  Parameter : IDENT COLON IDENT;
6  ConstraintType : PERM | PROH;
7  SectetPLExp: (MappingExp)? PredicateExp;
8  MappingExp: LET (ObjectReferences) IN;
9  ObjectReferences: ObjectReference (COMMA ObjectReference)*;
10 ObjectReference: IDENT EQUAL MappingVarType DOT MAP LPAREN IDENT RPAREN;
11 MappingVarType: SUBJECT | DELEGATOR | DELEGATEE | ATTRIBUTEREQUESTOR;
12 PredicateExp: PredicateImpliesExp (IMPLIES PredicateImpliesExp)*;
13 PredicateImpliesExp: PredicateAndExp (OR PredicateAndExp)*;
14 PredicateAndExp: Predicate (AND Predicate)*;
15 Predicate: (UnaryExp|BinaryExp)| "(" PredicateExp ")";
16 UnaryExp: PropertyCallExp (NotEmpty |ForAllExp);
17 BinaryExp: EqualityExp;
18 EqualityExp: additiveExp ((Not_EQUAL|EQUAL|GT|GTE|LT|LTE) additiveExp);
19 additiveExp: MultipicativeExp ((PLUS|MINUS)MultipicativeExp)*;
20 MultipicativeExp: SimpleExp ((MUL|DIV|MOD) SimpleExp)*;
21 SimpleExp: STRING|CONSTANTVALUE|PropertyCallExp|ContextFunctionExp;
22 PropertyCallExp: ModelPropertyCallExp (DOT ModelPropertyCallExp)*;
23 ModelPropertyCallExp: IDENT | SelectExp | SelectOneExp ;
24 SelectExp: SELECT LPAREN BooleanExp RPAREN;
25 SelectOneExp: SELECTONE LPAREN BooleanExp RPAREN;
26 ForAllExp: FORALL LPAREN BooleanExp RPAREN;
27 BooleanExp: BRelationalExp ((OR|AND) BRelationalExp)*;
28 BRelationalExp: IDENT ((EQUAL|NOT_EQUAL|GT|GTE|LT|LTE) BSimpleExp);
29 BSimpleExp: VariableReference | CONSTANTVALUE | STRING;
30 VariableReference: IDENT (DOT IDENT )?;
31 ActionExp: Action (SEMI Action)*;
32 Action: MappingVarType DOT IDENT LPAREN Arguments RPAREN;
33 Arguments: STRING|CONSTANTVALUE (COMMA (STRING|CONSTANTVALUE))*;
34 ContextFunctionExp: IDENT DOT IDENT LPAREN Arguments RPAREN ;
```

Fig. 11.11. Abstract Syntax of Sectet-PL

DELEGATOR (the delegator of the web service, cf. Section) or the DELEGATEE (the entity, to whom rights are delegated). A PredicateExp (line 12) defines the structure of the associated SECTET-PL constraint. It enforces the priority rules for the logical operators by organizing them in a recursive way (lines 12-14). For a detailed specification of the SECTET-PL grammar, please refer to [24].

11.5 Extending the Reference Architecture

The enforcement of Dynamic Constraints occurs through the same Reference Architecture which was presented in Chapter 8. Nervertheless, three adaptations were needed:

1. a specification of the general semantics of exectable policies for dynamic access control policies and their elements based on the XACML 2.0 specification. In Chapter 8 XACML was used to express some kind of "security compliance policies".
2. an adaptation of the message protocol between the PEP and the PDP in order to support queries on dynamic auhtorization checks based on roles (XACML-request and -replies).
3. an extension of Sun's XACML reference implementation of the PDP to cope with a hierarchical form of XPath expressions which can refer to multiple data sources such as XML database, parameters from the XACML Request etc (available at [184]).

Subsequently we briefly describe all three extensions, for a detailed account on the implementation, please refer to [24].

11.5.1 Access Control, Delegation and Privacy Policies

We base the extensions for Access Control Policies on the Abstract Syntax of XAML 2.0 as presented in Chapter 8 (cf. Figure 8.8 p. 132). For the implementation of Role Based Access Control, we fully rely on the XACML profile for RBAC [100]. Figure 11.12 shows the conceptual extensions we added to the XACML language in order to implement dynamic authorization conditions.

We subsequently briefly sketch the general semantics of the policy and its elements in the context of the XACML 2.0 specification and will give a short account on the specialized semantics of the corresponding policy and its elements. For brevity, certain attributes, namespaces and policy elements are omitted.

Role Policy Set

For every role in the Role Model, an XACML policy set called *Role Policy Set* (RPS) is created. Figure 11.13 shows an example RPS for the role CharteredAccountant in simplified XACML syntax. The root element Policy

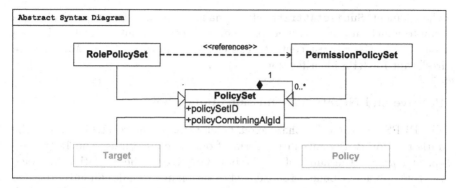

Fig. 11.12. Abstract Syntax of SECTET-PL

```
1  <PolicySet PolicySetId="RPS:CharteredAccountant" PolicyCombiningAlgId="deny-overrides">

2    <PolicySetIdReference>NPPS:CharteredAccountant</PolicySetIdReference>

3    <PolicySet PolicyCombiningAlgId="permit-overrides">
4      <PolicySetIdReference>PPPS:CharteredAccountant</PolicySetIdReference>
5      <PolicySetIdReference>DenyPolicy</PolicySetIdReference>
6    </PolicySet>

7    <Target>
8      <Subjects>
9        <Subject>
10         <SubjectMatch MatchId="string-equal">
11           <AttributeValue  DataType="string">CharteredAccountant</AttributeValue>
12           <SubjectAttributeDesignator  AttributeId="role" DataType="string"/>
13         </SubjectMatch>
14       </Subject>
15     </Subjects>
16     <Resources><AnyResource/></Resources>
17     <Actions><AnyAction/></Actions>
18   </Target>

19 </PolicySet>
```

Fig. 11.13. An Example Role Policy Set

Set contains two attributes. The `PolicySetId` points to the associated role, the combining algorithm is set to "deny-overrides" which is meant to logically enforce the precedence of negative permissions over the positive permissions.

In our case we assume that a set of negative permissions was specified for the role. They are referenced through `NPPS:CharteredAccountant` inside a `PolicySetIdReference` element. Positive permissions are specified in an inner policy through the same mechanism. Notice that the combining algorithm is set to permit-overrides, requiring only one out of many PPPS to return a positive result. In case none of the PPPS returns true, a general DenyPolicy will be applicable.

The `Target` element block inside the RPS specifies the role. According to the XACML profile for RBAC, the role name is specified with an `Attribute-Value` element given inside the `Subjects` element block. This makes the RPS applicable to any XACML Request targetting the role `CharteredAccountant`.

The element `SubjectAttributeDesignator` searches for a particular attribute which in our case is a role. This subject attribute is matched to an attribute in the request context. The elements `Resources` and `Actions` are irrelevant for RPS identification.

Positive and Negative Permissions Policy Set

The PPPS generated for `CharteredAccountant` in Figure 11.14 contains the authorization constraints in the form of one or more `Rules`. The `Target` element contains the name of the Web service and of the operation to which the rule applies. A `Condition` element additionally specifies an authorization constraint. If the authorization constraint is met by the subject of the Web service, it will be granted access. The PPPS references PPPS of roles that are direct or indirect super classes.

```
1  <PolicySet PolicySetId="PPPS:CharteredAccountant" policyCombiningAlgorithm = permit-overrides">

2    <PolicySetIdReference>PPPS:TaxAdvisor.JuniorAccountant</PolicySetIdReference>
3    <PolicySetIdReference>PPPS:TaxAdvisor</PolicySetIdReference>

4    <Policy PolicyId="Permissions:Role:CharteredAccountant" CombiningAlgorithm="permit-overrides">

5      <Rule Effect="Permit">
6        … Rule & Condition specifying Sectet-PL Constraint …
7      </Rule>

8    </Policy>
9  </PolicySet>
```

```
1   <Rule RuleId="1" Effect="Permit">
2     <Target>
3       <Subjects> <AnySubject/> </Subjects>
4       <Resources>
5         <Resource>
6           <ResourceMatch MatchId ="anyURI-equal">
7             <AttributeValue DataType="anyURI">
8               http://a.b.c.d:8081/TaxFileService
9             </AttributeValue>
10            <ResourceAttributeDesignator AttributeId="resource-id" DataType="anyURI"/>
12          </ResourceMatch>
13        </Resource>
14      </Resources>
15      <Actions>
16        <Action>
17          <ActionMatch MatchId ="string-equal">
18            <AttributeValue DataType="string">
19              http://wsserver.munsys.xsoap:getTaxFile
20            </AttributeValue>
21            <ActionAttributeDesignator AttributeId="action-id" DataType="string"/>
22          </ActionMatch>
23        </Action>
24      </Actions>
25    </Target>

26    <Condition FunctionId="string-is-in">
27      <Apply FunctionId= "custom-xpath-set-values">
28        <SubjectAttributeDesignator AttributeId=/TaxAdvisor/
29        [id='/Request/Subject/Attribute[@AttributeID=TA_ID]']/Client/SSN/text() />
30      </Apply>
31      <Apply FunctionId= "custom-xpath-one-and-only-one">
32        <ActionAttributeDesignator AttributeId=/Request/Action/Attribute
33        [@AttributeId=CLI_ID]/text()/>
34      </Apply>
35    </Condition>
36  </Rule>
```

Fig. 11.14. Example Positive Permission Policy Set (Top) and Rules (Bottom)

In our Role Model, CharteredAccountant inherits from the Junior Accountant and TaxAdvisor, therefore the PPPS includes a reference to the respective PPPS inside PolicySetIdReference (cf. Figure 11.14). The rules nested inside the Policy element specify the conditions under which the Web service operation will be accessible. The Condition element defines authorization constrains in the form of XACML functions for X-Path, X-Query, Date, Time etc.

Figure 11.14 shows the detailed context Definition for the PPPS. The rule's Target in a PPPS (or NPPS respectively) contains the name of the Web service inside the Resource element block, which corresponds to TaxFileService and the particular operation in the Action element block which in our case is getTaxFile.

The function SECTINO:function:1.0:custom-xpath-set-values evaluates the ID of the role interweaving the values from the XACML Request (TA_ID) and from the business logic (via an internal web service e.g. accessing a physician's database). Basically, our algorithm transforms logical operators in SECTET-PL to equivalent XACML logical operator functions, navigation expressions to their equivalent X-Path or X-Query expressions. The map function is transformed to an internal X-path expression on the XACML Request, extracting the subjectId.

The NPPS for a role is only generated, if a negative constraint is specified in the Access Model. A NPPS is generated according to the same rules that apply to the PPPS with two exceptions: the inner policy specifies the rule which denies access if applicable and an NPPS references no other policies, which means that negative permissions are not inherited. Context Definition and Authorization Constraint are specified in the same way as for PPPS.

Delegation Policies

Delegation Policies are executable artefacts based on XACML that configure the security components in the Reference Architectures of partners participating in a delegation scenario. The XACML profile for rights delegation ([79]) extends the core specification with types for the *Delegation Policies*. Figure 11.15 shows these extensions.

The profile introduces a block of elements called Delegates inside the Target block qualifying the policy as a delegation policy. The Delegate element defines a a role, UserID or a complex object which is allowed to delegate access rights specified by Subject, Resource and Action elements (e.g., a CharteredAccountant is allowed to add a TaxFile).

The Delegate element refers to someone authorized by an administrative policy to issue policies (e.g., a CharteredAccountant is allowed to delegate the right of a CharteredAccountant to add a TaxFile).

A policy may contain a PolicyIssuer element describing the source of an Access or a Delegation Policy. The absence of the element qualifies an

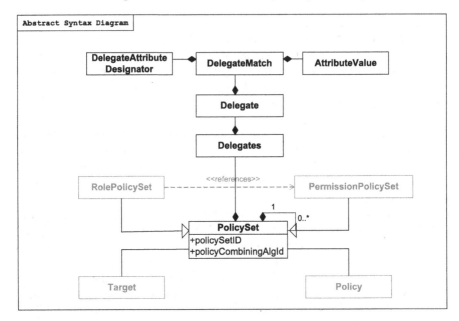

Fig. 11.15. XACML Extensions for Delegation Policies

Access or a Delegation Policy as a trusted policy and therefore, it is considered trustworthy and its origin is not verified by the PDP. A policy is considered unauthorized and discarded if he authority of the policy issuer cannot be traced back to a trusted policy during the "chain check", where the authorization component at the target's domain starts analyzing the last policy in the chain.

The validation process is performed based on request-reply protocol using administrative requests contain informationing about the policy issuers and the access context or the situation defined as "A set of properties delineated by the `Attributes` elements of an access request context."

As specified in the profile, the Delegation Policy files can restrict delegation by means of `Condition` and `IndirectDelegatesCondition` [79].

Restricted Delegation specified with SECTET-PL are transformed to Delegation Role Policy Sets following the structure for Role Policy Sets as defined for Access Policies in Section 11.5.1. The only difference is the role name appearing in the `Delegates` element section (Figure 11.16).

Figure 11.17 shows an example Delegation Poisitve Permission Policy Set for a `CharteredAccountant`. He is allowed to delegate the right of a `CharteredAccountant` to add a `TaxFile` to a `JuniorAccountant` working in the same a `workgroup`.

```
<PolicySet PolicySetId="DRPS:CharteredAccountant" policyCombiningAlgorithm="deny-overrides">
  <Target>
    <Delegates> <Delegate> <DelegateMatch MatchId="string-equal">
      <AttributeValue DataType="string"> CharteredAccountant </AttributeValue>
      <DelegateAttributeDesignator AttributeId="delegatorRole" DataType="string"/>
    </DelegateMatch> </Delegate> </Delegates>
    <Subjects> <AnySubject/> </Subjects>
    <Resources> <AnyResource/> </Resources>
    <Actions> <AnyAction/> </Actions>
  </Target>

  <PolicySet Combining Algorithm = "permit-overrides">
    <PolicySetIdReference>DPPPS:CharteredAccountant</PolicySetIdReference>
    <PolicySetIdReference>DenyPolicy</PolicySetIdReference>
  </PolicySet>
  <PolicySetIdReference>DNPPS:CharteredAccountant</PolicySetIdReference>
</PolicySet>
```

Fig. 11.16. An Example Delegation Role Policy Set

```
<PolicySet PolicySetId="DPPPS:CharteredAccountant" PolicyCombiningAlgId="...">

<Policy PolicyId ="Delegation:Permissions:Role:CharteredAccountant" CombiningAlgorithm="...">

  <Rule RuleId="1" Effect="Permit">
    <Target>
     <Subjects> <Subject> <SubjectMatch MatchId="string-equal">
       <AttributeValue DataType="string"> JuniorAccountant </AttributeValue>
       <SubjectAttributeDesignator AttributeId="DelegateeRole" DataType="string"/>
     </SubjectMatch> </Subject> </Subjects>
     <Resources> <Resource> <ResourceMatch MatchId ="anyURI-equal">
       <AttributeValue DataType="anyURI">
         http://a.b.c.d:8081/TaxFileService
       </AttributeValue>
       <ResourceAttributeDesignator AttributeId="resource-id" DataType="anyURI"/>
     </ResourceMatch> </Resource> </Resources>
     <Actions> <Action> <ActionMatch MatchId ="string-equal">
       <AttributeValue DataType="string">
         http://wsserver.TaxFileService.xsoap:addTaxFile
       </AttributeValue>
       <ActionAttributeDesignator AttributeId="action-id" DataType="string"/>
     </ActionMatch> </Action> </Actions>
     <Delegates> <AnyDelegate> </AnyDelegates>
    </Target>
    <Condition FunctionId="string-equal">
      <Apply FunctionId="custom-xpath-one-and-only-one">
        <DelegateAttributeDesignator AttributeId="/TaxFileService/
        CharteredAccountant [iD='/Request/Subject/Attribute[@AttributeID=delegatorId]'
        ]/workgroup/text()" DataType="http://www.w3.org/2001/XMLSchema#string"/>
      </Apply>
      <Apply FunctionId= "function:1.0:custom-xpath-one-and-only-one">
        <SubjectAttributeDesignator AttributeId="="/TaxFileService/
        CharteredAccountant [iD='/Request/Subject/Attribute[@AttributeID=delegateeId]'
        ]/workgroup/text()" DataType="http://www.w3.org/2001/XMLSchema#string"/>
      </Apply>
    </Condition>
  </Rule>
 </Policy>
</PolicySet>
```

Fig. 11.17. An Example Delegation Positive Permission Policy Set

11.5.2 Protocol Extensions

XACML request and replies are based on the abstract syntax for request and
response as defined in Figures 8.14 and 8.16 in Chapter 8 (cf. pp. 138) with
a slight modification: in case of a successful authentication the PEP assigns

```
 1  <Request>
 2    <Subject>
 3      <Attribute AttributeId="subject-id" DataType="XMLSchema#string">
 4        <AttributeValue>pete.lomac@xy.com</AttributeValue>
 5      </Attribute>
 6      <Attribute AttributeId="role" DataType="XMLSchema#string">
 7        <AttributeValue>TaxAdvisor.CharteredAccountant</AttributeValue>
 8      </Attribute>
 9    </Subject>
10    <Resource>
11      <Attribute AttributeId="resource-id" DataType="portId">
12        <AttributeValue>TaxFileService</AttributeValue>
13      </Attribute>
14      <Attribute AttributeId="action-id" DataType="resource-ID">
15        <AttributeValue>TaxFileService</AttributeValue>
16      </Attribute>
17    </Resource>
18    <Action>
19      <Attribute AttributeId="action-id" DataType="operation-ID">
20        <AttributeValue>getTaxFile</AttributeValue>
21      </Attribute>
22      <Attribute AttributeId="P" DataType="Client">
23        <Client age="27" dob="09-12-78" id="John Doe" >
24          <contact> <FullName firstname="John" lastname="Doe"/> </contact>
25          <address>
26            <city>Innsbruck</city>
27            <state>TIROL</state>
28          </address>
29        </Client>
30      </Attribute>
31    </Action>
32  </Request>
```

Fig. 11.18. Modified Request for Access Decision (PEP to PDP)

a role to the requester according to the credentials provided and queries a Policy Decision Point (PDP) to allow (or deny) access to web services. This is why a role attribute is passed along with the request (lines 6-8 in Figure 11.18). The PDP bases the access decision on user attributes and informs his PEP about the response.

Administrative Requests between the various Policy Decision Points in a distributed delegation scenario are formed as specified in the XACML specification [79].

11.5.3 PDP Extensions

A Policy Decision Point refers to a software component which makes the Allow/Deny decisions as a last step in the authorization. In general, accessing a data element or executing a service is controlled by the authorization process. This is a multi step operation in which user attributes are examined to determine whether the rules allow this requestor (in this particular role) to access the item or execute the service. The requestor identities available for authentication are used by the application to request more information about the requestor.

XACML offers a multiplicity of functions which can be used within the policies for decision making. In addition to standard functions, it also provides a possibility for the definition of new functions, data types, and combining algorithms. The XACML implementation by Sun Microsystems Inc. provides these extension points (please, refer to [184]). We have extended the Sun's implementation in the following two dimensions.

Hierarchical XPath Expressions

The SECTET-PL expressions can refer to different data sources such as parameters of the (web) service, internal representations in the DocumentModel etc. Because of this reason, the SECTET-PL expressions cannot be transformed to ordinary XPath expressions. We have developed a hierarchical form of XPath expressions which can refer to multiple data sources such as an XML database, parameters from the XACML Request etc. Given the SECTET-PL expressions, an hierarchical XPath expression is composed of several XPath expressions that are nested with each other. The result of one expression is used to evaluate the value of the other expression. Figure 11.19 shows a hierarchical XPath expression (Box A) which is composed of the two X-Path epressions (Box B). The expression refers to a requester who was assigned the role **CharterdAccountant** and mandates **Clients** with a specific address.

These expressions are separated over a simple inverted comma. The value of the internal XPath must be processed first in order to evaluate the result of the outer XPath. The internal expression refers to the XACML Requests and selects the subjectId of the caller of the service. The outside XPath expression looks in the XML database for a **TaxAdvisor** and using the **TA_ID** (evaluated using the internal XPath expression) locates the clients and correspondingly delivers their addresses. The depth of the nesting is limited theoretically to the size of the main memory.

Extended Functions

In order to interpret hierarchical XPath expressions, a list of functions is added to the PDP. These functions take the hierarchical XPath expressions as input, perform the intended function and output values of known types. In the following, a list of these functions is given.

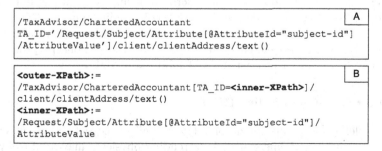

```
/TaxAdvisor/CharteredAccountant                                    A
TA_ID='/Request/Subject/Attribute[@AttributeId="subject-id"]
/AttributeValue']/client/clientAddress/text()
```

```
<outer-XPath>:=                                                    B
/TaxAdvisor/CharteredAccountant[TA_ID=<inner-XPath>]/
client/clientAddress/text()
<inner-XPath>:=
/Request/Subject/Attribute[@AttributeId="subject-id"]/
AttributeValue
```

Fig. 11.19. Hierarchical X-Path Expressions in Sectet-PL

- full-node-match: two strings in XACML Bags are examined for equality and a boolean result is returned. The sequence of the individual elements is not thereby of importance.
- custom-xpath-set-values: a bag of values can be returned based on the hierarchical XPath expression.
- custom-xpath-one-and-only-one-int: a single integer value is returned based on the hierarchical XPath expression
- custom-xpath-one-and-only-one-double: a single double value is returned based on the hierarchical XPath expression
- custom-xpath-one-and-only-one: a single value is returned based on the hierarchical XPath expression

11.6 Sectet-PL Transformations

Constraints specified in models with SECTET-PL are tranformed into XACML policy files with the help of a Java-based tool. This transformation component uses Antlr [3], a compiler program for the syntax analysis of the constraints. After the syntax analysis, an Abstract Syntax Tree is generated which is checked against the model information. Model information, captured in the sub models of the Interface View – namely in the Role Model, the Interface Model and the Document Model – is specified through references to XMI files. The models are built using a UML based Modeling Tool and exported via XMI files. The prototype implements a DOM parser to extract model information from the XMI files. After successful syntax and semantic analysis, generated XACML code can be viewed and can be transformed to XACML policy files. Moreover, constraints can be saved for later usage. For details on the SECETET-PL-Code Generator, please refer to [23].

11.7 Modeling Advanced Use Cases with Sectet-PL

In this Section we briefly describe approaches on how to handle a couple of advanced security scenarios by systematically extending the SECTET-Framework. This Section does not describe full implementations but rather addresses key issues of Model Driven Security Engineering in an industrial context, many of them subject to current research and prototypical application. Nevertheless, we sketch a viable path to proof-of-concept prototypes, that may be useful, or at least relevant in an industrial setting.

11.7.1 Break-Glass Policy (BGP)

BGP is defined as an authorization scheme to allow access to a patient's medical record in case of emergency. An attending physician may need to bypass routine access control restrictions to guarantee timely treatment without any delay due to administrative or technical complexities (e.g., [173, 116]). The purpose of BGP is to allow emergency access to the system, in cases where given rights are not sufficient to access the data. The associated constraint formalizes the BGP using external obligation operations (like e.g., audit). This ensures that, in case of an emergency access, all actions of the requester are audited. External functions (like e.g., audit) come in the form of an "obligation" and return a boolean values.

11.7.2 4-Eyes-Principle

The *4-Eyes-Principle* is a form of *Multiple Authorization*, which requires two users with a common interest to enter the system simultaneously. One of the users accesses the data whereas the other user monitors the access in order to ensure data confidentiality and integrity during access (see e.g., [202, 182]). In healthcare scenarios, the 4-Eyes-Principle requires the patient to be present, when a physician accesses her medical record. Physician's access is logged during the visit by some trusted *Proxy Service*. Enforcement of the 4-Eyes-Principle is usually performed indirectly (as in e.g., [146]): a *Tracing and Auditing Authority* is responsible for notifying and storing any communication between the data owner and the requesting service into the logging database, thereby guaranteeing *Accountability* of data access at anytime. *Logging and Auditing* capabilities permit the patient to set her privacy policy based on access history and identify potential abuse.

11.7.3 Usage Control (UC)

UC is a data-object specific authorization and access monitoring technique concerned with permissions, restrictions, continuity and resumption of services. It is implemented and logged at the user's platform within her domain. Data usage is controlled by the data service. For example, a requirement in such a scenario could state that

"Access to a medical record is allowed for 5 times only
and should last for 48 hours, after its first access".

11.7.4 Qualified Signature

The case of the *Qualified Signature* seems to be somewhat blurred. *Integrity* and the *Qualified Signature* in principle rely on the same cryptographic primitives (e.g., the hashing of values). This may suggest a specializaiton of the Security Objective *Integrity*.

But there is a fundamental difference in the business semantics of both requirements, and, in order to preserve this fundamendal difference at the level of the language structure, we introduced it as a specialisation of the new category of *Domain Policy* enforcing *Availability*. We motivate this with the intuition that in delivering a Qualified Signature a natural person makes fully qualified identity information available.

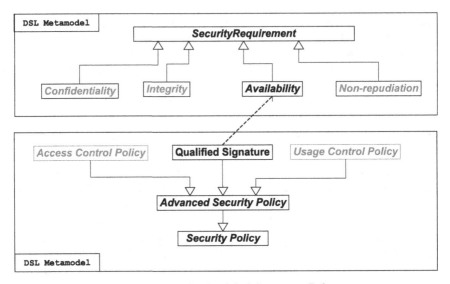

Fig. 11.20. The Qualified Signature-Policy

Abstract Syntax

The abstract class `DomainPolicy` inherits from the class `AdvancedSecurity-Policy` and enforces `Availability` (Figure 11.2 on p. 162).

A `QualifiedSignature` is associated to one or more `Domain_Roles`, which are defined in the Role Model, referenced through the proxy-class `Domain_RoleRef`, and a `DocumentRef`.

Concrete Syntax. Annotating the `DocumentType` part of a `Message` so that it complies with the requirement of `QualifiedSignature` can occur in one of two ways by setting the appropriate context and associating it to the corresponding element in the respective model.

The constraint box stereotyped «DomainPolicy» can be associated to either an element of the Document Model, like the `MessageBody` element in Figure 11.21, or to the `Action` element in the GWfM specifying the name of the `Interface` (Figure 11.22), of the `Operation`(s) (although not shown in Figure 11.22) and of the `Input` and the `Output` `Message`s (also hidden).

In the first case, the context is set to the instance of the Message Ǔ `processedAS`. It links a `DocumentType` to a `Domain_Role`, which is associated to a `Partner_Role` which represents an actor – a `Partner_Role` – in the GWfM. The hierarchy of local roles is opaque to Partners in the Global Workflow.

The `CompositeSecurityAttribute` `QualifiedSignature` indicates that the `Document` has to be signed personally by holders of the roles `Chartered-Accountant` and `JuniorAccountant`, two roles of the `TaxAdvisor`'s internal role hierarchy.

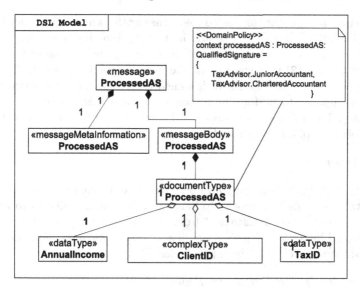

Fig. 11.21. Qualified Signature - As Specified in the Document Model

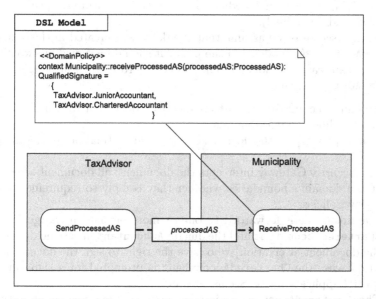

Fig. 11.22. Qualified Signature - As Specified in the Global Workflow Model

In the second case (Figure 11.22), the constraint box is associated to an Action in the GWfM. Specifically located in the Partition of the Partner_Role, it provides the Interface, whose Operation is invoked by the Partner_Role who has to provide the Qualified Signature. The constraint is attached to the `Action ReceiveProcessedAS`, which offers the `Opera-tion` Ű whose name is not shown in the `Action`, but according to best practice is named according to complementary sending `Action` of the `Sender` (`sendProcessedAS`) that waiting for the message coming from the `TaxAdvi-sor`. In both cases, the document is signed before leaving the domain bound-aries (as opposed to performing a signature during the execution of a local workflow). The gateway intercepts the document, and prompts the holders of the respective roles to sign the document.

Model Dependencies

A `DomainPolicy` is assigned to a `DocumentType` or one or more of its parts – a `DataType`. This corresponds to `Message`-information, referred to with the help of a proxy-class `DocumentRef` from the security meta-model. It is meant to be signed by a natural person holding a `Domain_Role` or a `Partner_Role`, as usual through reference by a proxy-class.

Enforcing the Qualified Signature-Policy

The following scenario describes how the Qualified Signature-Policy is enforced at the origin (this is actually where the Qualified Signature as specified in the Policy should be applied).

For this scenario, we assume that the document created in the domain of the `TaxAdvisor`. As modeled in the policy it should be signed by two officials before it can leave the domain. The following procedure will be triggered in the `TaxAdvisor`'s domain:

1. An employee `JuniorAccountant` creates a document to which the policy of a Qualified Signature applies.
2. The employee post the document to its final destination (e.g., `Municipa-lity`).
3. The Security Gateway intercepts the document: all document are checked at the domain's boundaries whether they comply to requirements of Se-curity Policies.
4. The document is forwarded to one or more officials in charge (e.g., the `CharteredAccountant` and the `JuniorAccountant` in case he did not sign the document at creation) who have the right to sign the document.
5. In our case the `CharteredAccountant` is prompted for a signature by a special application – a "Secure Viewer".
6. The `CharteredAccountant` signs the document by plugging his electronic ID card into the card reader which is connected to the his PC.
7. The PEP sends the document to the final destination.
8. The PEP at the destination's endpoint checks the document for compli-ance to the Security Policy which was aggreed upon beforehand – in this case the signature of the `CharteredAccountant`. In case of non compliance the document is discarded and a notification sent back to the originator.

Part III

A Case Study from Healthcare

health@net – A Case Study from Healthcare

Co-authored by
Thomas Schabetsberger[1], Richard Mair[1], Florian Wozak[1],
and
Basel Katt[2], Frank Innerhofer-Oberperfler[2], Markus Mitterer[2]

This Chapter is co-authored by Thomas Schabetsberger, Richard Mair and Florian Wozak from our project partner CEMIT as well as Basel Katt, Frank Innerhofer-Oberperfler, and Markus Mitterer – all three are colleagues from our research group Quality Engineering at the University of Innsbruck.

Thomas Schabetsberger, Richard Mair, and Florian Wozak – the leading architects of the health@net project – contributed material to Sections 12.1 and 12.2. Frank Innerhofer-Oberperfler and Markus Mitterer performed the Security Analysis (Section 12.3), whereas Basel Katt elaborated the Security Concept for Phase 2a and 2b (Section 12.5).

We organized this Chapter as follows: we present some background information on electronic healthcare in Section 12.1. We introduce the project health@net in Section 12.2. The core of the present Chapter is the systematic integration of complex security considerations based on the ProSecO approach and their realization with the SECTET-framework: in Section 12.3 we present results of a Security Analysis based on the ProSecO approach. This is the starting point for the health@net Security Concept which is elaborated in Section 12.4. The integration at the conceptual and the implementation level into the SECTET-framework is presented in Section 12.5.

---

[1] Healt@net (CEMIT), Austria {thomas.schabetsberger, richard.mair, florian.wozak} @healthatnet.at

[2] University of Innsbruck, Austria, {basel.katt, frank.innerhofer-ober perfler, markus.mitterer} @uibk.ac.at

12.1 Background

12.1.1 The Electronic Healthcare Record

The Electronic Health Record (EHR) stands for a concept aiming at the digital integration of healthcare information currently scattered over a myriad of traditional paper-based archives, databases holding health records, and clinical information systems distributed across multiple security domains of many stakeholders of the healthcare industry.

As a matter of fact, the status-quo comes at great costs to national economies, paired with an unsatisfactory level of service quality, possibly even leading to fatal errors resulting in erroneous treatment or wrong medication (e.g., [127, 155, 105]). Trying to systematically resolve these system-inherent weaknesses, a growing number of countries are working towards the realization of national EHR systems (e.g., [105, 85]). By now, leveraging the popularity of standards related to web services – based on the paradigm on Services Oriented Architectures – these initiatives have set the implementation of powerful infrastructures supporting inter-operability for trans-organizational healthcare services (e.g., [84]) at the top of their agenda. The EHR specifically refers to a consolidated, time and location independent electronic representation of a patient's healthcare related information.

Theoretically, the central promise of the EHR is the ability of each patient to retain exclusive control of his records. This means that he should be deciding who is allowed to view, store and/or change his records. However, for all practical purposes, the EHR will not replace every single patient file or record practioners may be keeping to track the treatment of their patients. For the time being EHR will only include so-called "discharge notes", medical statements issued after completion of a treatment.

The EHR is supposed to significantly boost cost-efficiency of healthcare systems [72]. In Austria, the introduction of the ecard system (Österreichische Gesundheits-Chipcard) for general practitioners provided the technical prerequisites for a nation-wide integration of healthcare providers into an electronic newtork (e.g., [208] and [198]).

12.1.2 National E-Health Initiatives

Currently, several national projects worldwide are engaged in similar endeavours at a very large scale most notably the Regional Health Information Organizations (RHIO) currently being formed in the USA, the British connecting for health initiative, and the Danish medcom and sundhed.dk projects. The IHE industry initiative does appreciate this trend and has put great effort in the formulation of integration profiles to standardize cross enterprise health data exchange like the XDS (cross enterprise document sharing) and XDS-I (cross enterprise image sharing) profiles [120].

In 2005, the Austrian Ministry of Health started the E-Health Initiative [4], a voluntary stakeholder group with a wide range of representatives from healthcare institutions, academia and industry, which delivered a recommendation for a national e-Health strategy in December 2005, which is currently in a consultation process. Key element of the recommendation is the establishment of a national electronic health record for all citizens, organized as a distributed system where all data is stored at the institutions where it is produced, but with the possibility for other institutions to access relevant information in a standardized way. The sharing of information is to be achieved through metadata indices (comparable to the IHE registry), but also here, the federation of distributed indices (residing at the main care providers) is a central design criterion.

12.1.3 Technical Standards for Healthcare

"Integrating the Healthcare Enterprise" (IHE) [4] is an initiative involving stakeholders of the healthcare industry aiming at the improvement of information exchange between information systems in various domains of the healthcare industry. IHE chiefly coordinates efforts pushing further development of established standards like DICOM and HL7, to address specific clinical needs in support of optimal patient care.

IHE drafted a common framework defining how to support basic interoperability needed for local and regional health information networks. Integration profiles define the detailed specifications on how these standards can be implemented for a specific medical domain. IHE developed a basic set of integration profiles aiming at:

1. supporting Cross-Enterprise Document Sharing (XDS) for document content interoperability. The technical framework for the IT infrastructure [191] comprises nine profiles. One of them – XDS – describes the registration, the distribution and the access to electronic healthcare data over healthcare related institutions [192]. XDS stands for a specification facilitating the exchange of documents between various medical institutions.
2. providing a security framework enforcing confidentiality, authenticity and integrity of patient care data,
3. facilitating cross-domain patient identification management to ensure consistent patient information and effective searches for EHRs.

IHE implementations of these standards are supported, documented, and tested by industry partners.

12.1.4 The Austrian Data Privacy Law

To reach compliance with the Austrian data privacy law, all trans-institutional access to health data has to be mandated by the patient in the form of an informed consent.

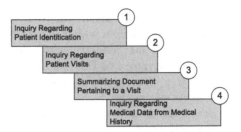

Fig. 12.1. 4-step-model

Therefore, a working group of Austrian data privacy experts [198] designed a conceptual model, the so called "4-step model for the request and the transmission of patient data" (Figure 12.1).

The model covers implementation aspects related to data privacy laws, as well as safety and security regulations. The model is set up and formalized in the form of a contract, which can be joined by healthcare providers.

Based on this generic model, participating institutions agree to access data from other institutions according to a specific 4-step process:

1. first searching for institutions that know about the patient,
2. secondly by searching for case information at specified institutions in accordance with the patient will,
3. thirdly accessing selected discharge summaries on the patient,
4. and finally retrieving parts of the patient record (like reports, lab results, or image data).

With this patient-consent centered framework, trans-institutional access to data is made possible even without amendments to the data privacy legislation. In accordance with these key elements for a national electronic health record, the health@net project team started with the design of a distributed IT architecture.

12.2 health@net

12.2.1 Project Mission

The efforts to implement a centralized management system for healthcare records in so-called "Independent Health Record Banks" [176] failed due to the overwhelming data volume and unbearable costs. Assimilating these insights, the project health@net set out to champion the concept of a "Distributed Electronic Healthcare Record": in opposition to all former approaches, healthcare data should not be migrated centrally onto servers of a single data processing center, but remain on the information systems of its "producers" – the various stakeholders of the healthcare industry.

Rather, patient records, distributed across various domains, should be made accessible to authorized requesters in the form of a single consolidated but "virtual" healthrecord. Practically stated, the technical goal of the project health@net is the realization of an information system providing a logically consolidated view on all distributed healthcare records of a patient. The system targets the stakeholders of the healthcare industry.

12.2.2 Organizational Setting

health@net, is set up as a research project involving academic and industrial partners. The project is mainly carried out by the following **key-partners**:

1. ITH icoserve GmbH, as the main industrial partner with extensive experience and know how in the area of Clinical Information Systems,
2. the Private Universität für Gesundheitswissenschaften, Medizinische Informatik und Technik (UMIT) as the key academic player,
3. and the Center of Excellence for Medicine and IT GmbH (CEMIT), a joint venture involving public agencies and the UMIT, managing the consortium and providing marketing know how.
4. Leopold-Franzens-Universität Innsbruck, with its research group "Quality Engineering" as a consultant on various matters of software and security engineering

The branch office of health@net is located with the CEMIT Competence Center.

Various regional as well as national stakeholders in healthcare as well as academic institution addtionally contribute to health@net as **cooperation partners**. Among them:

Users of clinical information systems and software

1. Tiroler Landeskrankenanstalten GmbH (Tilak), the management holding for the six largest hospitals in Tirol, with a budget of over 430 Million Euros,
2. Bezirkskrankenhaus Reutte, one of the major public hospitals in Tyrol,
3. Ärztekammer für Tirol, the Tyrolean chamber representing medical professionals,
4. Medizinische Universität Innsbruck, the biggest medical university in western Austria.

Research Institutions

1. Technische Universität Graz, as a consultant on various engineering topics

Developers of clinical information systems and software

1. ACP IT Solutions, a major provider of IT-solutions with an annual trunover of over 280 million Euros.

2. Professional Clinical Software GmbH, a vendor of clinical software, part of the TBS-Group, the leading european vendor of medical technology.

Standardization initiatives and bodies

1. E-health Intitiative Österreich, an Austrian consortium consisting of approx. 100 persons aiming at the elabortaion of a national startegy for the application of Information- and Communication Technologies in healthcare.
2. Arge ELGA, a working group set up by the Austrian Ministry for Heath, Familiy and Youth in charge of steering the planning and the implementation process of the Electronic Health Record (ELGA – German acronym for EHR, cf. Section 12.1.1).

Social Insurance Agencies

1. Sozialversicherungs-Chipkarten GmbH, a subsidiary of the Federation of Carriers of Social Insurance, aiming at the implementation and the management of a national information system supporting eletronic processes and transactions for servcies and activities related to social insurance.

The research group Quality Engineering (QE) of the Institute of Computer Science (University of Innsbruck, Prof. Dr. Ruth Breu) and the Institute for Health Information Systems (IIG) (University for Health Sciences, Medical Informatics and Technology (UMIT), Prof. Dr. Elske Ammenwerth), jointly assume leadership in matters of security in health@net.

12.2.3 Architectural Concept

In the project's inception phase it became obvious, that a full support of co-operative healthcare needs substantially more than a mere directed electronic transfer of textual information. Although web portals may offer support for image and multimedia information, the activity of collecting information on a patient becomes very inconvenient: healthcare institutions intending to cooperate quite certainly may all have their own web portal (and most probably with different look and feel). The big challenge that emerged lay in the need of an intuitive but systematic access to relevant health information from other institutions. The concept of a "Shared Electronic Health Record" seemed to be the way to go for.

Design Criteria

In accordance with these key elements for a national electronic health record, the health@net project team started with the design of a distributed IT architecture, based on principles of GRID technology [212] and in coordination with the Austrian GRID effort. The following design criteria were identified as key to success:

1. a distributed storage of health data,
2. a high level of security against misuse and attacks through reliance on authenticated web services,
3. an absolute respect of patient consent and features to grant and retract access permissions to documents by the patient himself.

All functionalities are conceived as Web services in a Service Oriented Architecture (SOA).

Target Architecture

Based on these requirements and following the architecural guidelines of IHE-XDS health@net elaborated an architecural concept supporting the exchange of information across institutional boundaries. A distributed system of Web services supports decentralized management of records (leaving data at the location of production). Health information is made accessible via a distributed chain of indices.

Figure 12.2 shows the components of the core system architecture [99]:

1. The Access Node (AN) acts as a Gateway to the system from the outside. Queries to PLI, DMDI are only generated by AN and have to be signed. Clients are checked, and permissions enforced.
2. The Document Clearing (DC) processes all documents from the internal system of an institution before making them available in the system.
3. The Document Registry (DR) is the physical or virtual repository for medical documents. It delivers documents only if the request is signed by trusted DMDI.

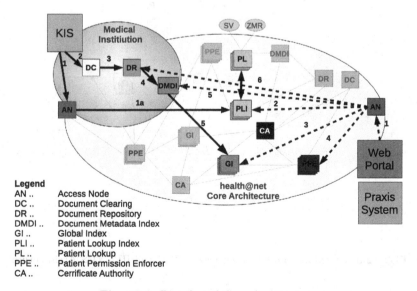

Legend	
AN ..	Access Node
DC ..	Document Clearing
DR ..	Document Repository
DMDI ..	Document Metadata Index
GI ..	Global Index
PLI ..	Patient Lookup Index
PL ..	Patient Lookup
PPE ..	Patient Permission Enforcer
CA ..	Cerrificate Authority

Fig. 12.2. Distributed Core Architecture

4. The Document Meta Data Index (DMDI) contains document meta-data and links to the Document Repository (DR). It holds document based permissions, authorizes and signs queries about specific documents (the mDMDI acts as master and the sMDMDI as the slave DMDI).

5. The Global Index (GI) registers DMDI servers, which have specific information about a patient (MPID).

6. The Patient Permission Enforcer(PPE) holds and enforces global permissions for every patient. Permissions can be individually overridden at the document level.

7. The Patient Lockup (PL) holds all demographic data of patients and maps them to the Master Patient Identifier (MPID). It is connected to the PPE.

8. The Patient Lockup Index (PLI) processes queries for patients from the AN, and forwards them to the PL before communicating results back. The PL service is not queried directly due to security considerations. Only service which requires no patient consent are granted access.

9. The Master Patient ID(MPID) is a unique patient ID within the health@net grid. It identifies individual patients and merges together various national and regional identifiers. It is intended only for internal use.

Depending on their functionality the Web services are logically allocated to different abstract components. Figure 12.3 illustrates the aggregation of services into logical components of the core architecture.

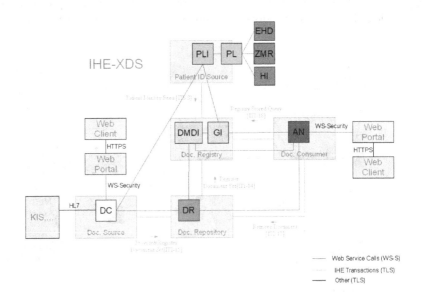

Fig. 12.3. Distribution of Web services on Nodes of IHE-XDS Architecture

Basic Use Cases

Figure 12.2 also shows the two basic use cases that were implemented in Phase 1:

Retrieving a Document

The uses case for document retrieval (shown in dashed lines in Figure 12.2) triggers the following procedure: the AN, single point of entry into the health@net network, first receives a request from the web portal (1). After authenticating the web portal's message, it queries the MPID of the patient by sending an encrypted request to the PLI (2). The PLI will check the MPID using the PI. Upon getting the patient's ID the AN asks the registry service (GI) about the locations that maintain this specific patient's record (3). The GI checks authentication of the request and sends back the list of DMDI and PPE locations. At this stage the consent of the patient is checked by sending a request to the PPE (Patient Permission Enforcer) (4). This component stores global permissions of patients. Using rules stored in the PPE, it ensures that the request is granted access to the record of this specific patient. Consequently, the PPE sends back an encrypted response to the AN using the latter's private key. The AN forwards this response to the list of DMDI(s) received by the GI (5). The DMDI, which holds document's meta-data, authenticates the request and ensures that it is sent by the PPE. After authenticating the response, the DMDI sends all locations of repositories. Finally the AN requests the document from the list of received repositories (6).

Adding a Document

The uses case for adding a document (shown in solid lines in Figure 12.2) is executed as follows: a document is initially added by entering the web portal. The request first is re-directed to the AN (1) in order to get the Patient's MPID (1a). After reception of the MPID, a request to add a new document is sent to the DC (Document Clearing) of the system. Document Clearing stores the document in the DR (3) and adds the corresponding meta-data in the DMDI(s) (4). GI(s) are updated by the DMDI about the new document and its corresponding DMDI(s)(5).

Anticipating security considerations covered in the next Section, it is worth mentioning that in this early stage of the design, each Web service was already considered as a security domain of its own. Nevertheless, the communication between service components was only secured in an ad-hoc manner at a very low technical level through Secure Sockets Layer (SSL).

Current Project State

By the end of 2007, a first software release intended for pilot installations was completed. This early implementation focused on the transmission of textual information. The original IHE XDS framework had to be extended by additional components in order to cater for the distributed and federated design – functionality that was on the IHE roadmap for 2007. The verification of IHE compliance was reached at the 2007 IHE Europe connect-a-thon.

Current work deals with scalability on the one hand, preparing the backbone architecture to cope with large volume data sets from medical imaging. Built on a planned high-bandwidth network between regional health institutions, transparent access to relevant health data across health organizations will become a reality. On the other hand, security issues will come to the fore. During implementation of the first release, security issues were only dealt with at a very basic level. Basic transport-layer encryption mechanisms were used to enforce data confidentiality and integrity from one node to the next. The system's security architecture basically relied on Role Based Access Control for the restriction of access to data by (Web) services. The integration of application-level user roles into the security architecture is part of the current release (cf. Section 12.4).

Security considerations in healthcare networks have to cope with many complex issues that cannot be dealt with such primitive security controls. For the sake of examples, one can think of topics such usage control on remote clients (e.g. a document is accessible for 5 days on client only), endpoint security (e.g., attacks on client through malicious software), as well as advanced application level security requirements (e.g., 4-eyes-principle).

12.3 health@net – Security Analysis

12.3.1 Introduction

In this chapter we will give an overview and a practical example on how to identify security objectives and refine security requirements for a Service Oriented Architecture based on the ProSecO method presented in Chapter 6.

Subsequently we will not focus on the entire security management process but just on the two steps of security objective identification and security requirements engineering. In Section 12.3.2 we will shortly introduce the scope of analysis and the context of our case study. Section 12.3.3 explains the identification of security objectives. Section 12.3.4 focuses on the engineering of detailed security requirements. Finally we give an small conclusion.

12.3.2 Functional System View

Scope of Analysis

The starting point for the ProSecO security analysis process is a basic Global Functional Model that depicts important business and technical objects and the partners involved in the Service Oriented Architecture. The

Global Functional Model provides the frame to identify dependencies among the various processes, information objects and services. The analysis of security concepts like Security Objectives and Security Requirements is executed on the basis of these modeled elements and dependencies.

The health@net network allows several partners and institutions (e.g. hospitals, physicians, patients) to share electronic patient records. Security is of uttermost importance for the acceptance of such a network and therefore it provides a good case for our example.

In practice in such a scenario we have a high number of heterogeneous partners in the network. These partners have differing expectations on security and have also different levels of maturity in their security. What we will explain in this chapter is how the security objectives of all partner can be elaborated and how they are concretised.

Global Functional Model

To demonstrate the security requirements engineering process we use only a reduced schematic example of the health care network (see Figure 12.4). This condensed model consists of a *Health Care institution*, which may for example be a hospital or a general practitioner. This institution is involved in the business processes *Read Health Record* and *Write Health Record*, that both access the information object *Health Record*. The underlying services that provide the functionality are *Retrieve Health Record* and *Commit Health Record*. Each access to the health care network requires authorisation, which is provided by the *Authorisation Engine* service and in case of permission the medical document is delivered by or stored in the *Document Repository*.

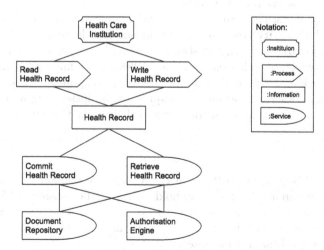

Fig. 12.4. Schematic Global Functional Model

12.3.3 Identification of Security Objectives

General Approach

The distinction between high level security objectives and more detailed and fine-grained security requirements is important to be able to focus and prioritise the analysis from an overall perspective. The overall process of security objectives definition is inspired by work on Goal-oriented requirements engineering [199].

The identification of security objectives is an important step in the security analysis process. Security Objectives should be defined in general from a business point of view. They serve the purpose to provide clear and understandable communication of the main security goals. In our point of view it is important to derive these security objectives not from a technical perspective (i.e. IT perspective) but to define the goals from a professional perspective of the involved partners or stakeholders.

Sources for Security Objectives may be manifold and include internal corporate policies, contractual and/or legal obligations, they may stem from the overall security strategy of a partner or the need to classify and protect information.

The process of identification of Security Objectives is therefore not straightforward but is composed of different activities. It may on one hand be necessary to do an analysis of the legal regulations and constraints to achieve compliance. On the other hand the IT department could bring overall objectives to the table that might stem from frameworks like COBIT [123] or ITIL [149]. It could furthermore be necessary to conduct interviews and discussions with stakeholders that might have serious privacy and/or information protection considerations.

A variety of methods can provide guidance and tools to identify the knowledge and the security concerns of the various stakeholders. Peltier's FRAP methodology [161] is identifying stakeholders and puts information assets under their ownership. This enables the utilisation of knowledge from users that are working every day with the analysed components. The OCTAVE approach [27] describes various techniques like brainstorming and interview techniques to identify areas of concern and their impact on the organisation.

Case Study

Gathering all Security Objectives in the health care domain is a challenging task, since requirements of all stakeholders have to be considered. Extraordinary significant regulations have been stated in text of a law, but beside those there exist several additional sources which must be traced. The following sources were used for this purpose:

- Legal Requirements for the Exchange of Patient Data in Austria
- International Standards

- Functional Requirements of the involved stakeholders
- System Requirements

Based on this pool a further filtering for security related objectives has been performed. The resulting amount of objectives do sometimes overlap with others in their meaning and for that reasons is makes sense to group them together. Such general security objective groups are sufficiently described in the literature by several professionals and we stick here to the work of Donald G. Firesmith [88]. Firesmith proposed 12 mayor Security Objectives, which are listed in the following (see Table 12.1):

Type of Security Objective
Identification Requirements
Authentication Requirements
Authorisation Requirements
Immunity Requirements
Integrity Requirements
Intrusion Detection Requirements
Non-repudiation Requirements
Privacy Requirements
Security Auditing Requirements
Survivability Requirements
Physical Protection Requirements
System Maintenance Security Requirements
Availability Requirement (supplementary added)

Table 12.1. Security Objectives (adapted from [88])

As this list does not contain explicitly the objective "Availability" what is a quality issue to Firesmith but fundamental in the health care domain, this objective was supplementarily added. To summarise the present results, we have a schema for grouping the Security Objectives and a list of sources which refer to the requirements of the involved stakeholders. Based on this knowledge a Security Objective Matrix is created that indicates which source has any impact to a concrete Security Objective group. This information is not always observable easily and may be obtained by methods like literature analysis, brainstorming and interviews with domain experts.

The resulting matrix consists of crosses, where each indicates that a specific source has some bearing to this group of Security Objective (see Figure 12.5).

At the end sources with overlapping content can be consolidated and described in the context of the health care domain. With this approach most of the Security Objectives proposed by Firesmith were obtained, except two of them. Non of the sources are affecting the Security Objective 'Intrusion Detection' and 'System Maintenance Security', so these are considered to be suggestions for an extended security control. When examining the security

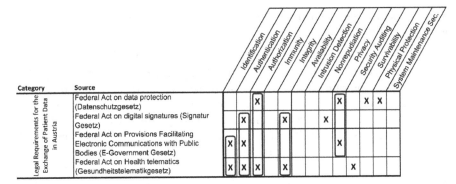

Fig. 12.5. Security Objective Matrix

meta-model it can be realized that each Security Objective is related to a Model Element. This object represents any type of class from the Global Functional Model (see Figure 12.4) and demonstrates which part of the enterprise is involved in this Security Objective.

For further explanations we will concentrate on two specific Security Objectives

- **Authorisation of parties (SO-1)** All involved individuals and computers obtain according to their physical role permissions and privileges. Care must be taken that each party can only perform functionality appropriate to their real task.
- **Integrity of the health record (SO-2)** Users of the health care network must be sure that information is properly processed and stored.

Our first Security Objective SO-1 can be attached to the Model Element *Health Care Institution*, as it is an organisational task to ensure authorisation of all involved roles and systems. The second Security Objective SO-2 is related to the *Health Record*, as integrity always deals with information. These Security Objectives do not just affect the Model Elements to which they are attached but they propagate to dependent elements. furthermore their intention is inherited. When examining our Global Functional Model (see Figure 12.4) we can expand the obtained Security Objectives to other Model Elements following the dependency graph top down. For our example this means that SO-1 is affecting all other elements and SO-2 all services, as the former is the root element and the latter the top element of all services.

12.3.4 Engineering of Security Requirements

General Approach

Starting from the initially identified Security Objectives more detailed and elaborated Security Requirements have to be defined. The scope of analysis for defining Security Requirements is defined by the dependencies of the model elements, i.e. the dependency graph.

Security requirements elicitation in general is a non-trivial task that imposes a lot of responsibility on the security analyst. It is no straightforward process that leads to unambiguous requirements, but instead it is a process driven by experience and a very good understanding of security related issues by the analyst.

There are a variety of methods that can help to identify the necessary requirements and derive them in a top-down or bottom-up approach. A bottom-up approach might be based on the checklists and threat catalogues that are delivered by national and international standards like British Standard 7799-3:2006 [60], NIST 800-30 [181], France's EBIOS [75], Germany's Baseline Protection Manual[61] or Spanish Administrations MAGERIT [145].

Based on the potential threats that might realize in our scope of analysis we could formulate Security Requirements that describe the prevention of those threats. In this way we follow an approach to define security requirements by considering misuse cases or attacker goals [179, 73, 140].

Examples for security requirements based on such a negative statement might be: *Prevent man-in-the-middle attacks on this communication channel* or *Prevent automatic password guessing by delayed timeouts after 3 attempted logins*. It is clear, that such an approach leads to rather technical requirements that may focus on the communication or even cryptographic level of abstraction [98, 97].

On the other hand we follow a top down approach refining security requirements of higher levels into security requirements in the context of model elements of lower levels. For example a Security Objective "Ensure Availability of Core Services" might be refined to the more detailed requirements *Ensure 99,99 % uptime* or *Maximum tolerable service failure must not exceed 4 hrs.*

Techniques that are employed in the definition of more detailed security requirements are interview-techniques that are proposed by OCTAVE [27] or by standards like ISO 27001 [121]. The relevant stakeholders from the business lines know best what can go wrong if the underlying IT infrastructure fails, while the IT specialists have the necessary understanding what could fail technically. Both perspectives are required to implement a business oriented security strategy.

Example Case

In our case the definition of security requirements is tailored toward service oriented architectures in the sense, that our scope of analysis on a global level is the realization of a service oriented architecture with the business processes and information objects as the main concepts of analysis. Since our enterprise model is only a static model of the dependencies of the various elements, we use sequence diagrams to analyse the possible paths of information flow throughout the SOA (see Figure 12.6).

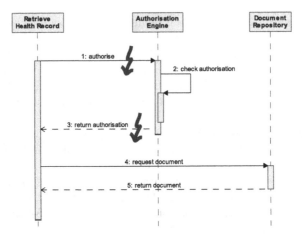

Fig. 12.6. Schematic Sequence Diagram

That way we are able to identify potential weak points in the communication between services and potential attack scenarios. We use such scenarios to define security requirements that are based on concrete threats.

What is important in the security analysis process is that every security requirement must be traceable to its original security objective. This allows a priorisation and analysis of risks from a business perspective by considering potential business impacts.

The exemplary elaboration of security requirements is based on the objective SO-1. The following requirements were created in a bottom-up approach by examining the Germany's Baseline Protection Manual [61]. In this way the Authorisation objective can be split up into the following requirements.

- Permissions must be assigned correctly and promptly (SR-1): The allocation of permissions must be done with extraordinary diligence, that users actually possess only permissions which are necessary to fulfil their tasks. In case of a role modification of an employee the permissions must be changed promptly.
- Avoid man-in-the-middle attacks (SR-2): Any authorised communication channel cannot be taken over by another computer or individual.
- On-time authorisation (SR-3): Any authorisation attempt must be processed within a defined time frame to allow fluent communication.

12.3.5 Conclusion

The process of identifying and defining security objectives and requirements is a non-trivial task that imposes a lot of responsibility on the shoulders of the security analyst. It is important to solve possibly conflicting requirements (e.g. availability vs. confidentiality) to have very good communication skills and a

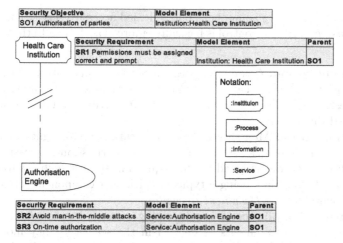

Fig. 12.7. Example Security Requirements

broad understanding and know-how about the organisational and technical architecture of an organisation.

The approaches explained and mentioned in this chapter can only give a guidance but still require a lot of experience and a variety of social and technical skills from the analyst. Also the checklists can give a hint as to what security requirements might be considered but every Service Oriented Architecture will have its own special objectives that stem from the various interests of the cooperating institutions, departments or partners.

12.4 health@net – Security Concept

Based on the security analysis presented in the previous Section, the health@net team elaborated a security concept based on *Role Based Access Control*. Compliance with IHE profiles was a prime objective: e.g., authentication and authorization are performed in strict conformance to the IHE-ATNA profile [191] (i.e., based on certificates and bi-directional). Security concerns were integrated according to a security concept split into three phases.

12.4.1 Phase 1: Service-level Security

In Phase 1 authorization is enforced based on roles, but these roles are exclusively assigned to services. Enforcement components in the target architecture simply make sure that services can only be invoked by a registered and authenticated health@net service (or component) node according to specific rules. For example, a *Document Source* may be allowed to invoke services of a *Document Repository* component but is denied access to services of a *Document Consumer*. Access control is basically enforced according to the following procedure:

1. **Authentication.** A node requesting a service is authenticated through a "Service Certificate" (e.g., X509 v3). The certificate is sent along with the request. It specifies the service's role in an attribute, and is issued by a trusted third party.
2. **Authorization.** After successful authentication, access rights are checked based on permissions assigned to the role (permission-role assignment), which in turn was assigned to the requesting subject (subject-role assignment) – The subject being a typical health@net component service (e.g., documentQuery of *Document Repository*).
3. **Security Compliance.** Every incoming message has to comply to specific security requirements as defined in the security policy model (i.e., signed and encrypted message elements). Enforcement is realized based on machine-readable policies stored in repositories. These policies are generated from the specific policy model and configure enforcement components to perform the respectice checks.

12.4.2 Phase 2a: Static, Process-level Security

Phase 2 provides for the extension of access control to process-level user roles: after having granted access to the requesting service node, the "application-level" role of the user (e.g., physician, nurse, pharmacist etc.) that originated the access request is checked. Due to the large variety of different documents that together represent the virtual healthcare record of a patient, and the variety of associated access rights, it is necessary to support very fine-granular access rules. For example, a pharmacist may only be able to read the prescription but not a doctor's discharge notes.

As in phase 1, access control is based on the RBAC model. Authentication is realized with the help of the e-card which is available to all citizens in Austria. After authentication, the user will be assigned a certificate including personal data, information about his person, his profession and his rights. On access, this certificate will be checked against rules stored in a local repository for the corresponding requested component or service.

12.4.3 Phase 2b: Dynamic, Process-level Security

In phase 2b, access control is enhanced so to integrate checks on dynamic, context-dependent parameters. Access rights defined in Security Policies may depend on parameters that have to be checked at run-time:

- **Location dependent access:** e.g., a pharmacist may be allowed to read a prescription only within the perimeter of the pharmacy.

- **Time dependent access:** e.g., a patient may want to define a timeframe for a physician to access his records, whereas there is be no such tme constraints for the family doctor to access his record.
- **Contextual information:** e.g., a right to read a diagnosis may be granted only in presence of the patient in question.

12.5 Realizing Security with the Sectet-Framework

As already shown through the running example from e-government, SECTET is a framework for Model Driven Security. In the example, the framework supported the design, the implementation and the management of secure inter-organizational workflows in a peer-to-peer environment (i.e. without central control). The technical architecture was based on the paradigm of Service Oriented Architectures.

Due to its genericity, the SECTET-Framework covers a large set of component-based applications from a broad variety of domains such as e-government, e-health, e-education etc. Case studies from healthcare and e-government provided the opportunity to apply the framework in real life scenarios [25, 106, 57, 108].

In this Section, we discuss extensions and adaptations to the SECTET-Domain Architecture necessary to cater for the integration of security concerns into the health@net scenario. Security requirements are based on the findings of the security analysis (Section 12.3) and operationalize the security concept (Section 12.4).

12.5.1 Conceptual Background

We base our conceptual understanding of the health@net problem context on the definition of three related *Domains*: the *Problem Domain*, the *Security Domain* and the *Application Domain*. This structure should help us identify the differences to the running example used throughout this book and to adapt and extend the SECTET-framework accordingly.

Problem Domain

The architectural structure of the application context basically defines the *Problem Domain*. An e-governement application differs from a typical e-tendering, e-commerce or e-healthcare scenario by exhibiting a set of specific architecural patterns. For example, we noticed that most scenarios in e-government were defined in terms of documents flowing from one security-domain to the next without central co-ordination. The original SECTET-framework was designed to mainly support scenarios from e-government. The framework accordingly supported solutions for a *Problem Domain* defined as "security-critical inter-organizational workflows".

In healthcare, specifically in IHE-based scenarios, the problem revolves more around modeling distributed patient records and related security issues. This requires some adaptation of the original SECTET-Framework. This becomes evident when raising the level of model abstraction towards business level semantics. However, as we will see subsequently the problem setting in phase 1a (securing the service-level) is very similar to the one encountered when we considered inter-organizational workflows.

In health@net, the Problem Domain is defined as the area of *scenarios providing access to privacy-sensitive, distributed records*. In this context, the notion of *Privacy* in the definition points to the requirement that patients must retain legal ownership and control over their records, even when "delivered" onto untrusted hosts. The specification of so-called Usage Control Policies requires the integration of a Security Model going beyond the capabilities of the RBAC model. This is accounted for by the integration $UCON_{ABC}$ security model. The enforcement of such policies necessitates the extension of the technical infrastructure as well as process-level adaptations. Nevertheless, we will not elaborate on this point as this is part of some future agenda of the health@net project. We sketched some of these extensions in Chapter 11.

Application and Security Domain

The problem domain relates an *Application Domain* (Figure 12.8) – here defined as *"accessing distributed patient records"* – to a *Security Domain*.

The Security Domain captures industry and application specific security concerns through abstract *Security Requirements* (Box A in Figure 12.8) which are enforced by concrete *Security Policies* (Box B). Security Policies (e.g., emergency access, 4-eyes-principle, and patient privacy) are based on a specific *Security Model* (Box C) introducing security related semantics into the models.

The *Application Domain* introduces the specific application context to which Security Policies refer.

The *Document Model* (Box D) represents the view onto the consolidated patient record. The latter may be accessed by roles according to their access permissions. Roles are defined in the *Role Model* (Box E).

12.5.2 Model Views

As already stated in Section 12.5.1 the Problem Domain for the phases 2a and 2b cannot be defined in terms of a network of partners realizing a virtual, decentralized workflow by calling services and exchanging documents as was the case for the running example. Instead, we have to consider a scenario where partners need access to a consolidated view of a document whose parts are distributed over multiple security domains. Each domain keeps control over the parts it produced and actually contributes to the "virtual" patient record. This implies an almost static view onto the Application Domain.

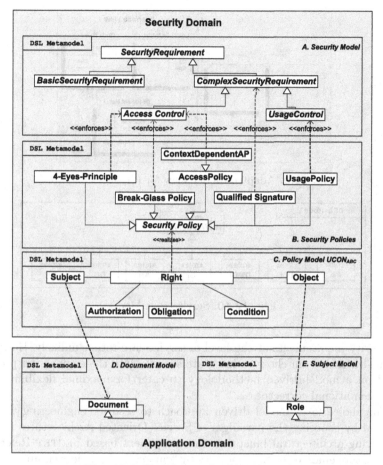

Fig. 12.8. Health@net Problem Domain

Therefore, when considering application level security concerns as planned in phases 2a and 2b of the health@net security concept, we primarily use the three models of the Interface View to model the application scenario (cf. Figure 12.9). However, service-level security remains a matter of securing the flow of documents between service components. This necessitates to rely on the Global Workflow Model for security design.

Subsequently we will show how the various models are used in phase 1 of the health@net Security Concept (cf. Section 12.4). Phases 2a and 2b are covered in Section 12.6.

Phase 1 – Service-level Security

Service-level security is primarily designed, modeled and configured during the initial implementation process. Once the system is up and running, changes

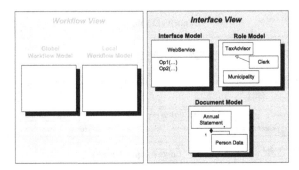

Fig. 12.9. Adapted Model View for Phases 2a and 2b

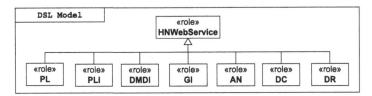

Fig. 12.10. Service Role Model

to security requirements at the level of services are rather unlikely. However, the health@net team chose to integrate security into the engineering process based on a model-driven methodology to cater for maximal flexibility and implementational correctness.

The choice for a model driven approach to security engineering was facilitated by choosing the paradigm of Service Oriented Architectures for the underlying architectural blueprint: the component based SECTET Reference Architecture enforces security policies by "embedding" services components in a security infrastructure, whose components act as a single point of access to service components from the outside. The design of loosely-coupled components supports an independent implementation of functionality and security.

In the *Interface View* every component of the health@net core architecture (cf. Figure 12.2 on p. 195) is modeled as a role that offers services with specific properties and access rules.

The *Role Model* defines the roles that tries to get access to offered service in a rather flat hierarchical structure (Figure 12.10).

The *Document Model (DM)* is a class diagram that describes the datatypes used in each component for its clients. Those will be seen as documents, not objects and will be interpreted in context of XML schemas. Figure 12.11 shows the DM for `Registration Data` flowing from the DMDI to the GI.

The Interface Model (IM) consists of all services/functions that should be visible to outside the boundaries of the components. The parameters used in these functions are either primitive datatypes or types defined in the document model. The Interface Model is independent from the context in which the

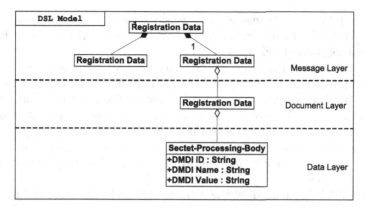

Fig. 12.11. Exemplary Document Model Registration Data

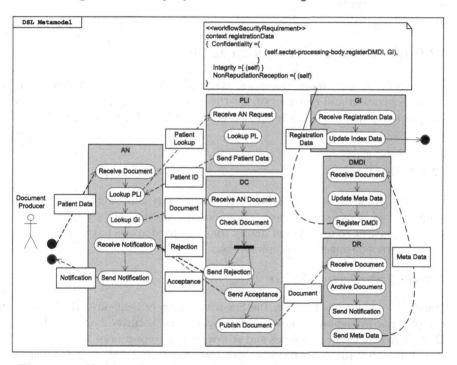

Fig. 12.12. Updating Patient Data: Document Flow in the Target Architecture

services will be invoked. The IM is not shown here. However, interfaces are also modeled in the Global Workflow (cf. Figure 12.12).

The Access Model describes the constraints, under which each role is allowed to invoked specific service in a component.

Figure 12.12 illustrates a Global Workflow Model that captures the document flow between the different service components in the target architecture.

In Phase 1 the security model only considers security requirements at the service level. The Figure exemplarily shows a Basic Security Policy for the document `Registration Data`

In the context of Phase 1 of the Security Concept, each service component will be represented by a `Partner Role`. This means that every service component represents a security domain of its own and is modeled as an Activity Partition in the UML-Activity Diagram. Documents are passed as parameters of Web service calls. According to the interaction paradigm of Web services, service invocation is modeled as a bilateral interaction through an Object Flow between two roles. Security policies are associated with Documents modeled as Object Nodes.

The models are parsed by the Transformation Component and machine-readable XACML files configuring the security components wrapping each service components are generated.

12.6 health@net - Phases 2a & 2b

In this section we present use cases, the health@net Security Architecture, policy generation and distribution for the enforcement of Advanced Security Policies as defined in Phases 2a and 2b. Henceforth, we focus on Authorization Policies.

12.6.1 Use Cases

Figure 12.13 shows use cases related to static and dynamic authorization. For simplicity, we consider only cases where doctors are the only actors who need access to patient records. Other actors who may need access to patient records are insurers, pharmacists and nurses etc.

Default Access Control Policies

During the deployment phase, the Security Engineer configures the security components by deploying generated policies. The Security Engineer defines Default Access Control Policies and stores them in repositories. When a General Actor tries to access records, his access rights are checked according to permissions specified. All access is generally reported and logged for potential auditing.

Patient Privacy Policies

In addition to what is specified in Default Access Control Policies, a Patient can define his own privacy rules. He can specify fine granular policies to restrict access to his records to specific actors or to further restrict access to specific contextual parameters (e.g., time, location etc.). For the sake of practicability,

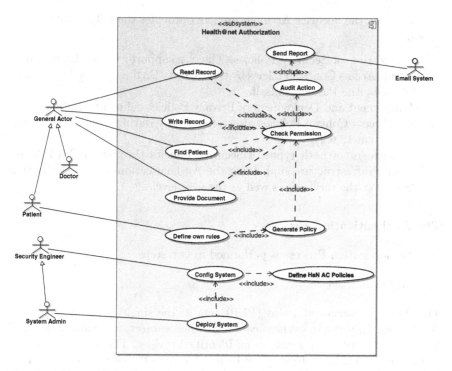

Fig. 12.13. Use Cases Related to Static and Dynamic Authorization (Phase 2a & 2b)

there will be a set of predefined rules in a templates-like style that patients can choose as Privacy Policies ("opt-in" or "opt-out"). In case a patient does not specify any Privacy Policy, only Default Access Control Policies defined by the service provider are applicable.

12.6.2 Security Architecture

The Security Architecture is designed as a Service Oriented Architecture in a way to meet the Security Requirements and Objectives that were defined beforehand. Early in the design process, the health@net team made the following decisions:

1. Authentication and single sign-on should be based on the SAML protocol.
2. The authorization model should primarily be based on Role Based Access Control and eventually be extended to the $UCON_{ABC}$ model.
3. Identity management should happen through certificates: user and service components are assigned digital certificates bound to the role assigned to the subject.

Generally, the Security Architecture (SA) provides the following functionalities:

1. Specification of Security Policies. The SA supports both: the design of Default Access Control Policies by the Security Engineer as well as Privacy Polices by the Patient himself.
2. Management and Deployment of Privacy Policies defined by Patients. Default Access Control Policies are stored locally during initial deployment (cf. Section 12.6.2).
3. Enforcement of both types of Security Policies through an XML-based security infrastructure supporting the Authentication and Authorization Process at the services- as well as the user level.

The Authentication Process

The Authentication Process is performed in two steps.

User Authentication

The Policy Enforcement Point (PEP) acts as the single point of entry into the domain. In order to authenticate the calling subject, the call is redirected to a trusted third party acting as an Identity Provider. The latter asserts the identity of the calling subject when he first log in to the system (e.g., with his E-Card). The Identity Provider extracts the identity and subject attributes required for authorization, and returns them as SAML protocol assertions to the PEP.

Service Authentication

Inside the Security Architecture, Service Components representing Security Domains use certificates to authenticate each other. The Policy Enforcement Point identifies calling Service Components and extract their attributes. This includes its Service Component-role and additional meta-information. This information is integrated into certificates assigned to every Service Component during deployment or reconfiguration.

The Authorization Process

Figure 12.14 shows the Security Architecture for the enforcement of access control which consists of a two-step policy enforcement: (1) Cryptographic- and (2) Authorization Policy Enforcement; Cryptographic Policy Enforcement checks security requirements related to Basic Security Policies and leverages basic cryptographic controls like digital encryption and signature to enforce Confidentiality, Integrity, and Non-repudiation. Authorization Policy Enforcement enforces application-level access control taking User-roles and handling

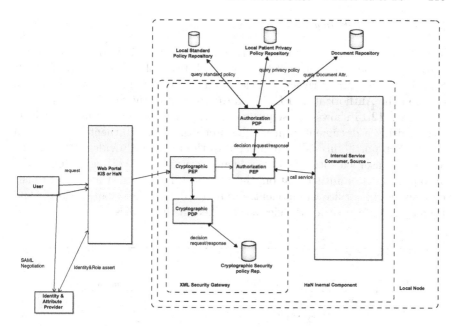

Fig. 12.14. Security Architecture

Advanced Security Policies (e.g., 4-Eyes-Principle). Enforcement may neces-
sitate process-level adaptations.

Both steps rely on three components: a Policy Enforcement Point- (PEP), a
Policy Decision Point (PDP), and a Policy Repository. The PDPs are based on
SUN's XACML reference implementation, whereas the PEPs implementation
technology depends on the target architecture's platform. For a Web services
based target architecture using the AXIS framework [189], the PEP can be
integrated as a "Handler". The Policy Repository can be a plain database or
an encrypted local file system.

When a component gets a request, the XML security gateway intercepts
the call. A user's request is basically handled according to the following procedure.

1. Cryptographic Policy Enforcement

The security gateway first performs checks on cryptographic security requirements: it queries the cryptographic PEP with a request. The latter forwards a
request for decision to the cryptographic PDP. The PDP retrieves the corresponding policy from the Policy Repository, evaluates the request and returns
a decision response to the PEP; based on the response the PEP either blocks
or forwards the request together with information on caller identity and role
(of both the user and the requesting service component) to the Authorization PEP.

2. Authorization Policy Enforcement

The Authorization PEP will in turn query the related PDP for an access control decision. Its PDP will have to check two policies: the static Default Security Policy and Privacy Policies defined by Patients. Upon a positive decision the Authorization PEP forwards the call to the Service Component. Figure 12.15 shows the sequence diagram for the requesting procedure. Before firing a document request, the user logs in and authenticates himself to the Web portal; his call is redirected to the Identity Provider (IP). The IP asserts the user's identity and his role and returns the SAML assertion to the Web portal. After authentication, the Web portal forewards the request to the corresponding Service Component. Security Components wrap the latter and thereby enforce Security Policies as specified in the models.

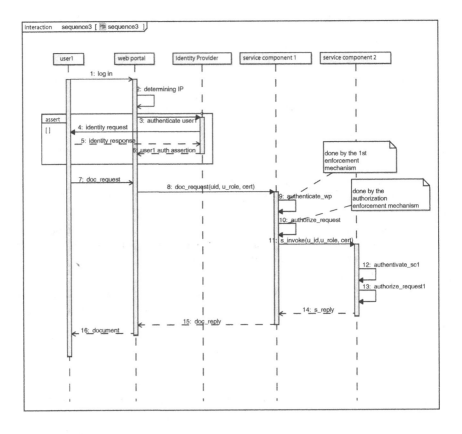

Fig. 12.15. Processing a Service Request

XACML Policy Generation

Models are translated into executable XACML Policies. The XACML language can address either multiple "subjects" with one policy or handle a set of policies for a single request. This allows to build a single policy referring to both types of subjects involved, namely the User-role and the Service Component-role.

Figure 12.16 shows the model for XACML policy language. The core element of a Policy is the Target. It consists of a Subject, a Resource, an Action and an Environment. The latter represents the attributes of one or more Subject(s) trying to commit an Action on a Resource in context of specific Attributes of the Environment.

A Rule consists of a Target, a Condition and an Effect resulting from an evaluation. An Effect can be either a "permit" or a "deny". A Rule is evaluated with respect to a specific Target.

A Policy consists of a Rule, a Target, and a PolicySet. A PolicySet can have one or more Policies. In this case a combination algorithms defines the behaviour in case more than one Policy is applicable to a specific request.

All information needed for the generation of XACML policies is captured in models of the Interface View. Figure 12.17 shows a class diagram that contains a part of the Document Model. Roles are defined with (1) specific attributes (e.g., ID, LOINC_CODE [15] etc.), (2) the Document exchanged and stored (in form of the "Clinical Document Architecture" (CDA))[115], and (3) Constraints to access the Document by the specific Role.

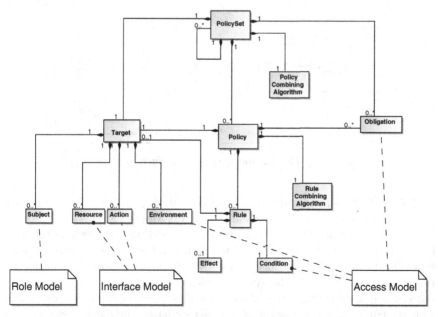

Fig. 12.16. XACML Policy Language Model

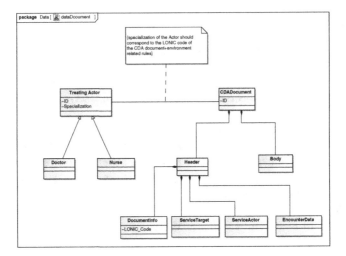

Fig. 12.17. Document Model

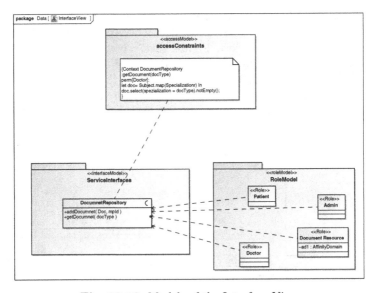

Fig. 12.18. Models of the Interface View

Figure 12.18 exemplarily shows the rest of the models in the Interface namely the Role-, the Interface- and the Access Model.

As was mentioned before access control in health@net is based on the Role Based Access Control: Users are assigned Roles and Roles are assigned Permissions. Public healthcare authorities are responsible for informally defining the Roles to be considered in the system. Roles correspond to the various stakeholders in healthcare scenarios (doctors, nurses, pharmacists etc..). User-Role assignement is based on digital or even paper-based certificates. However in this book, we will only consider digital certificates based on public key certificates.

Administrators of local nodes (corresponding to a stakeholder's security domain or a `Partner_Role` in the GWfM) will model these hierarchical roles into models as shown in the Role Model. The Interface Model represents the services that are offered by the various Components and Users. Figure 12.18 exemplarily shows services provided by the *Document Repository* components. The model illustrates the use of a Constraint applied when the corresponding role is trying to execute the service. The Constraint states that the specialization of the User-role Doctor should correspond to the type of document that is to be accessed. The type of the document is extracted using the LOINC code [15] – universal identifiers for laboratory and clinical documents – in the clinical documents strucured according to the ANSI-standard Clinical Document Architecture (CDA) [115].

Figure 12.19 summarizes the steps for model tranfomation. XACML policies are generated based on the UML models according to the rules of a Domain Specific Language (DSL) which is structured through meta-models. In a first step, DSL's meta-models are specified. Based on the DSL, an Instance Model is designed and finally – based on Model-to-Code transformation functions – the XACML policies are generated.

Policy Distribution

Especially in peer-to-peer architectures, the distribution of policies represents a major challenge.

In health@net we have two distinct policies for authorization decisions: Default Access Control Policies are created by the service provider holding an administrative role. They contain the rules for Security Policies as defined

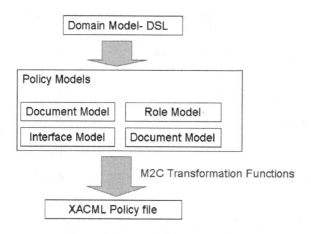

Fig. 12.19. Model Tranformations

for Phase 1 and 2a of the Security Concept (Services Level- and Static Access Control). On the other hand, Patient Privacy Policies are defined by the Patient as defined for Phase 2b of the Security Concept (Dynamic Access Control). The policies of the first type will be stored locally, at the location they were created. The distribution of the second type of policies is not so trivial and is based on a specific protocol. There are three possible approach to handle the distribution of Patient Privacy Policies:

1. a central server stores Patient Privacy Policies. Upon request the central server is asked to provide the suitable policy (as depicted in Figure 12.20).
2. A Policy Management System that is similar to a Public Key Infrastructure (PKI). In this approach each policy is signed by a trusted third party and distributed to the users that need them. That means each request should be accompanied with the corresponding trusted and signed policy.
3. The third option is "Instant Policy Distribution": policies are stored locally at the nodes where the patient's document is stored.

The first approach exhibits two shortcommings. First, it represents a single point of failure. Second, it may cause significant delays as a bottle-neck for request processing: the remote policy repository that has to be queried by service components for each incomming request. These problems are solved by the second approach. However a new problem arises: possible state inconsistencies

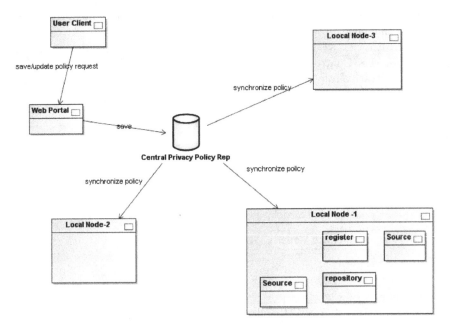

Fig. 12.20. Central Server Architecture

between the various local copies of the same policies may occur. Especially the lack of a reference point for conflict resolution and policy synchronization does not make it a viable approach.

Although the third approach solves the problems posed by the first and the second approach, it requires a complex system for policy management (policy issuing, updating, revoking and storing functionalities). This makes it a heavy investment. Cost considerations lead the health@net to opt for a hybrid approach combining the first and the second approach. Accordingly, Privacy Policies are first stored on a central server. In a second step, the central server publishes and distributes the policies to the components. Thus, every component has a copy of this policy. Figure 12.21 shows the workflow for this adapted "Instant Policy Distribution" done by the central server after the patient creates his Patient Privacy Policy and stores it on the server.

As illustrated in the figure the Patient will use a Policy Generation Tool to generate his Patient Privacy Policy. He will then send his policy to the central server which first queries the *Registry* service for the locations of all

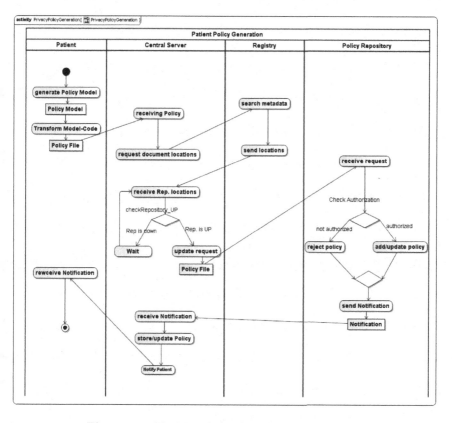

Fig. 12.21. Workflow for Instant Policy Distribution

local nodes in question. The *Registry* service stores and maintains the health record of this Patient. After receiving a set of locations of relevant local nodes, the central cerver updates or stores the policy of the patient in the respective Policy Repositories of local nodes.

Part IV

Appendices

A

Mapping Tables

A.1 Mapping Table for Inbound Policy File

Inbound Policy File (XACML) Abstract Syntax		Security Policies Metamodel		Remarks
Target Element	Attribute	**Source Element**		
Rule	RuleId	GWfMetamodel:ObjectNode		Name of document instance
	Effect	"permit"		set to "permit" by default
Rule.Condition		*BasicSecurityPolicy*		Container element
Rule.Condition.Apply.AttributeValue		Sender		Role name of invoking party
Rule.Condition.Apply.AttributeValue		Receiver		Role name of providing party
Rule.Condition		Confidentiality		Container element
Rule.Condition.Apply.AttributeValue		Receiver		Public key provider for encryption
Rule.Condition.Apply.Apply.AttributeSelector	RequestContextPath	DocumentRef & Confidentiality		Composite X-Path expression according to production rule
Rule.Condition		Integrity		Container element
Rule.Condition.Apply.AttributeValue		Sender		Private key provider for signature
Rule.Condition.Apply.Apply.AttributeSelector	RequestContextPath	DocumentRef & Integrity		Composite X-Path expression according to production rule
Rule.Condition		NonRepudiationOfSending		Container element
Rule.Condition.Apply.AttributeValue		Sender		Receiver identified through resource section of Policy target
Rule.Condition.Apply.Apply.AttributeSelector	RequestContextPath	DocumentRef & NonRepudiationOfSending		Composite X-Path expression according to production rule
Rule.Condition		NonRepudiationOfReception		Container element
Rule.Condition.Apply.AttributeValue		Receiver		Sender identified through resource section of Policy target
Rule.Condition.Apply.Apply.AttributeSelector	RequestContextPath	DocumentRef & NonRepudiationOfReception		Composite X-Path expression according to production rule
Policy	PolicyId	GWfMetamodel:Action		Interaction name, Action with outgoing object flow
	RuleCombininAlgId	"permit-overrides"		Default value
Target				Container element
Target.Subjects.Subject.SubjectMatch.\ AttributeValue		Sender		Invoking party of Interaction
Target.Subjects.Subject.SubjectMatch. \ SubjectAttributeDesignator	AttributeID	"subject-id"		Default value
Target.Resources.Resource.ResourceMatch. \ AttributeValue		Receiver		Servcie provider
Target.Resources.Resource.ResourceMatch. \ ResourceAttributeDesignator	AttributeID	"resource-id"		Default value
PolicySet	PolicySetId	GWfMetamodel:Activity		Name of GWf
PolicySet.Target.Resources.Resource.\ ResourceMatch.AttributeValue		GWfMetamodel:Activity		Name of GWf
PolicySet.Target.Resources.Resource.\ ResourceMatch.ResourceAttributeDesignator	AttributeID	"resource-id"		Default value
PolicySet.PolicySet.Target.Resources.Resource.\ ResourceMatch.AttributeValue		DocumentRef		Name of documentType
PolicySet.PolicySet.Target.Resources.Resource.\ ResourceMatch.ResourceAttributeDesignator	AttributeID	"resource-id"		Default value
PolicySet	PolicySetId	GWfMetamodel:Activity		Name of GWf
PolicySet.Target.Resources.Resource.\ ResourceMatch.AttributeValue		GWfMetamodel:Activity		Name of GWf
PolicySet.Target.Resources.Resource.\ ResourceMatch.ResourceAttributeDesignator	AttributeID	"resource-id"		Default value
PolicySet.PolicySet.Target.Resources.Resource.\ ResourceMatch.AttributeValue		DocumentRef		Name of documentType
PolicySet.PolicySet.Target.Resources.Resource.\ ResourceMatch.ResourceAttributeDesignator	AttributeID	"resource-id"		Default value
Target				Container element
Target.Subjects.Subject.SubjectMatch.\ AttributeValue		Sender		Invoking party of Interaction
Target.Subjects.Subject.SubjectMatch. \ SubjectAttributeDesignator	AttributeID	"subject-id"		Default value
Target.Resources.Resource.ResourceMatch. \ AttributeValue		Receiver		Servcie provider
Target.Resources.Resource.ResourceMatch. \ ResourceAttributeDesignator	AttributeID	"resource-id"		Default value

Fig. A.1. Mapping Table for Inbound Policy File

A.2 Mapping Table for Outbound Policy Files

Outbound Policy Template Abstract Syntax		Security Policy Metamodel	Remarks
Target Element	Attribute	Source Element	
schema	targetNamespace	RoleRef, GWfMetamodel:Action, DocumentRef	Unique Id identifying Template RoleRef identifies validity domain
element	name	DocumentRef	References the document instance in interaction
	type	DocumentRef	References document container definition
element.complexType	name	DocumentRef	Document container definition
element.complexType.annotation.appinfo./ BasicSecurityPolicy.Confidentiality./ ElementName		DocumentRef	Document node to be encrpyted
element.complexType.annotation.appinfo./ BasicSecurityPolicy.Confidentiality./ ElementName.Roles.Role		Receiver	Role providing service
element.complexType.annotation.appinfo./ BasicSecurityPolicy.Integrity./ ElementName		DocumentRef	Document node to be signed
element.complexType.annotation.appinfo./ BasicSecurityPolicy.Integrity./ ElementName.Roles.Role		Sender	Role invoking service
element.complexType.annotation.appinfo./ BasicSecurityPolicy.NRSender./ ElementName		DocumentRef	Document node to comply with non-repudiation of sending
element.complexType.annotation.appinfo./ BasicSecurityPolicy.NRSender./ ElementName.Roles.Role		Sender	Role invoking service
element.complexType.annotation.appinfo./ BasicSecurityPolicy.NRReceiver./ ElementName		DocumentRef	Document node to comply with non-repudiation of reception
element.complexType.annotation.appinfo./ BasicSecurityPolicy.NRReceiver./ ElementName.Roles.Role		Receiver	Role providing service

Fig. A.2. Mapping Table for Outbound Policy Files

A.3 Mapping Table for BPEL Files

BPEL Abstract Syntax		Sectet Metamodel		Remarks
Target Element	Attribute	Source Element	Attribute	
Root Element				
process	name	GWfMetamodel:ActivityPartition	name	Composite string, with name of Activity
		GWfMetamodel:Activity		prefixing name of ActvityPartition
	targetNamespace	*refer to name attribute*	name	*refer to name attribute*
Synchronuous Interaction Pattern				
partnerLink	name	SecurityMetaModel:Sender		Partner_role of service requester
	partnerLinkType	GWfMetamodel:ObjectNode		"PLType" appended to name
	myRole	RoleModelMetaModel:Partner_Role		"Provider" appended to name
Providing a Synchronous Service				
receive	name	GWfMetamodel:ObjectNode		"receive" string prefix to ObjectNode
				of incoming ObjectFlow
	partnerLink	SecurityMetaModel:Sender		
	portType	SecurityMetaModel:Sender		Composite string, e.g.,
		SecurityMetaModel:Receiver		SenderRole_ReceiverRole
	operation	GWfMetamodel:ObjectNode		String "send" prefixed to name of ObjectNode
	variable	GWfMetamodel:ObjectNode		
	createInstance	GWfMetamodel:ControlFlow		If first activity to be created in
				Bpel process, set to "yes"
reply	name	GWfMetamodel:ObjectNode		"reply" string prefix to ObjectNode
				of outgoing ObjectFlow
	partnerLink	SecurityMetaModel:Sender		Same as for receive activity
	portType	SecurityMetaModel:Sender		Same as for receive activity
		SecurityMetaModel:Receiver		
	operation	GWfMetamodel:ObjectNode		Same as for receive activity
	variable	GWfMetamodel:ObjectNode		Name of ObjectNode of outgoing
Synchronous Service Invocation				Bpel process, set to "yes"
invoke	name	SecurityMetaModel:Sender		"callback" string prefix to Sender
	partnerLink	SecurityMetaModel:Sender		Same as for receive activity
	portType	SecurityMetaModel:Sender		Composite string, with string
		SecurityMetaModel:Receiver		"Callback" appended, e.g.:
				SenderReceiverCallback
	operation	GWfMetamodel:ObjectNode		String "send" prefixed to ObjectNode
	inputVariable	GWfMetamodel:ObjectNode		ObjectNode of ObjectFlow going out
	outputVariable	GWfMetamodel:ObjectNode		ObjectNode of ObjectFlow comming back
Asnchronuous Interaction Pattern				
partnerLink	name	SecurityMetaModel:Sender		Partner_role of service requester
	partnerLinkType	GWfMetamodel:ObjectNode		"PLType" appended to name
	myRole	RoleModelMetaModel:Partner_Role		"Requester" appended to name
		GWfMetamodel:ObjectFlow		in case of outgoing ObjectFlow
				otherwise append "Provider" string
	PartnerRole	RoleModelMetaModel:Partner_Role		see myRole
		GWfMetamodel:ObjectFlow		
Providing an Asynchronous Service				
receive	name	GWfMetamodel:ObjectNode		"receive" string prefix to ObjectNode
	partnerLink	SecurityMetaModel:Sender		
	portType	SecurityMetaModel:Sender		Composite string, e.g., SenderReceiver
		SecurityMetaModel:Receiver		
	operation	GWfMetamodel:ObjectNode		String "send" prefixed to ObjectNode
	variable	GWfMetamodel:ObjectNode		
	createInstance	GWfMetamodel:ControlFlow		If first activity to be created in
Asynchronous Service Invocation				Bpel process, set to "yes"
invoke	name	SecurityMetaModel:Sender		"callback" string prefix to Sender
	partnerLink	SecurityMetaModel:Sender		Same as for receive activity
	portType	SecurityMetaModel:Sender		Composite string, with string "Callback"
		SecurityMetaModel:Receiver		appended, e.g.: SenderReceiverCallback
	operation	GWfMetamodel:ObjectNode		String "send" prefixed to ObjectNode
	inputVariable	GWfMetamodel:ObjectNode		ObjectNode of ObjectFlow going out
				to Sender defined in receive activity
Messages				
variable	name	GWfMetamodel:ObjectNode		All ObjectNodes with ObjectFlow
	messageType	GWfMetamodel:ObjectNode		going into or comming from ActivityPartition
Wrapping elements				
partnerLinks		no mapping		Wrapper element, one element for
				every Partner_Role BPEL file
sequence		no mapping		Wrapper element, one element for
				every Partner_Role BPEL file
variables		no mapping		Wrapper element, one element for
				every Partner_Role BPEL file

Fig. A.3. Mapping Table for BPEL Files

A.4 Mapping Table for BPEL Files (continued)

BPEL Abstract Syntax		Sectet Metamodel		Remarks
Target Element	Attribute	Source Element	Attribute	
Asnchronuous Interaction Pattern				
partnerLink	name	SecurityMetaModel:Sender		Partner_role of service requester
	partnerLinkType	GWfMetamodel:ObjectNode		"PLType" appended to name
	myRole	RoleModelMetaModel:Partner_Role		"Requester" appended to name
		GWfMetamodel:ObjectFlow		in case of outgoing ObjectFlow
				otherwise append "Provider" string
	PartnerRole	RoleModelMetaModel:Partner_Role		see myRole
		GWfMetamodel:ObjectFlow		
Providing an Asynchronous Service				
receive	name	GWfMetamodel:ObjectNode		"receive" string prefix to ObjectNode
	partnerLink	SecurityMetaModel:Sender		
	portType	SecurityMetaModel:Sender		Composite string, e.g., SenderReceiver
		SecurityMetaModel:Receiver		
	operation	GWfMetamodel:ObjectNode		String "send" prefixed to ObjectNode
	variable	GWfMetamodel:ObjectNode		
	createInstance	GWfMetamodel:ControlFlow		If first activity to be created in
Asynchronous Service invocation				Bpel process, set to "yes"
invoke	name	SecurityMetaModel:Sender		"callback" string prefix to Sender
	partnerLink	SecurityMetaModel:Sender		Same as for receive activity
	portType	SecurityMetaModel:Sender		Composite string, with string "Callback"
		SecurityMetaModel:Receiver		appended, e.g.: SenderReceiverCallback
	operation	GWfMetamodel:ObjectNode		String "send" prefixed to ObjectNode
	inputVariable	GWfMetamodel:ObjectNode		ObjectNode of ObjectFlow going out
Messages				to Sender defined in receive activity
variable	name	GWfMetamodel:ObjectNode		All ObjectNodes with ObjectFlow
	messageType	GWfMetamodel:ObjectNode		going into or cooming from ActivityPartition
Wrapping elements				
partnerLinks		no mapping		Wrapper element, one element for
				every Partner_Role BPEL file
sequence		no mapping		Wrapper element, one element for
				every Partner_Role BPEL file
variables		no mapping		Wrapper element, one element for
				every Partner_Role BPEL file

Fig. A.4. Mapping Table for BPEL Files (continued)

A.5 Mapping Table for WSDL Files

WSDL Abstract Syntax		Sectet Metamodel	Remarks
Target Element	Attribute	Source Element	
Root Element			
wsdl:definitions	targetNameSpace	GWfMetamodel:ActivityPartition	Wrapper element, one element for every Partner_Role BPEL file
Type Definitions			
types			Container element
types.xsd:schema			Container element
types.xsd:schema.xsd:import	namespace	GWfMetamodel:ObjectNode	According to production rules for every ObjectNode
	definitions	GWfMetamodel:ObjectNode	According to production rules for every ObjectNode
Message Definitions			
message	name	GWfMetamodel:ObjectNode	Append "Request" oder "Response"
message:part	name	"payload"	Default value
	element	GWfMetamodel:ObjectNode	Namespace prefix set to namespace of import declaration
PortType Definition (Synchronous)			Chosen when incomming ObjectFlow comes from same Action that ObjectFlow returns to
portType	name	SecurityMetaModel:Sender	Composite string, e.g.,
		SecurityMetaModel:Receiver	SenderReceiver
portType.operation	name	GWfMetamodel:ObjectNode	String "send" prefixed to ObjectNode
portType.operation.input	message	GWfMetamodel:ObjectNode	In case of incomming ObjectNode
portType.operation.output	message	GWfMetamodel:ObjectNode	In case of outgoing ObjectNode
PortType Definition (Asynchronous)			Chosen when ObjectFlow returns to Action with no outgoing ObjectFlow
portType	name	SecurityMetaModel:Sender	Two elements generated, the second appended.
		SecurityMetaModel:Receiver	Composite portType with string "Callback"
		GWfMetamodel:ObjectNode	String, e.g., "TaxAdvisorMunicipality_processedAS"
portType.operation	name	GWfMetamodel:ObjectNode	Two elements generated, the second as callback operation. String "send" prefixed to ObjectNode
portType.operation.input	message	GWfMetamodel:ObjectNode	If Incomming ObjectNode
portType.operation.output	message	GWfMetamodel:ObjectNode	If Outgoing ObjectNode
PartnerLinkType Definition			
plnk:partnerLinkType	name	GWfMetamodel:ObjectNode	"PLType" appended to name
plnk:partnerLinkType.plnk:role	name	SecurityMetaModel:Sender	One role declaration for each, Sender
		SecurityMetaModel:Receiver	and Receiver
	portType	SecurityMetaModel:Sender	*Synchronous invocation:*
		SecurityMetaModel:Receiver	Composite string, with string "Callback" appended, e.g.: SenderReceiverCallback
			Asynchronuous invocation:
			SecurityMetaModel:Sender
			SecurityMetaModel:Receiver
PartnerLinkType Definition			
plnk:partnerLinkType	name	GWfMetamodel:ObjectNode	"PLType" appended to name
plnk:partnerLinkType.plnk:role	name	SecurityMetaModel:Sender	One role declaration for each, Sender
		SecurityMetaModel:Receiver	and Receiver
	portType	SecurityMetaModel:Sender	*Synchronous invocation:*
		SecurityMetaModel:Receiver	Composite string, with string "Callback" appended, e.g.: SenderReceiverCallback
			Asynchronuous invocation:
			SecurityMetaModel:Sender
			SecurityMetaModel:Receiver

Fig. A.5. Mapping Table for WSDL Files

References

1. AndroMDA,
   http://www.andromda.org/.
2. Eclipse - an open development platform,
   http://www.eclipse.org/.
3. Enterprise JavaBeans Technology,
   http://java.sun.com/products/ejb/.
4. Integrating the Healthcare Enterprise,
   http://www.ihe.net/.
5. MagicDraw UML,
   http://www.magicdraw.com/.
6. Netbeans 6.1,
   http://www.netbeans.org/.
7. Oracle BPEL Process Manager,
   http://www.oracle.com/appserver/bpel_home.html.
8. Rational Rose,
   http://www-306.ibm.com/software/awdtools/developer/rose/.
9. WebSphere Integration Developer,
   http://www-306.ibm.com/software/integration/wid/.
10. Wikipedia. http://en.wikipedia.org/wiki/Web_service [Last Modified 14 July 2008].
11. Information Technology Security Evaluation Criteria, 1991. Version 1.2.
12. Common Criteria for Information Technology Security Evaluation, Part 1: Introduction and General Model, 1999. Version 2.1, CCIMB-99-031.
13. SHVT Manual, Fraunhofer Institute for Secure Telecooperation, 2004.
14. Business Process Modeling Notation (BPMN) Information, 2006. Available online: http://www.bpmn.org.
15. Logical Observation Identifiers Names and Codes (LOINC ©), 2008. LOINC Version 2.22 and RELMA Version 3.23.
16. Trusted Computer System Evaluation Criteria, Dec. 1985. DOD 5200.28-STD.
17. ISO/IEC 13888-1. Information Technology - Security Techniques - Non- repudiation - Part 1: General. Technical report, 1997.
18. ISO/IEC 13888-3. Information Technology - Security Techniques - Non- repudiation - Part 3: Mechanisms Using Asymmetric Techniques. Technical report, 1997.

19. W. M. P. van der Aalst. Verification of Workflow Nets. In G. Balbo, editor, *Application and Theory of Petri Nets 1997*, volume 1248, pages 407–426. Springer Verlag, 1997.

20. W. M. P. van der Aalst, A. Kumar, and H. M. W. Verbeek. Organizational Modeling in UML and XML in the Context of Workflow Systems. In *Proceedings of the 2003 ACM Symposium on Applied Computing (SAC)*, pages 603–608, 2003.

21. W. M. P. van der Aalst and M. Weske. The P2P Approach to Interorganizational Workflows. In Moira C. Norrie, editor, *CAiSE*, volume 2068, pages 140–156. Springer, 2001.

22. W.M.P. van der Aalst. Loosely Coupled Interorganizational Workflows: Modelling and Analyzing Workflows Crossing Organizational Boundaries. *Information and Management*, 37(2):67–75, 2000.

23. M. Alam. SECTETPL : A Predicative Language for the Specification of Access Rights. Technical report, 2006. URL: http://qe-informatik. uibk.ac.at/muhammad/TechnicalReportSECTETPL.pdf.

24. M. Alam. *Model Driven Realization of Dynamic Security Requirements in Distributed Systems*. PhD thesis, Leopold-Franzens-Universität Innsbruck, 2007.

25. M. Alam, M. Hafner, and R. Breu. Modeling Authorization in an SOA based Application Scenario. In *IASTED Conference on Software Engineering*, pages 79–84, 2006.

26. M. Alam, M. Hafner, and R. Breu. Model-Driven Security Engineering for Trust Management in SECTET. *Journal of Software, Academy Publisher*, 2(1), 2007.

27. C. J. Alberts and A. J. Dorofee. *Managing information security risks: the OCTAVE approach*. Pearson Education, 2002.

28. B. Alhaqbani and C. Fidge. Access Control Requirements for Processing Electronic Health Records. In A. H. M. ter Hofstede, B. Benatallah, and H.-Y. Paik, editors, *Business Process Management Workshops*, volume 4928 of *Lecture Notes in Computer Science*, pages 371–382. Springer, 2007.

29. A. Anderson. Core and hierarchical role based access control (RBAC) profile of XACML v2.0. Oasis standard, OASIS, 2005.

30. A. Anderson and H. Lockhart. SAML 2.0 profile of XACML v2.0. Oasis standard, OASIS, 2005.

31. R. J. Anderson. *Security Engineering: A Guide to Building Dependable Distributed Systems*. Wiley, 2001.

32. S. Anderson. Web Services Secure Conversation Language (WS-Secure Conversation), February 2005. Technical report, 2005.

33. S. Anderson. Web Services Trust Language (WS-Trust), February 2005. Technical report, 2005.

34. T. Andrews and et al. Business Process Execution Language for Web Services, Version 1.1. Technical report, BEA, IBM, Microsoft, SAP, Siebel, 2003.

35. A. Arkin. Business Process Modeling Language (BPML). Specification, pbmi.org, 2002.

36. A. Arkin, S. Askary, B. Bloch, F. Curbera, Y. Goland, N. Kartha, S. Thatte, P. Yendluri, and A. Yiu. Web Services Business Process Execution Language Version 2.0. Technical report, 2005. http://www.oasis-open.org/committees/download.php/14616/wsbpel-specification-draft.htm.

37. B. Atkinson, G. Della-Libera, S. Hada, M. Hondo, P. Hallam-Baker, J. Klein, B. LaMacchia, P. Leach, J. Manferdellie, H. Maruyama, A. Nadalin, N. Nagaratnam, H. Prafullchandra, J. Shewchuk, and D. Simon. Web Services Security (WS-Security) - Version 1.0. Specification, IBM Corp., Mircosoft Corp., VeriSign, Inc., 2002.

38. V. Atluri, W. Huang, and E. Bertino. A Semantic Based Execution Model for Multilevel Secure Workflows. *International Journal of Computer Security*, 8(1):3–41, 2000.

39. V. Atluri and W-K. Huang. Enforcing Mandatory and Discretionary Security in Workflow Management Systems. *Journal of Computer Security.*, 5(4):303–339, 1997.

40. S. Bajaj. Web Services Policy 1.2 - Framework (WS-Policy) W3C Member Submission 25 April 2006. Technical report, W3C, 2006.

41. S. Bajaj, G. Della-Libera, and B. Dixon. Web Services Federation Language (WS-Federation), version 1.0. Technical report, BEA, IBM, Microsoft, RSA Security and VeriSign, 2002.

42. K. Ballinger and D. Box. Web Services Metadata Exchange (WS-MetadataExchange). Technical report, 2004.

43. M. Bartel, J. Boyer, and B. Fox. XML-Signature Syntax and Processing, W3C Recommendation 12 February 2002. Technical report, W3C, 2002.

44. D. Basin, J. Doser, and T. Lodderstedt. Model Driven Security for Process-Oriented Systems. In *Proc. 8th ACM Symposium on Access Control Models and Technologies.* ACM Press, 2003.

45. D. Basin, J. Doser, and T. Lodderstedt. Model driven security: From UML models to access control infrastructures. *ACM Trans. Softw. Eng. Methodol.*, 15(1):39–91, 2006.

46. R. Bastos and D. Ruiz. Extending UML activity diagram for workflow modeling in production systems. pages 3786–3795, 2002.

47. T. Bellwood, S. Capell, and L. Clement. UDDI Version 3.0.2, UDDI Spec Technical Committee Draft, Dated 20041019. Technical report, OASIS, 2004.

48. M. Ben-Or, O. Goldreich, S. Micali, and R. Rivest. A fair protocol for signing contracts. *IEEE Transaction on Information Theory*, 36(1):40–46, 1990.

49. M. Bernauer, G. Kappel, and G. Kramler. Comparing WSDL-Based and ebXML-Based Approaches for B2B Protocol Specification. In *ICSOC*, pages 225–240, 2003.

50. M. Bernauer, G. Kappel, G. Kramler, and W. Retschitzegger. Specification of Interorganizational Workflows - A Comparison of Approaches. In *Proceedings of the 7th World Multiconference on Systemics, Cybernetics and Informatics*, pages 30–36, 2003.

51. E. Bertino, E. Ferrari, and V. Atluri. The Specification and Enforcement of Authorization Constraints in Workflow Management Systems. *ACM Transactions on Information and System Security*, 1(2):65–104, 1999.

52. R. Bilorusets, D. Box, and L. F. Cabrera. Web Services Reliable Messaging Protocol (WS-ReliableMessaging), February 2005. Technical report, 2005.

53. M. Bishop. *Computer Security: Art and Science*, chapter 25. Addison-Wesley, December 2002.

54. T. Bray, J. Paoli, C. M. Sperberg-McQueen, and E. Maler. Extensible Markup Language (XML) 1.0 (Second Edition). W3C Recommendation 6 October, World Wide Web Consortium, 2000.

55. R. Breu, M. Breu, M. Hafner, and A. Nowak. Web Service Engineering - Advancing a New Software Engineering Discipline. In D. Lowe and M. Gaedke, editors, *Web Engineering, Proceedings of the 5th International Conference, ICWE 2005*, volume 3579 of *Lecture Notes in Computer Science*, Sydney, Australia, 2005. Springer.

56. R. Breu, K. Burger, M. Hafner, and G. Popp. Towards a Systematic Development of Secure Systems. *Special Issue of the Information Systems Security Journal*, 13(3):1–12, 2004.

57. R. Breu, M. Hafner, and B. Weber. Model Driven Security for Interorganizational Workflows in e-Government. In *TCGOV*, pages 122–133, 2005.

58. R. Breu, G. Popp, and M. Alam. Model-based development of access policies. *Journal for Software Tools and Technology Transfer (STTT)*, 9:457–470, 2007.

59. A. D. Brucker, J. Doser, and B. Wolff. An MDA framework supporting OCL. *j-eceasst*, 5, 2006.

60. BSI - British Standards Institution. BS 7799-3:2006 Information security management systems - Part 3: Guidelines for information security risk management, 2006.

61. BSI (Federal Office for Information Security). IT Baseline Protection Manual, 2004.

62. L. F. Cabrera, G. Copeland, W. Cox, M. Feingold, T. Freund, C. Kaler, J. Klein, D. Langworthy, A. Nadalin, D. Orchard, I. Robinson, J. Shewchuk, and T. Storey. Web Service Coordination (WS-Coordination). Specification, BEA Systems, IBM Corp., Microsoft Corp., 2003.

63. L. F. Cabrera, G. Copeland, W. Cox, T. Freund, J. Klein, D. Langworthy, I. Robinson, T. Storey, and S. Thatte. Web Services Business Activity Framework (WS-BusinessActivity). Specification, BEA Systems, IBM Corp., Microsoft Corp., 2004.

64. L. Felipe Cabrera, G. Copeland, and M. Feingold. Web Services Atomic Transaction (WS-AtomicTransaction), Version 1.0. Technical report, 2005.

65. L. M. Camarinha-Matos, H. Afsarmanesh, M. Ollus, and L. M. Camarinha-Matos. *Virtual Organizations. Systems and Practices*. Springer-Verlag, 1. edition edition, 2005.

66. L. M. Camarinha-Matos, H. Afsarmanesh, M. Ollus, L. Matos, and M. Camarinha. *Virtual Organizations. Systems and Practices*. Springer-Verlag, 1. edition edition, 2005.

67. S. Cantor, J. Kemp, R. Philpott, and E. Maler. Assertions and Protocols for the OASIS Security Assertion Markup Language (SAML) V2.0. Oasis standard, OASIS, 2005.

68. F. Casati, E. Shan, U. Dayal, and M.-C. Shan. Business-oriented management of web services. *Commun. ACM*, 46(10):55–60, 2003.

69. D. W. Chadwick and A. Otenko. RBAC Policies in XML for X.509 Based Privilege Management. In *SEC '02: Proceedings of the IFIP TC11 17th International Conference on Information Security*, pages 39–54, Deventer, The Netherlands, The Netherlands, 2002. Kluwer, B.V.

70. R. Chinnici, M. Gudgin, J.-J. Moreau, J. Schlimmer, and S. Weerawarana. Web Service Description Language (WSDL) Version 2.0 Part 1: Core Language. W3C Working Draft 10 November, World Wide Web Consortium, 2003.

71. J. Clark, C. Casanave, K. Kanaskie, B. Harvey, J. Clark, N. Smith, J. Yunker, and K. Riemer. ebXML Business Process Specification Schema Version 1.01. Specification, UN/CEFACT and OASIS, 2001.

72. Commission of the European Union. e-Health - making healthcare better for European citizens: An action plan for a European e-Health Area [online]., 2004. Available at: http://europa.eu/eur-lex/en/com/cnc/2004/com2004_0356en01.pdf [Accessed 4. October 2006].

73. R. Crook, D. C. Ince, L. Lin, and B. Nuseibeh. Security Requirements Engineering: When Anti-Requirements Hit the Fan. In *RE '02: Proceedings of the 10th Anniversary IEEE Joint International Conference on Requirements Engineering*, pages 203–205, Washington, DC, USA, 2002. IEEE Computer Society.

74. A. Datta, A. Derek, J. C. Mitchell, and D. Pavlovic. A derivation system and compositional logic for security protocols. *Journal of Computer Security*, 13:423–482, 2005.

75. DCSSI, Direction centrale de la sécurité des systèmes d'information. EBIOS: Expression des Besoins et Identification des Objectifs de sécurité, June 2005. Version 2.0.

76. M. Donner. From the Editors: Whose Data Are These, Anyway? *IEEE Security & Privacy*, 2(3):5–6, 2004.

77. A. Dussart, B. Aubert, and M. Patry. An Evaluation of Inter-Organizational Workflow Modeling Formalisms. *J. Database Manag.*, 15(2):74–104, 2004.

78. C. Eckert. *IT-Sicherheit*. Oldenbourg, München [u.a.], 2004.

79. E. Rissanen (ed.). XACML v3.0 Administration and Delegation Profile Version 1.0 Working Draft 19, 10 Oct 2007. Technical report, OASIS open 2005, 2007.

80. Active Endpoints. ActiveBPEL Open Source Engine Project, 2008. http://www.active-endpoints.com/active-bpel-engine-overview.htm.

81. T. Erl. *Service-Oriented Architecture : A Field Guide to Integrating XML and Web Services*. Prentice Hall PTR, 2004.

82. R. Eshuis and R. Wieringa. A formal semantics for UML activity diagrams – Formalising workflow models, 2001.

83. P. Giorgini et al. *ST–Tool: A CASE Tool for Modeling and Analyzing Trust Requirements*. Springer LNCS 3477, 2005.

84. R. Vogl et al. Architecture for a distributed national electronic health record in Austria. In *Proc. EuroPACS 2006: The 24th International EuroPACS Conference*, pages 67–77, 2006.

85. T. Schabetsberger et al. From a Paper-based Transmission of Discharge Summaries to Electronic Communication in Health Care Regions. *Int. Journal of Medical Informatics*, 75, 3-4:209–215, 2006.

86. M. Farwick. Generating Local BPEL Processes from Global Workflows Expressed in UML2 Activity Diagrams. B.s. thesis, Dept. Computing Science, University of Innsbruck, 2007.

87. D. F. Ferraiolo and D. R. Kuhn. Role Based Access Control. In *Proc. 15th National Computer Security Conference*, 1992.

88. D. Firesmith. Engineering Security Requirements. *Journal of Object Technology*, 2(1):53–68, 2003.

89. The Apache Foundation. Apache WSS4J, http://ws.apache.org/wss4j/ .

90. M. Fowler. *Refactoring. Improving the Design of Existing Code*. Addison-Wesley, 1999.

91. Bundesamt für Sicherheit in der Informationstechnologie. SOA Security Compendium,

http://www.bsi.bund.de/literat/studien/soa/soa-security-kompendium.pdf, 2008.

92. D. Frankel. *Model Driven Architecture*. John Wiley & Sons, 2003.

93. E. Freudenthal, E. Keenan, T. Pesin, L. Port, and V. Karamcheti. DisCo: A Distribution Infrastructure for Securely Deploying Decomposable Services in Partly Trusted Environments. Technical report, 2001.

94. E. Freudenthal, T. Pesin, L. Port, E. Keenan, and V. Karamcheti. dRBAC: Distributed Role-based Access Control for Dynamic Coalition Environments. In *Twenty-second IEEE International Conference on Distributed Computing Systems (ICDCS), Vienna, Austria, 2002*, 2002.

95. A. L. Opdahl G. Sindre, D. G. Firesmith. A Reuse-Based Approach to Determining Security Requirements. In *Proc. 9th International Workshop on Requirements Engineering: Foundation for Software Quality (REFSQ'03)*, June 2003.

96. T. Garfinkel, M. Rosenblum, and D. Boneh. Flexible OS Support and Applications for Trusted Computing. In *Proceedings of the 9th Workshop on Hot Topics in Operating Systems HotOS-VIII*, 2003.

97. M. Gerber, R. von Solms, and P. Overbeek. Formalizing information security requirements. *Information Management & Computer Security*, 9(1):32–37, 2001.

98. M. Gerber and Rossouw von von Solms. From Risk Analysis to Security Requirements. *Computers & Security*, 20:577–584, 2001.

99. G. Göbel, R. Penz, T. Schabetsberger, M. Springmann, and F. Wozak. Health@net- service architecture of sehr, system description and technical use cases. Technical report, 2008.

100. D. Gollmann. *Computer Security*. John Wiley & Sons, 1998.

101. P. W. P. J. Grefen, K. Aberer, H. Ludwig, and Y. Hoffner. CrossFlow: Cross-Organizational Workflow Management for Service Outsourcing in Dynamic Virtual Enterprises. *IEEE Data Engineering Bulletin*, 24(1):52–57, 2001.

102. E. Gudes, M. S. Olivier, and R. P. van de Riet. Modelling, specifying and implementing workflow security in Cyberspace. *Journal of Computer Security*, 7(4):287–315, 1999.

103. M. Gudgin, M. Hadley, N. Mendelsohn, J.–J. Moreau, and H. F. Nielsen. SOAP Version 1.2 Part 1: Messaging Framework. W3C Recommendation 24 June, World Wide Web Consortium, 2003.

104. M. Gudgin, M. Hadley, N. Mendelsohn, J.–J. Moreau, and H. F. Nielsen. SOAP Version 1.2 Part 2: Adjuncts. W3C Recommendation 24 June, World Wide Web Consortium, 2003.

105. T. Gunter and N. Terry. The Emergence of National Electronic Health Record Architectures in the United States and Australia: Models, Costs, and Questions. *Journal of Medical Internet Research*, 7(1):e3, 2005.

106. M. Hafner, B. Agreiter, R. Breu, and A. Nowak. SECTET: An Extensible Framework for the Realization of Secure Inter-Organizational Workflows. *Journal of Internet Research*, 16(5), 2006.

107. M. Hafner, M. Alam, and R. Breu. Towards a MOF/QVT-based Domain Architecture for Model Driven Security. In *Proceedings of the 9th International Conference on Model Driven Engineering Languages and Systems (Models 2006)*, Genova, Italy, 2006.

108. M. Hafner, M. Breu, R. Breu, and A. Nowak. Modelling Inter-organizational Workflow Security in a Peer-to-Peer Environment. In *ICWS '05: Proceedings of the IEEE International Conference on Web Services (ICWS'05)*, pages 533–540, Washington, DC, USA, 2005. IEEE Computer Society.

109. M. Hafner, R. Breu, and B. Weber. Model Driven Security for Inter-Organizational Workflows in E-Governement. In A. Mitrakas, P. Hengeveld, Despina. Polemi, and J. Gamper, editors, *Secure eGovernment Web Services*, chapter 14. Idea Group, Inc., 2007.

110. M. Hafner, M. Memon, and M. Alam. Modeling and Enforcing Advanced Access Control Policies in Healthcare Systems with SECTET. In H. Giese, editor, *LNCS Volume on Models in Software Engineering Workshops and Symposia at MoDELS 2007 Nashville, TN, USA, September 30 – October 5, 2007 Reports and Revised Selected Papers*. Springer, 2007.

111. C. Hailey, R. Laney, J. Moffett, and B. Nuseibeh. Security requirements engineering, a framework for representation and analysis. *to appear in IEEE Transactions on Software Engineering*, 2007.

112. A. Hall and R. Chapman. Correctness by Construction: Developing a Commercial Secure System. *IEEE Software*, 19(1):18–25, /2002.

113. P. Hallam-Baker and S. H. Mysore. XML Key Management Specification (XKMS 2.0). Technical report, W3C, 2005. URL: http://www.w3.org/TR/2005/REC-xkms2-20050628/.

114. B. Hartman, D. J. Flinn, K. Beznosov, and S. Kawamoto. *Mastering Web Services Security*. Wiley, 2003.

115. HL7.org. HHL7 Version 3 Standard: Clinical Document Architecture (CDA), Release 2. Ansi/hl7 cda, r2-2005, 2005.

116. J. Hu and A. Weaver. Dynamic, Context-Aware Access Control for Distributed Healthcare Applications, August 2004.

117. V. Hu, D. Ferraiolo, and D. Kuhn. Assessment of Access Control Systems. Technical Report NISTIR 7316, National Inst. of Standards and Technology, US Department of Commerce, September 2006.

118. W.K. Huang and V. Atluri. SecureFlow: A secure Web-enabled Workflow Management System. In *ACM Workshop on Role-Based Access Control*, 1999.

119. T. Imamura. XML Encryption Syntax and Processing, W3C Recommendation 10 December 2002. Technical report, W3C, 2002.

120. Integrating the Healthcare Enterprise. Health@net- service architecture of sehr, system description and technical use cases. Trial implementation version, 2004. Available at: http://healthcare.xml.org/resources/IHE_ITI_Cross-enterprise_Doc_Sharing_2004_08-15.pdf.

121. ISO (International Organization for Standardization). ISO/IEC 27001 Information technology – Security techniques – Information security management systems – Requirements, 2005.

122. ISO/IEC 13888-2. Information technology - security techniques - non- repudiation - part 2: Mechanisms using symmetric techniques. Technical report, 1998.

123. IT Governance Institute. Control Objectives for Information and related Technology (COBIT) 4.1, 2007.

124. P. Jiang, Q. Mair, and J. Newman. Using UML to Design Distributed Collaborative Workflows: from UML to XPDL. In *WETICE '03: Proceedings of the Twelfth International Workshop on Enabling Technologies*, page 71, Washington, DC, USA, 2003. IEEE Computer Society.

125. J. Jürjens. *Secure Systems Development with UML.* Springer Verlag, 2004.
126. N. Kavantzas, D. Burdett, and G. Ritzinger. Web Services Choreography Description Language Version 1.0 W3C Working Draft 27 April 2004. Working draft, W3C, 2004.
127. L. Kohn, J. Corrigan, and M. Donaldson. *To Err is Human: Building a Safer Health System.* Washington DC, National Academy Press, 2000.
128. S. Kremer, O. Markowitch, and J. Zhou. An Intensive Survey of Fair Non-Repudiation Protocols. *Computer Communications,* 25:1601–1621, 2002.
129. F. Leymann and D. Roller. *Production workflow: concepts and techniques.* Prentice Hall PTR, Upper Saddle River, NJ, USA, 2000.
130. M. Li and R. Poovendran. Enabling Distributed Addition of Secure Access to Patient's Records in A Tele-Referring Group. In *IEEE-EMBS 2005: Proceedings of the 27th IEEE EMBS Annual International Conference",* pages 308–317. IEEE, 2005.
131. M. Little. Transactions and Web Services. *Communications of the ACM,* 46(10):49–54, 2003.
132. T. Lodderstedt. *Model Driven Security from UML Models to Access Control Architectures.* PhD thesis, Albert-Ludwigs-Universität Freiburg im Breisgau, 2003.
133. T. Lodderstedt, D. A. Basin, and J. Doser. SecureUML: A UML-Based Modeling Language for Model-Driven Security. In J.-M. Jézéquel, H. Hußmann, and S. Cook, editors, *UML,* volume 2460 of *Lecture Notes in Computer Science,* pages 426–441. Springer, 2002.
134. P. Louridas. Some Guidelines for Non-repudiation Protocols. *Computer Communication Review,* 30(4), October 2000.
135. Azzurri Ltd. JET Tutorial Part 1 (Introduction to JET) [online]., 2005. Available at: http://www.eclipse.org/articles/Article-JET/jet_tutorial1.html [Accessed 4. October 2006].
136. M. Alam and R. Breu and M. Hafner. Modeling Permissions in a (U/X)ML World. In *IEEE ARES 2006.* ISBN: 0-7695-2567-9.
137. K. Mantell. From UML to BPEL. Technical report, IBM-developerWorks, 2003.
138. O. Markowitch and Y. Roggeman. Probabilistic non-repudiation without trusted third party. In *Second Conference on Security in Communication Networks'99,* Amalfi, Italy, 1999.
139. D. Masys, D. Baker, A. Butros, and K. E. Cowles. Giving patients access to their medical records via the internet. *Journal of the American Medical Informatics Association,* 9:181–191, 2002.
140. J. McDermott and C. Fox. Using abuse case models for security requirements analysis. *Computer Security Applications Conference, 1999.(ACSAC'99) Proceedings. 15th Annual,* pages 55–64, 1999.
141. J. Mendling and M. Hafner. From Inter-Organizational Workflows to Process Execution: Generating BPEL from WS-CDL. *Journal of Enterprise Information Management,* 2006.
142. A. J. Menezes, P. C. van Oorschot, and S. A. Vanstone. *Handbook of Applied Cryptography.* CRC, 1996.
143. IBM & Microsoft. Security in a Web Services World: A Proposed Architecture and Roadmap,. A joint security whitepaper from IBM Corporation and Microsoft Corporation. April 7, 2002, Version 1.0. Technical report, IBM & Microsoft, 2002.

144. J. A. Miller, M. Fan, A. P. Sheth, and K. J. Kochut. Security in Web-Based Workflow Management Systems.

145. Ministerio de Administraciones Públicas. Methodology for Information Systems Risk Analysis and Management (MAGERIT version 2), 2006.

146. M. Casassa Mont, S. Pearson, and P. Bramhall. Towards Accountable Management of Identity and Privacy: Sticky Policies and Enforceable Tracing Services. In *DEXA '03: Proc. of the 14th Int. Workshop on Database and Expert Systems App.*, page 377, Washington, DC, USA, 2003. IEEE Computer Society.

147. T. Moses. Core and hierarchical role based access control (RBAC) profile of XACML v2.0. Oasis standard, OASIS, 2005.

148. E. Newcomer and G. Lomow. *Understanding SOA with Web Services*. Addison-Wesley Professional, 2004.

149. OCG (Office of Government Commerce). Best Practice for Security Management., 1999. The ITIL Infrastructure Library.

150. University of Southern California. RFC - 793 Transmission Control Protocol, Darpa Internet Program, Protocol Specification, 1981.

151. OMG. MDA Guide Version 1.0.1, omg/2003-06-01. Technical report, The OMG, 2003.

152. OMG. MOF 2.0/XMI Mapping, Version 2.1.1. Technical report, 2007.

153. The OMG. UML 2.0 OCL Specification, ptc/03-10-14. 2003.

154. The OMG. Meta Object Facility (MOF) 2.0 Core Specification. OMG Available Specification, 2005.

155. Committee on Quality of Health Care in America. Inst. of Medicine. *Crossing the Quality Chasm: A New Health System for the 21st Century*. Washington DC Nat. Acad. Press, 2001.

156. M. O'Neill. *Web Services Security*. McGraw-Hill Osborne Media, 2003.

157. openArchitectureWare.org. openArchitectureWare [online]., 2005. Available at: http://www.openarchitectureware.org/ [Accessed 19. February 2008].

158. Republik Österreich. Bundesgesetz über elektronische Signaturen (Signaturgesetz – SigG), 1999.

159. Cover Pages. Web Services Metadata Exchange (WS-MetadataExchange) for Service Endpoints, http://xml.coverpages.org/ni2004-03-05-a.html, 2008.

160. J. Park and R. Sandhu. The UCON ABC Usage Control Model. *ACM Transactions on Information and Systems Security*, 7:128–174, 2004.

161. T. R. Peltier. *Information security risk analysis*. Auerbach, 2001.

162. C. Pfleeger and S. Pfleeger. *Security in Computing*. Prentice Hall, 2003.

163. F. Innerhofer-Oberperfler R. Breu and A. Yautsiukhin. Quantitative Assessment of Enterprise Security Systems. submitted.

164. D. Raptis, T. Dimitrakos, B.A. Gran, and K. Stølen. The CORAS Approach for Model-based Risk Management applied to e-Commerce Domain. In *Proc. CMS-2002*, pages 169–181, 2002.

165. S. Rinderle and P. Dadam. Schema Evolution in Workflow Management Systems. *Informatik Spektrum*, 26(1):17–19, 2003. (in German).

166. A. Rodriguez, E. Fernandez-Medina, and M. Piattini. Capturing Security Requirements in Business Processes Through a UML 2.0 Activity Diagrams Profile. In *Proc. ER Workshops 2006*, pages 32–42, 2006.

167. J. Rosenberg and D. L. Remy. *Securing Web Services with WS-Security: Demystifying WS-Security, WS-Policy, SAML, XML Signature, and XML Encryption*. Sams Publishing, 2004.

168. R. Ross, S. Katzke, A. Johnson, M. Swanson, G. Stoneburner, and A. L. Rogers. Recommended Security Controls for Federal Information Systems. Technical report, National Institute of Standards and Technology, 2005. NIST Special Publication 800-53.

169. R. Sandhu, E. Coyne, H. Feinstein, and C. Youman. Role-based access control models. *IEEE Computer*, 29(2), 1996.

170. R. S. Sandhu, V. Bhamidipati, and Q. Munawer. The ARBAC97 model for role-based administration of roles. *ACM Transactions on Information and Systems Security (TISSEC)*, 1(2):105–135, 1999.

171. R.S. Sandhu, E.J. Coyne, H.L. Feinstein, and C.E. Youman. Role Based Access Control Models. *IEEE Computer 29(2), IEEE Press*, pages 18–47, 1996.

172. M. Schumacher, E. Fernandez-Buglioni, D. Hybertson, F. Buschmann, and P. Sommerlad. *Security Patterns : Integrating Security and Systems Engineering (Wiley Software Patterns Series)*. John Wiley & Sons, March 2006.

173. Joint NEMA/COCIR/JIRA Sec. and Priv. Committee. Break-Glass - An Approach to Granting Emergency Access to Healthcare Systems. http://www.nema.org/prod/med/security/.

174. E. Seidewitz. What Models Mean. *IEEE Softw.*, 20(5):26–32, 2003.

175. Service Central de la Sécurité des Systèmes d'Information. Expression of Needs and Identification of Safety Objectives (EBIOS). online, 1997.

176. A. Shabo, P. Vortman, and B. Robson. Who's afraid of lifetime electronic medical records? In *Proceedings of the Towards Electronic Health Records conference 2001.*, 2001.

177. S. Shah. *Hacking Web Services (Internet Series)*. Charles River Media, 2006.

178. R. Shirey. Security Architecture for Internet Protocols: A Guide for Protocol Designs and Standards, Internet Draft, November 1994.

179. G. Sindre and A. L. Opdahl. Eliciting security requirements with misuse cases. *Requirements Engineering*, 10(1):34–44, January 2005.

180. T. Stahl and M. Völter. *Modellgetriebene Softwareentwicklung*. dpunkt.verlag GmbH, Heidelbeg, 1. auflage edition, 2005.

181. G. Stoneburner, A. Goguen, and A. Feringa. *Risk Management Guide for Information Technology Systems*. National Institute of Standards and Technology, special publication 800-30 edition, July 2002.

182. T. Straub. Usability Challenges of PKI. Master's thesis, University of Darmstadt, Germany, 2005.

183. B. Suh and I. Han. The IS risk analysis based on a business model. *Information & Management*, 41(2):149–158, December 2003.

184. Sun Microsystems, Inc. Sun's XACML Implementation [online]., 2005. Available at: http://sunxacml.sourceforge.net/index.html [Accessed 19. February 2008].

185. F. Swiderski and W. Snyder. *Threat Modeling*. Microsoft Press, 2004.

186. T. Tedrick. How to exchange half a bit. In D. Chaum, editor, *Advances in Cryptology: Proceedings of Crypto 83*, Advances in Cryptology: Proceedings of, pages 147–151. Plenum Press, New York and London, 1984.

187. T. Tedrick. Fair exchange of secrets. In GG. R. Blakley and D. C. Chaum, editors, *Advances in Cryptology: Proceedings of Crypto 84*, volume 196 of *Lecture Notes in Computer Science*, pages 134–138. Springer-Verlag, 1985.

188. The Apache Software Foundation. The Apache Ant Project, http://ant.apache.org/.

189. The Apache Software Foundation. Web Services Axis, http://ws.apache.org/axis/.
190. The Eclipse Foundation. JDT - Java Development Tools, http://www.eclipse.org/jdt/.
191. Integrating the Healthcare Enterprise. IHE, 2005, IT Infrastructure Technical Framework vol.1 (ITI TF-1) Integration Profiles [online]. Technical report, 2005. Available from: http://www.ihe.net/Technical_Framework/upload/ihe_iti_tf_2.0_vol1_FT_2005-08-15.pdf [Accessed 5. October 2006].
192. Integrating the Healthcare Enterprise. IHE, 2005, IT Infrastructure Technical Framework vol.1 (ITI TF-2) Transactions [online]. Technical report, 2005. Avaliable from: http://www.ihe.net/Technical_Framework/upload/ihe_iti_tf_2.0_vol2_FT_2005-08-15.pdf [Accessed 5. October 2006].
193. The OMG. UML 2.0 Infrastructure Specification, ptc/03-09-15. OMG Adopted Specification, The OMG, 2003.
194. The OMG. *MOF/QVT Final Adopted Specification, http://www.omg.org/docs/ptc/05-11-01.pdf*, volume ptc/05-11-01. 2005.
195. The OMG. Unified Modeling Language: Superstructure, version 2.0, formal/05-07-04. Technical report, The OMG, 2005.
196. The OMG. Common Object Request Broker Architecture (CORBA) Specification, Version 3.1. OMG Available Specification, 2008.
197. M. R. Thompson, A. Essiari, and S. Mudumbai. Certificate-based authorization policy in a PKI environment. *ACM Trans. Inf. Syst. Secur.*, 6(4):566–588, 2003.
198. Sozialversicherungs-Chipkarten Betriebs und Errichtungsgesellschaft m.b.H. Stufenmodell für die Anforderung und Übermittlung von Patientendaten [online]., 2005. Available at: http://www.chipkarte.at/esvapps/page/page.jsp?p_pageid=220&p_ menuid=59290&p_id=5 [Accessed 4. October 2006].
199. A. van Lamsweerde. Goal-Oriented Requirements Engineering: A Guided Tour. In *5th IEEE International Symposium of Requirements Engineering*, pages 249 – 262, 2001.
200. H. M. W. Verbeek, A. Hirnschall, and W. M. P. van der Aalst. XRL/Flower: Supporting Interorganizational Workflows using XRL/Petri-net Technology. In *Web Services, E-Business, and the Semantic Web, CAiSE 2002 International Workshop (WES 2002)*, pages 93–108, 2002.
201. J. Viehmann. Fair Non-Repudiation. M.s. thesis, Dept. Computing Science, University of Innsbruck, 2007.
202. G. Vogt. Multiple Authorization – A Model and Arch. for Increased, Practical Security. In *Proc. of the IFIP/IEEE 8th Int. Symp. on Integrated Network Management (IM 2003)*, pages 109–112, Colorado Springs, USA, March 2003. IFIP/IEEE, Kluwer Academic Publishers.
203. M. Völter. What is a Domain Specific Language? Posted on Blog Friday, September 28, 2007. URL: http://voelterblog.blogspot.com/2007_09_01_archive.html.
204. W3C. Web Services Addressing (WS-Addressing), W3C Member Submission 10 August 2004. Technical report, W3C, 2004.
205. w3.org. Hypertext Transfer Protocol – HTTP/1.1, 1999.
206. J. Wainer, P. Barthelmess, and A. Kumar. W-RBAC - A Workflow Security Model Incorporating Controlled Overriding of Constraints. *International Journal of Cooperative Information Systems*, 12(4):455–485, 2003.

207. S. Weerawarana, F. Curbera, F. Leymann, T. Storey, and D. F. Ferguson. *Web Services Platform Architecture: SOAP, WSDL, WS-Policy, WS-Addressing, WS-BPEL, WS-Reliable Messaging, and More*. Prentice Hall PTR, 2005.

208. Wikipedia. Elektronische Gesundheitskarte [online]., 2008. Available at: http://de.wikipedia.org/wiki/Elektronische_Gesundheitskarte [Last Modified 14 July 2008].

209. C. Wolter, H. Plate, and C. Hebert. Collaborative Workflow Management for eGovernment. In *DEXA '07: Proceedings of the 18th International Conference on Database and Expert Systems Applications*, pages 845–849, Washington, DC, USA, 2007. IEEE Computer Society.

210. C. Wolter and A. Schaad. Modeling of task-based authorization constraints in BPMN. In *Business Process Management*, volume Volume 4714/2007, pages 64–79. Springer Berlin/Heidelberg, 2007.

211. C. Wolter, A. Schaad, and C. Meinel. Task-based entailment constraints for basic workflow patterns. In *SACMAT '08: Proceedings of the 13th ACM symposium on Access control models and technologies*, pages 51–60, New York, NY, USA, 2008. ACM.

212. F. Wozak, E. Ammenwerth, M. Breu, R. Penz, T. Schabetsberger, R. Vogl, and M. Wurz. Medical Data GRIDs as Approach towards Secure Cross Enterprise Document Sharing (Based on IHE XDS). *Studies in Health Technology and Informatics*, 124, 2006.

213. J. Zhou and D. Gollmann. A Fair Non-repudiation Protocol. *Proceedings of the IEEE Symposium on Research in Security and Privacy*, pages 55–61, 1996.

Index

SECTET Model Views, 96
SECTET-Reference Architecture, 121
SECTINO, 66
4-Eyes-Principle, 37, 183
4-step model, 192

Security Micro-process, 81

Access Control, 86
Access Control Policies, 100
Advanced Security Policies, 36, 93, 100, 162
Apache Ant, 155
Apache Axsi, 42
application level, 74
Architectural Blueprint, 121
Attacks, 38
Authentication, 125
Authorization Policy Enforcement, 216
Availability, 161

Baseline Protection, 89
Basic Security Policies, 93, 99, 114, 116, 122
Basic Security Policy, 31
BPML, 24
BPSS, 25
Break-Glass Policy, 37, 182
business level, 74

Case Study, 200
Choreography, 23, 24
Code Artifacts, 55
Code Generation, 154

Component Configuration, 130
Computer security, 27
Confidentiality, 93, 127
Confidentiality Policy, 99
Cross-Enterprise Document Sharing, 191
Cryptographic Policy Enforcement, 215

Delegation of Rights, 36
Delegation Policies, 177
Dependency Graph, 83
Deployment Process, 157
Description Layer, 22
Discovery Layer, 22
Discretionary Access Control, 33
Document Model, 98, 107, 172
Domain, 52, 53
Domain Architecture, 47, 56
Domain Definition, 93
Domain Policies, 100
Domain Role, 77
Domain Specific Language, 93
Domain Specific Languages, 52
DSL Meta-models, 100
Dynamic Access Control Policy, 36
Dynamic Constraints, 164
Dynamic RBAC, 165

e-government, 65
E-Health Initiative, 191
ebXML, 24
Eclipse IDE, 155
Electronic Health Record, 190
Engineering Process, 156

Formal Approaches, 90
Framework, 8, 57
Functional Meta Model, 75
Functional System View, 73, 74, 198

Generation of Security Artefacts, 141
Generation of Services Artefacts, 142
Global Business Process, 76
Global Functional Meta-model, 75
Global Functional Model, 199
Global System Meta Model, 75
Global View, 74
Global Workflow Model, 103
Global Worklfow, 94

net, 192, 193
    Access Model, 211
    Application Domain, 208
    Architectural Concept, 194
    Authentication Process, 214
    Authorization Process, 214
    Basic Use Cases, 197
    Default Access Control Policies, 212
    Design Criteria, 194
    Document Model, 210
    Interface Model, 210
    Interface View, 210
    Model Views, 208
    Organizational Setting, 193
    Patient Privacy Policies, 212
    Problem Domain, 207
    Project Mission, 192
    Role Model, 210
    Security Analysis, 198
    Security Architecture, 213
    Security Concept, 205
    Security Domain, 208
    Target Architecture, 195
    Use Cases Phase 2a, 212
Horizontal Transformations, 54
HTTP, 18

Inbound Policy File, 143
Information, 75
Institution, 75
institutions, 77
Integrity, 93, 127
Integrity Policy, 99
inter-organizational workflows, 8, 65

Interface Model, 98, 110, 111
Interface View, 97, 107

Level of Abstraction, 74
Level of Interaction, 74
Local Business Process, 77
Local Component, 78
Local Functional Meta-model, 77
Local System Meta Model, 75
Local View, 74
Local Workflow Model, 105
Local Worklfow, 94
Location, 78
Logging Unit, 126

Mandatory Access Control, 34
Messaging Layer, 21
Meta-model Based Transformations,
    150
Meta-Object Facility, 48
Model Driven Architecture, 50
Model Driven Security, 8, 51, 57
Model Driven Security Engineering, 5
Model Driven Software Development,
    47, 49
Model-to-Code Transformation, 54
Model-to-model Transformation, 55
Modeling Component, 8
Modularity, 72

Node, 78
Non-repudiation, 93, 128
Non-repudiation Policy, 99

Orchestration, 23
Outbound Policy Files, 144

Permission, 87
Permission Assignment Constraints, 164
physical level, 74
Policy Configuration Engine, 125
Policy Decision Point, 126
Policy Distribution, 219
Policy Enforcement Point, 123, 126
Policy Generation, 217
Privacy Policies, 170
Privacy Policy, 38
Problem Space, 51
ProSecO, 8, 71
Public Key Infrastructure, 126

Qualified Signature, 37, 70, 183
Quality of Service Layer, 22

RBAC, 162
Realization Process, 155
Reference Architecture, 9, 52, 122
Requirements Engineering, 73
Rights Delegation, 167
Risk, 80
Risk Analysis, 85
Role, 87
Role Based Access Control, 34
Role Model, 97, 108, 172

SAML, 44
scenario, 65
Sectet, 8
Sectet-PL, 164
Security Analysis, 38, 71
Security Components, 54, 123
Security Control, 40, 80
Security Control Engineering, 86
Security Layer, 22
Security Management, 89
Security Meta-model, 79
Security Micro-process, 73
Security Models, 32
Security Objective, 79, 201
Security Objectives, 29, 82, 200
Security Objetives, 93
Security Policies, 98
Security Policy, 30
Security Requirement, 38, 80
Security Requirements, 30, 69, 202
Security Requirements Engineering, 83
Security Transformations, 143
Service, 76
Service Components, 54, 123
Service Oriented Architecture, 3
Service Oriented Architectures, 15
Services Composition Layer, 23
Services Transformations, 145
Session Engine, 126
SOAP, 18
Software Process, 90
Solution Space, 51
Standards, 140
Static RBAC, 165

Supporting Security Components, 126

Target Architecture, 52, 54
TCP/IP, 18
Template Based Transformations, 149
Threat, 39, 80
Tool Chain, 153
Traceability, 73
Transformation Component, 9
Transformations, 141, 182
Transport Layer, 21

$UCON_{ABC}$, 35, 208, 213
UDDI, 18, 20
Unified Modeling Language, 48
Usage Control, 183
Usage Control Policies, 100
Usage Control Policy, 37
Use Cases, 68

Vertical Transformations, 55
Virtual Enterprise, 15
Vulnerability, 39

Web Services, 17
Web Services Security Standards, 23, 41, 44
Web Services Specification Stack, 20
Workflow Engine, 123
Workflow View, 97
WS-AtomicTransactions, 23
WS-BPEL, 24
WS-BusinessActivity, 23
WS-Coordination, 23
WS-Federation, 45
WS-ReliableMessaging, 22
WS-SecureConversation, 45
WS-Security, 41
WS-Trust, 45
WSDL, 18, 20
WSS4J, 42

X.509 certificate, 123
XACML, 44, 174
XACML-data-flow model, 121
XKMS, 45
XML-Digital Signature, 42
XML-Encryption, 42
XPath, 181